A gift has been made by:

Bobby Roberts

In honor of

CALS

THE WORLD'S LARGEST PRISON

MERCER
UNIVERSITY PRESS

Endowed by
TOM WATSON BROWN
and
THE WATSON-BROWN FOUNDATION, INC.

THE WORLD'S LARGEST PRISON

THE STORY OF CAMP LAWTON

JOHN K. DERDEN

MERCER UNIVERSITY PRESS | MACON, GEORGIA

MUP/H850

© 2012 Mercer University Press
1400 Coleman Avenue
Macon, Georgia 31207

First Edition

Books published by Mercer University Press are printed on acid-free paper that
meets the requirements of American National Standard for Information Sciences—
Permanence of Paper for Printed Library Materials.

Mercer University Press is a member of Green Press Initiative
(greenpressinitiative.org), a nonprofit organization working to help publishers and
printers increase their use of recycled paper and decrease their use of fiber derived
from endangered forests. This book is printed on recycled paper.
  Library of Congress Cataloging-in-Publication Data

Derden, John K.
 The world's largest prison : the story of Camp Lawton / John
K. Derden. -- 1st ed.
     p. cm.
 Includes bibliographical references and index.
 ISBN 978-0-88146-415-3 (hardback : alk. paper)
 1. Camp Lawton (Prison stockade) 2. United States--History--
Civil War, 1861-1865--Prisoners and prisons. 3. Georgia--
History--Civil War, 1861-1865--Prisoners and prisons. I. Title.
 E612.C26D47 2012
 973.7'7--dc23
                      2012021537

Contents

Preface

This is the story of Camp Lawton, the Civil War prison camp located near Millen, Georgia, on the site of what is known today as Magnolia Springs State Park. Although short lived and little remembered, the camp was once called "the largest prison in the world."[1] It was built late in the war by the Confederate government to house Union prisoners. This is also the story of the men who built, administered, and guarded the prison as well as those who were incarcerated there and those who died in it. And it is the tale of those who tried to liberate them.

My interest in Camp Lawton stems from a visit I made to the site long ago. In the summer of 1973, my wife Carolyn and I accepted teaching positions in Swainsboro, Georgia. I was to be an instructor in history at Emanuel County Junior College (now East Georgia College), and she was to teach for the Emanuel County School System. In the spring of 1974, I accompanied Carolyn and several other public school teachers and their students on a field trip to Magnolia Springs State Park, near Millen, Georgia. While performing my chaperoning duties, I noticed several markers and signs at the park indicating that this had once been the site of Camp Lawton, a Confederate prison camp for Union POWs. I am not a professionally trained historian of the American Civil War—my field is European history—however, like many others, the Civil War held a personal fascination for me, and I had read widely about it. I thought I knew a great deal about the war and, therefore, was surprised that I had never even heard of Camp Lawton. I determined to learn more about it when I got home.

To my surprise local citizens also seemed to know little or nothing about it. Initially, I could find no local traditions about the prison. So, following the well-worn historical process, I started to research the literature. The first source I consulted was William Best Hesseltine's classic, *Civil War Prisons: A Study in War Psychology*, in which I found brief mentions of Camp Lawton.[2] Hesseltine's book

---

[1] Winder to Cooper, 24 September 1864, United States, War Department, *The War of the Rebellion: A Compilation of the Official Records of the Union and Confederate Armies*, series 2, vol. 7 (Washington DC: Government Printing Office, 1880–1901) 869–70.

[2] William Best Hesseltine, *Civil War Prisons: A Study in War Psychology* (New York: Frederick Ungar Publishing, 1964) 154, 156f, 165, 169, 247, 251.

was valuable as well for the overview and context that it gave the Civil War POW story. Naturally, I also perused *The War of the Rebellion: A Compilation of the Official Records of the Union and Confederate Armies*, the 128-volume mother lode of all Civil War sources, looking for every reference I could find relating to Camp Lawton. In addition, I discovered that Billy Townsend of the Parks and Historic Sites Division, Georgia Department of Natural Resources, had conducted a survey of the site for interpretative purposes, and I was able to obtain a copy of his report.[3] Other sources informing my early researches included the host of accounts published by former Union POWs and directed to a Northern readership fascinated by the tales they had heard from returning POWs and read about in articles in the press. My examination of these initial sources only whetted my appetite because it revealed that there was a story to be told, very little had been done to tell it, and, yet, the sources were available to do so. As I gathered more sources, original and secondary, print and visual, I started to put together a narrative of the history of Camp Lawton.

I have always enjoyed speaking to the public and, believing that this story would prove intrinsically interesting not only for my students but also for local citizens, I developed a 35-mm slide presentation tracing the history of Camp Lawton. In the intervening years I have given this presentation numerous times through its succeeding iterations (now in a digital format) to groups all over the southern and eastern part of Georgia. I have even incorporated it into a tour of Sherman's March through East Central Georgia that I have given annually since the 125th anniversary in 1979. Ultimately, however, I could no longer avoid my growing collection of materials relating to Camp Lawton. They cried out for publication.

I wish to thank the many people over the years who have assisted, inspired, and encouraged me in this project, beginning with my current and former colleagues at East Georgia College, including Dr. James Dorsey, Dr. George Heaps-Nelson, Dr. James Stevenson, Dr. Reid Derr, and Dr. Willie Gunn; and East Georgia College librarians Carol Bray and Bettye Doyle. I must also mention former US Senator David Gambrell whose interest in, and writings on, Sherman's March through East Central Georgia stimulated me to document the Camp Lawton experience. Others who have provided essential help include the staff at Magnolia Springs State Park, particularly former park manager Bill Giles;

---

[3] Billy Townsend, "Camp Lawton: Magnolia Springs State Park" (Atlanta: Recreation and Programming Section, Parks and Historic Sites Division, Georgia Department of Natural Resources, July 1975).

local citizens, such as Donald Perkins and Robert Reeves, who have provided additional information, insight and feedback; descendants—D. Reid Ross, Terry and Margaret Ann Chatfield McCarty, Nina J. Raeth, and Doug Carter—of individuals who took part in the operation of the prison; and, most importantly, my family.[4] Of the latter, I particularly want to thank my parents John B. (CW4 US Army Retired) and Virginia Derden, whose choice of a military life provided a wonderful and stimulating childhood and sparked my initial interest in history, my wife Carolyn, and my sister-in law Julia Derden who graciously prepared the index for the book. Particular note should be made of Mark H. Dunkelman, author and prolific chronicler of the history of the 154th New York, who shared a number of unpublished manuscript accounts by regimental members who saw Camp Lawton. Finally, recognition is due to the late Dr. Warren F. Spencer, Professor of History at The University of Georgia, my mentor in graduate school. The collaboration among the Camp Lawton researchers and site property owners was extremely fruitful in advancing the writing of this history. Dr. Sue Moore, Professor of Anthropology at Georgia Southern University; Dr. Brent Tharp, Director of the Georgia Southern Museum; along with Kevin Chapman, Graduate Supervisor for the Camp Lawton/Magnolia Springs Project, and graduate students Matthew Newberry, Matthew Luke, Amanda Morrow, Mary Craft, and Christopher Kowalczyk welcomed me into the project and readily shared information regarding the archeological dig at the prison site. I only hope that I contributed as much to them as they did to me. The US Fish & Wildlife Service and the Georgia Department of Parks and Recreation were helpful as well.

Institutions that provided essential resources for this book include the Wilson Library of the University of North Carolina, Stetson Memorial Library of Mercer University, University of Georgia Libraries, New York State Archives, Beaufort National Cemetery, Vermont Historical Society, Minnesota Historical Society Archives, University of Iowa Libraries Special Collections, Georgia Department of Archives and History, Georgia Historical Society, Ohio Historical Society, the National Archives, Emory University Manuscript Archives and Rare

---

[4] Former Magnolia Springs State Park superintendent Bill Giles has edited two sourcebooks for the history of Camp Lawton: *Disease, Starvation & Death: Personal Accounts of Camp Lawton, the South's Largest Prison* (Magnolia Springs State Park GA: Lulu Press, 2005), and *"The World's Largest Prison": A Camp Lawton Compendium* (Magnolia Springs State Park GA: Café Press, 2004). *Disease, Starvation & Death* is listed as the second edition of the *Compendium*, but there are significant differences in content between the two books.

Book Library, the Virginia Historical Society, and Andersonville National Historic Site.

John K. Derden
Professor of History Emeritus
East Georgia College
Swainsboro, Georgia, 2012

NOTE TO READER. The numbering and nomenclature of military units within the text is done as follows: Regiments are designated by numerals and state of origin—i.e., 154th New York. Infantry units will not be specifically identified with the term "Infantry." Therefore, the reader should assume that the 2nd Georgia is an infantry unit. Artillery, mounted infantry, cavalry, reserve, and regular army units will be identified as such—i.e., 5th New York Heavy Artillery, 3rd US, 1st Georgia Reserves, etc.

Acknowledgments

This study represents the first attempt to put together a full-length, comprehensive history of Camp Lawton. As such, it owes much to several pioneers—to Billy Townsend of the Historic Preservation Division of the Georgia Department of Natural Resources, who constructed the first documented narrative history of the prison; to Dr. George A. Rogers and Dr. R. Frank Saunders, Jr., professors at Georgia Southern University, who published the first scholarly article on Camp Lawton; to Dr. Sue Mullins Moore, her student Kevin Chapman, and their associates who initiated the first extensive archaeological examination of the site; and to Bill Giles, who as manager of Magnolia Springs State Park developed interpretive materials for the site and published two collections of source documents for the prison. But, most of all, this narrative derives from the documents and accounts left by those who made that history, the Union and Confederate participants. To that end, I have attempted to let them tell the story in their own poignant, inimitable words.

As is the case with any historical work, this narrative represents only a milepost along the road to a more complete understanding of the history of Camp Lawton. Future archaeological findings augmented by new document and artifact discoveries will further illuminate the story. Hopefully, one impact of this publication will be to encourage those who may hold previously unpublished materials related to Camp Lawton to recognize their importance and make them accessible. A particular need is to unearth not only more POW accounts but also surviving letters or diaries of Confederate guards and prison staff. This latter side of the story, in human terms, has yet to be told. Finally, if this study stimulates local interest in the site, affixes Camp Lawton more prominently on the map of Civil War Georgia, and gives voice to those who were associated with its brief history, it will have accomplished its purpose.

THE WORLD'S LARGEST PRISON

THE STORY OF CAMP LAWTON

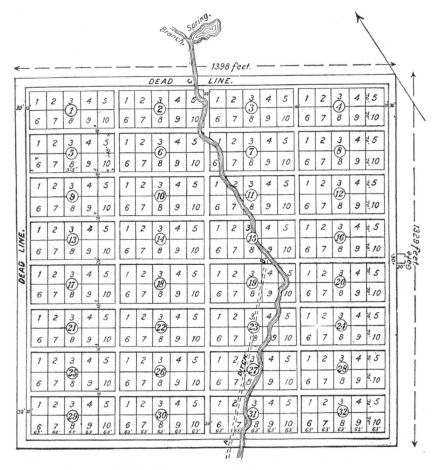

PLAN OF STOCKADE AT CAMP LAWTON.

A.—B. Artificial channel. Turn stream into for sinks. Old channel closed.
B.—C. Natural stream for bathing, washing, &c.
Each division will contain 1,000 men, and may contain 1,250.

On 26 September 1864, General Winder submitted this map to Confederate authorities in Richmond. This represents what he intended to build. Note the depiction of the wall line, deadline, stream, latrine ditch, and spring. The carefully designed streets and avenues were never laid out.

Above, *Frank Leslie's Illustrated Newspaper*, 14 January 1865, carried this view of
the exterior of Camp Lawton. Note the depiction of the gate, indicated by the
diagonal line in the wall just above the earthwork on the right.

Below, the same artist also drew the prison interior, using his imagination to
populate it. Note the fanciful dead line with guards standing within the
stockade on platforms across a shallow ditch. However, the large size of the
stockade is obvious, and the ovens are clearly depicted in the distance.

Harper's Weekly, 7 January 1865, scooped the story by publishing the first pictures of Camp Lawton drawn by an eyewitness artist correspondent. Visible are the sentry boxes and ladders, as well as a dim outline of one of the fortifications overlooking the prison (on the right-hand side of the picture on the elevation among the trees).

This *Harper's Weekly* illustration also gives some idea of the size of the Camp Lawton stockade interior. The brick ovens with places for the cauldrons are clearly visible as are the sentry boxes overlooking the prison walls. The artist saw the abandoned stockade; thus, the prisoners' dwellings were devoid of the items removed during the evacuation in late November. *Harper's Weekly*, 7 January 1865.

The burning of Millen Junction, so graphically described by Sherman's officers and represented here in a contemporary *Harper's Weekly* illustration, occurred on 3 December 1864. Millen was a strategic target because of its railroad junction and an emotional target because of the nearby Camp Lawton. The POWs colloquial name for Camp Lawton derived from the small railroad town. *Harper's Weekly*, 7 January 1865.

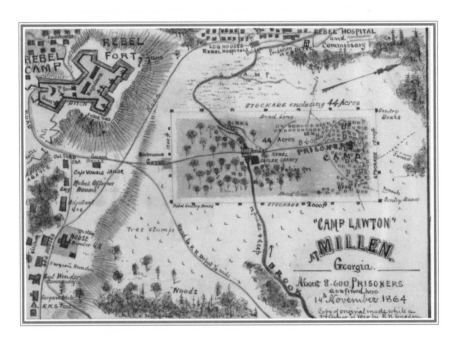

Dated 4 November 1864, this Sneden illustration is one of two bird's eye views of the prison and its supporting facilities, including labeled administrative buildings, the guards' camp and hospital, POW hospital, burial trenches, the road network, and the major earthwork on the south ridge. The absence of the depiction of the large spring is puzzling. The sinks (latrines) were located downstream from the bridge within the stockade. *Virginia Historical Society*

This Sneden image shows the stockade from the southeast. The gate is visible as is the earthwork on the south ridge. The placement of the earthwork in the left center of the painting relative to that of the stream does not agree with his other renderings. All of Sneden's paintings depict the stockade as rectangular, whereas General Winder's map and his measurements indicate it was nearly square. *Virginia Historical Society*

Sketch of the interior of Camp Lawton by Robert Sneden. Visible are the footbridge across the stream that ran through the stockade, the sutler's shanty next to it, brick ovens, the deadline, and the main area of POW occupancy on the far slope. Note also elements of Confederate infrastructure beyond the walls. POWs would be brought through the gate and marched across the footbridge to the far slope near the ovens where they would be settled. *Virginia Historical Society*

Another interior view of Camp Lawton by Sneden, revealing the basic layout within the stockade itself. The earthwork on the ridge south of the stockade is shown looming over the walls, giving Confederate officials there a clear view of the interior of the prison. *Virginia Historical Society*

Sneden sketch of one of the interior corners of the stockade. Clearly depicted are one of the brick ovens, the deadline, a collection of prisoner shebangs, and one of the guards' "pigeon roosts." *Virginia Historical Society*

Sneden illustrated his personal "shanty" in this painting that also details the brick ovens constructed for baking and boiling but which, according to POW accounts, were apparently never used for those purposes. Interestingly, Sneden's representations of the ovens differ in detail, as a close examination of his paintings reveals. *Virginia Historical Society*

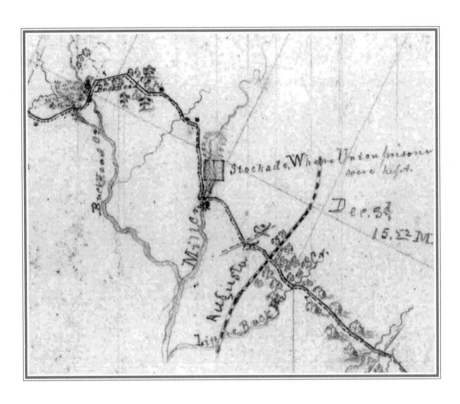

A detail of a map drawn by Sherman's topographical engineers as they passed through the area on 3 December 1864. The map shows the road and railroad network around the camp as well other features such as nearby streams. This depiction corroborates Winder's portrayal of the stockade as square.

The term "shebang" was commonly used to describe the huts built by prisoners. McElroy and comrades built this one at Camp Lawton. Note the buzzards that seem to be omnipresent in the skies in POW representations of the prisons. McElroy indicated that this was the most substantial shebang he ever built.

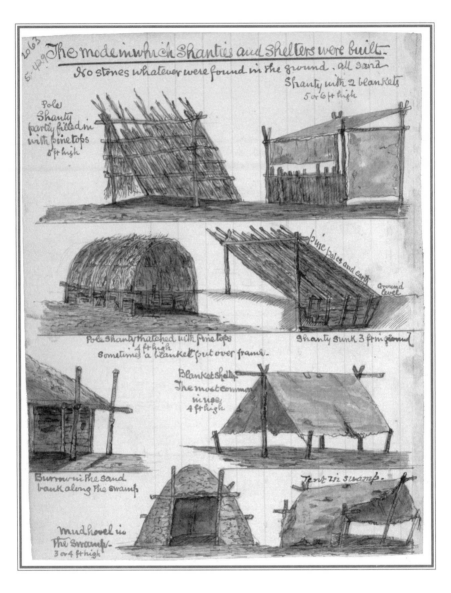

Although Sneden meant here to illustrate the shebangs at Camp Sumter, their Camp Lawton counterparts were no doubt similar. The variety in design and construction was dictated by the enterprise of the POWs and the availability of materials. Note the use of blankets, wood, mud, pine boughs, pine straw, and the earth itself. At Camp Lawton bricks stolen from those destined for the construction of the ovens were pilfered for POW use. *Virginia Historical Society*

Clothing was in short supply at Camp Lawton. Thus, there was a great deal of "sharp practice" to secure such articles. This illustration shows McElroy examining his "lucky find" in front of his shebang.

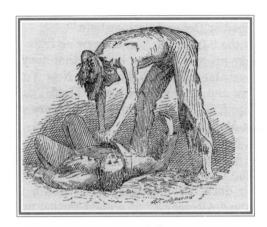

Above, the paucity of serviceable clothing among Camp Lawton POWs caused some to seek to resupply themselves through macabre means. This practice could spread infectious diseases.

Below, many POWs, and soldiers in the field for that matter, mentioned the constant struggle to deal with vermin—lice, fleas, etc. Here a POW is shown attempting to eradicate the problem by singeing his clothes over a fire. This temporary expedient no doubt also damaged the clothing and hastened its deterioration.

McElroy remembered cows' heads being brought into the prison from the slaughterhouse. For protein-starved POWs this was considered quite a treat.

Above, rations were delivered to the stockade by mule-drawn wagons, divided, and distributed to the POWs who were organized into divisions, hundreds, detachments, and messes.

Below, this illustration taken from the Camp Sumter experience represents just as well the situation at Camp Lawton, particularly when one considers the onset of cool fall weather combined with lack of weatherproof housing. Although Camp Lawton was only operational for about six weeks, many POWs associated it with freezing temperatures.

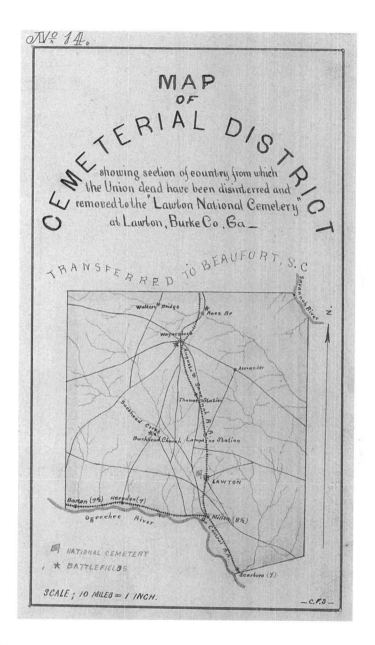

This map from the National Archives shows the location of the short-lived Lawton National Cemetery and the surrounding district from which the bodies of Union soldiers were collected following the war. *National Archives and Records Administration*

Two large timbers pulled from the stream bed c. 1970. Their location was in the proximity of where the western stockade wall crossed the stream. If from the Camp Lawton era, they could have been parts of the wall, segments of the latrine lining, or bridge timbers. They remain in storage. *Courtesy of Georgia Archives, Vanishing Georgia Collection*

Above, this US large cent recovered from the site testifies to the prison economy. With money in short supply, coins could be modified to suit the needs of those within the stockade. Photography by Amanda Morrow, Georgia Southern University. *Access to the collection courtesy of US Fish and Wildlife Service.*

Below, the obverse and reverse of Heintz and Henkle token. Although this grocery business was located in Columbus, Ohio, its token was possibly used as money at Camp Lawton. *Photography by Amanda Morrow, Georgia Southern University. Access to the collection courtesy of US Fish and Wildlife Service.*

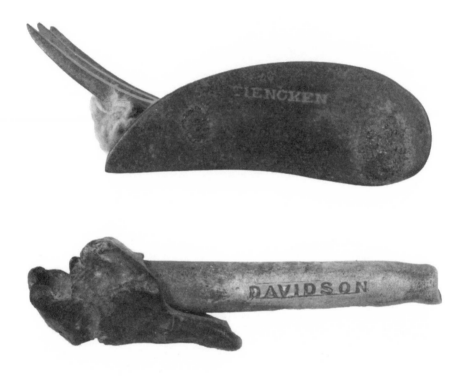

Above, one of the more poignant objects recovered by archaeologists was this tourniquet buckle with some of the webbing still attached.

Below, one of the more interesting and personal artifacts found on site was this pipe fashioned by the marriage of a clay stem and a lead bowl reflecting the enterprise of a POW who attempted to ameliorate his condition so that he could smoke. *Photography by Amanda Morrow, Georgia Southern University. Access to the collection courtesy of US Fish and Wildlife Service.*

Above, the presence of POWs from a New York regiment is reflected in this New York infantry button. Other types of military buttons have been recovered from the site. POW accounts indicate that uniform buttons were sought after items in the illicit trade among guards and POWs.

Below, the obverse and reverse of a German-made token featuring an image of George Washington also reflects the presence of ethnic German POWs. In addition, an 1862 Austrian pfennig has been recovered. Tokens, foreign coins, and other items were "monetized" by POWs in the prison economy. *Photography by Amanda Morrow, Georgia Southern University. Access to the collection courtesy of US Fish and Wildlife Service.*

Ultimately, the bodies of the Union dead from Camp Lawton were brought to the Beaufort National Cemetery (Beaufort SC), where they lie in peaceful and well-maintained surroundings. *John K. Derden*

Introduction

A Forgotten Story

A loud, piercing whistle, a chuffing engine, and billowing clouds of smoke rising above the treetops announced the arrival of another train from Savannah at Millen Junction. Trains were a daily occurrence at this small railroad town, but this one was different. It was the second week of October 1864, and the poorly maintained locomotive pulling a ramshackle collection of cars carrying its human cargo had spent almost the whole day puffing inland from Savannah on the war-worn tracks of the Georgia Central Railroad. Since early morning the locomotive had chugged across a landscape reflecting the signs of fall. The preponderance of evergreen Southern yellow pines in the forests through which the train steamed was counterbalanced by the interspersed stands of hardwood trees colored by the change of season. The locomotive's most difficult obstacle along the tracks was the slow climb over Parramore Hill, the highest point along the line between Savannah and the junction. After a brief stop in Millen to take on wood and water, the train built up a head of steam and renewed its journey, taking the right branch of the junction's "Y", and heading slowly up the tracks toward Augusta and its cargoes' destination in the piney woods. For that cargo—forlorn Union POWs and their almost equally forlorn guards—it was only another stage in what had already been a taxing journey.

About five miles north of Millen Junction, the train slowed to a stop, accompanied by the loud, prolonged hiss and clouds of released steam. The guards detrained, established a perimeter, and off-loaded the POWs. Formed into a loose column, they shuffled westward from the railroad through the woods to a large clearing prickly with the stumps of hundreds of freshly-cut trees where stood an enormous, just completed log stockade. For the next six weeks this prison pen was to be their home. They soon learned its name—Camp Lawton. For some, it was to be their last stop before they were exchanged and returned home to freedom; for others, it was to prove to be simply another way station in their continuing odyssey through the Confederate prison system; and for still others, it was to become their final resting place.

On 24 September 1864, Confederate Brigadier General John H. Winder, who was headquartered at Camp Sumter (Andersonville) near Americus, Georgia, sent a dispatch to Confederate Adjutant General Samuel Cooper, in Richmond, Virginia, announcing that he was temporarily at the site of a new prison, Camp Lawton, near Millen, Georgia, to oversee its completion.[1] "[I]t is, I presume, the largest prison in the world; it contains forty-two acres," he wrote to Cooper.[2] Size was important because the new prison camp was being constructed to provide additional housing for Union POWs. General Winder, who was Commissary General of Prisons in Alabama and Georgia, knew something about housing prisoners; for most of the war he had been in charge of managing POWs in and around Richmond, and he had spent the current summer at Camp Sumter trying to deal with an overcrowding situation that had spiraled wildly out of control with disastrous and fatal results. The new camp, he hoped, would help to alleviate these problems.

---

[1] Camp Sumter is now, and was then, more commonly known as Andersonville. All Confederate prisons had official camp names, but Union POWs, and even Confederate guards, often called them either by the name of the nearest railroad stop where prisoners were offloaded, or the closest town. Thus, for example, Camp Sumter became "Andersonville"; Camp Oglethorpe became "Macon"; and Camp Lawton became "Millen." Millen was often spelled phonetically in Union diaries. Thus, one finds "Milan" and "Millin" in addition to its correct spelling. Interestingly, at least one other Camp Lawton existed in Georgia during the Civil War. A letter (Sherod E. Roberts to Kiziah Roberts, 8 November 1861, transcribed by Spessard Stone) in the Hagan-Roberts Collection, Georgia Department of Archives and History, mentions a Camp Lawton in Savannah, where the 29th Georgia encamped for a time. Also, see the mention of this Camp Lawton in Cornelius R. Hanleiter's diary [Elma S. Kurz, ed., "The War Diary of Cornelius R. Hanleiter," *The Atlanta Historical Bulletin* 14, no. 3 (1969): 29-30]. Union POWs referred to Confederate prisons generically as "pens," "bullpens," "stockades," "hellholes," etc.

[2] Winder to Cooper, 24 September 1864, United States, War Department, *The War of the Rebellion: A Compilation of the Official Records of the Union and Confederate Armies*, series 2, vol. 7 (Washington DC: Government Printing Office, 1880–1901) 869–70.

At the height of its operation, Camp Lawton (named for the small community of Lawton along the railroad tracks to the east) held more than 10,000 POWs, served briefly as the headquarters of General John Winder, who had been promoted to Confederate Commissary-General of Prisons East of the Mississippi, featured a slaughter house and leather works, witnessed a mock election for US president in November 1864, and was the scene of attempts to recruit Union POWs for Confederate military service.[3] Yet, within two months of its opening, the "largest prison in the world" would be abandoned and burned, becoming one more artifact left derelict in the destructive path of Sherman's March to the Sea. Over the succeeding years, its hastily constructed, shoddy buildings and all physical evidence of its existence would disintegrate from the ravages of nature and man. By the turn of the century, only the heartwood stumps of the pines that had been cut to build the stockade, perhaps a few log cabins built as part of the prison infrastructure, and a series of deteriorating earthworks would remain to identify its location.[4] Today, Camp Lawton is virtually forgotten, its memory obscured by the site's later uses as a Civilian Conservation Corps (CCC) camp in the

---

[3] A long tradition holds that Camp Lawton was named for Confederate Quartermaster General A.R. Lawton. However, no official records document that fact. Since the community of Lawton (later to become Lawtonville) predated the Civil War—its post office being established in 1854—a logical assumption is that it is the source of the name. After all, Camp Sumter was named for the county in which it was located. However, there may be an indirect connection with General Lawton because, prior to the war, he was a well-known lawyer in Savannah and in 1849 (at the age of 31) was elected President of the Augusta and Savannah Railroad, the line that ran from Augusta to Millen. A number of stations along both the Georgia Central Railroad and the Augusta and Savannah Railroad were named for railway officials. Therefore, it is possible that the Lawton station was named for him, and the prison was named for the community. See Gerald J. Smith, Jr., "'Satisfaction Wherever He Served': The Career of Alexander Robert Lawton, 1818-1862" (master's thesis., Georgia Southern University, 1991).

[4] In the late 1970s, the author presented a program on Camp Lawton to the Millen Lions Club. After the meeting an elderly gentleman approached and said that as a young boy early in the twentieth century, his uncle had taken him up on one of the ridges overlooking the site of Camp Lawton and pointed out the remains of stumps of trees that he said had been cut to build the camp.

1930s, and as the beautiful state park and recreational area it has become today.

The reasons that Camp Lawton is significant are that its history illuminates some important aspects of the Civil War; among them, the treatment of Union POWs, the abilities and disabilities of the Confederacy in the last stages of the war, the impact of Sherman's March, divisions among the Confederate populace and leadership, the human toll of the conflict, and the amazing ability of the past to continue to surprise the present.

The operation of Camp Lawton is an integral part of the story of one of the saddest chapters in American military history, the handling of POWs during the Civil War. The treatment of POWs seems always tragic, but during the Civil War additional poignancy was derived from the fact that these were American soldiers imprisoning American soldiers.[5] An immense literature has grown up over the subject, much of it imbued with partisan cant, and the story of Camp Lawton is illustrative of this issue. In addition, the operation of Camp Lawton is reflective of the attrition that was beginning to take a significant toll on Confederate financial, communications, and transportation infrastructure as the conflict entered its latter stages. Camp Lawton had to be built, operated, and evacuated in the midst of the increasingly chaotic state of affairs within the Confederacy.

Moreover, Camp Lawton was directly in the path of Sherman's March to the Sea and, in fact, was one of the Union general's campaign objectives.[6] Several of Sherman's units marched by the abandoned camp, and a number of enlisted men and officers left diary accounts of their impressions. Included among these were artist correspondents whose drawings of the camp were to be published in Northern publications such as *Harper's Weekly* and *Frank Leslie's Illustrated Newspaper*. These illustrations and the accompanying articles were to inflame Northern

---

[5] A good analysis of the POW experience within the broader context of American history can be found in Paul J. Springer, *America's Captives: Treatment of POWs from the Revolutionary War to the War on Terror* (Lawrence: University Press of Kansas, 2010).

[6] William Tecumseh Sherman, *Memoirs of General W. T. Sherman*, 2 vols. (New York: Library of America, 1990) 2:667.

public opinion, already aroused by stories of abuse of Union POWs by the Confederacy.

Also, the construction and operation of the camp reveal a people divided over what to do with their enemy prisoners. Letters to the Confederate authorities in Richmond reacting to the prospect of the camp's construction reflect this concern, as do the conflicts among Confederate authorities regarding the necessity of an additional prison and the sources of manpower to staff it. These concerns were echoed in letters to Richmond dealing with other camps and the POW issue in general.

Further, the story of Camp Lawton is important because of the people involved—those who died and those who survived, those who were prisoners and those who were captors. Estimates of the number of POW deaths at the prison range from 450 to more than 1,600; yet, the prison guard, being comprised of old men and boys serving under difficult circumstances, suffered, as well. Because the participants usually tell the story best, whenever possible I have let them speak for themselves through their letters, reports, diaries, memoirs, and published accounts. As I have reproduced these accounts, I have corrected neither the spelling nor the grammar.

Finally, exciting recent document discoveries and ongoing archaeological investigations relating to Camp Lawton have illuminated and rekindled interest in its story, helping to answer some old questions, yet at the same time posing new ones.[7] The story of Camp Lawton is proving an excellent case study of the dynamism of history.

---

[7] In 1994, a remarkable collection of several hundred Civil War watercolors and drawings came to light along with the diary/memoirs of the artist, Robert Knox Sneden, a Union veteran. Acquired by the Virginia Historical Society, the materials in this collection, totaling 5,000 diary pages and 900-plus illustrations, indicated that Sneden had been incarcerated at Camp Lawton and contained several never-before-published views of the camp. Two books have resulted: Robert Knox Sneden, *Eye of the Storm: A Civil War Odyssey,* ed. Charles F. Bryan, Jr., and Nelson D. Lankford (New York: The Free Press, 2000); and *Images from the Storm: 300 Civil War Images by the Author of Eye of the Storm,* ed. Charles F. Bryan, Jr., James C. Kelly, and Nelson D. Lankford (New York: The Free Press, 2001). Also, Georgia Southern University initiated an archaeological examination of the site in 2010 ("An Archaeological Dig Being Conducted at Magnolia Springs State Park," *The Millen News,* 24 March 2010).

When an acquaintance heard about this book on Camp Lawton, he exclaimed, "How can you write a book on that; it was only open for two weeks." Well, it was actually six weeks, but the comment deserves a response. Although Camp Lawton was indeed short lived, the context of its creation, existence, and closing form an essential component of the story of Civil War military prisons. Moreover, virtually all of the issues relating to the Civil War POW experience are encapsulated in its story.

For all of these reasons, the story of Camp Lawton deserves to be told.

1

The Setting

Every story has a setting, and the history of Camp Lawton is no exception. The chronological setting is the American Civil War; the geographical setting is what, in 1864, was Burke County, Georgia (part of which is now Jenkins County), specifically the area around Magnolia Springs and the town of Millen.

The epicenter of the story was Magnolia Springs, which today is within the boundaries of a state park in Jenkins County. Magnolia Springs State Park lies astride US Route 25, five miles north of Millen, Georgia. The central feature of the park is a large artesian spring that flows as much as nine million gallons of water a day and feeds a stream of clear water that makes a gentle dogleg through the center of a shallow valley bordered by two low, pine tree-covered, parallel ridges. To the east of the park, the railroad connecting Millen with Augusta runs north and south along the same bed as it did in the Civil War. Even before the Civil War, Magnolia Springs was well known to local residents as a recreational spot because of the large spring and its stream of cool, crystal clear water surrounded by plentiful shade trees. Large numbers of people frequented the area for swimming and fishing and other social activities such as picnics and family reunions. Early accounts describe it as a place where the stream seemed to disappear underground, reappear after a short distance, then flow into a mill pond. The area around Magnolia Springs was mostly pine forest.[1]

---

[1] The brief survey history and descriptive material relating to Magnolia Springs State Park was derived primarily from Georgia Department of Natural Resources, State Park & Historic Sites Division, "Magnolia Springs State Park," http://www.gastateparks.org/info/magspr/ (accessed 7 November 2010), and "Millen," *The New Georgia Encyclopedia*, http://www.georgiaencyclopedia.org/nge/Article.jsp?id=h-2929 (accessed 7 November 2010).

In 1861, Magnolia Springs was a part of the large land holdings of Batt Jones and his wife, Caroline Elizabeth (Sapp). Both of their families, especially the Sapps, were prominent landowners and slaveholders and formed the upper crust of white plantation society in antebellum Burke County. Batt and Caroline's 1857 marriage forged a formidable union of these two families. Unfortunately, the marriage was brief because Batt died in 1862. Thus, it was to his widow, Caroline, that the Confederate government came in 1864 looking for a place to build a military prison. The Jones's holdings and those of their neighbors possessed all of the elements—land, water, timber, and labor—that would be needed to construct "the largest prison in the world."

The small town of Millen lies five miles south of Magnolia Springs State Park, and their respective roles in the Civil War are intertwined. Currently, Millen has a population of about 3,500, and is the seat of Jenkins County. Millen is located approximately 50 miles south of Augusta and 80 miles northwest of Savannah. Initially settled in 1835 and named Brinsonville, its location was a good one in that it was close to the Ogeechee River, one of the three navigable waterways in antebellum Burke County—the other two being the Savannah River and Brier Creek.[2] It was also located on one of the major roads leading into the interior of Georgia from Savannah. Thus, as Georgia moved its capital into the hinterland, first to Louisville (1796) and then to Milledgeville (1807), many travelers passed through the area. Moreover, as a novel and exciting mode of transportation technology was developed, the village became one of the regular stops on the new Georgia Central Railroad as its construction (1835–43) proceeded west from Savannah toward Macon.[3]

The advent of the railroad brought a name change, and Brinsonville was now known as "Seventy Nine" or "Old 79" due to its distance from Savannah. It then became "Millen's Junction" in 1854 when the Georgia Central Railroad and the Augusta and Savannah Railroad, which ran

---

[2] Albert M. Hillhouse, *A History of Burke County, Georgia: 1777–1950* (Jointly published by Swainsboro GA: Magnolia Press, 1985, and Spartanburg SC: Reprint Co., 1985) 102, 72.

[3] When completed to Macon, the Central Georgia Railroad was reputed to be the longest railroad in the world under single ownership: Richard E. Prince, *Central of Georgia Railway and Connecting Lines* (Millard NE: Privately printed, n.d.) 6.

from Millen to Augusta, intersected. The junction was named for McPherson B. Millen, a superintendent of the Georgia Central Railroad, and it remains the central feature of the town today. The town actually did not officially become Millen until 1881, when the Georgia legislature issued an act of incorporation naming it as such, thereby recognizing its well-established colloquial name.[4]

Although Millen was nothing more than a small railroad town before the Civil War, the existence of the junction there made it well known to travelers going to and from Macon, Savannah, and Augusta. But the junction was important in another sense, as well. Its connection to Macon, Savannah, and Augusta was to prove strategically important in a military sense, and its location within a productive agrarian region meant it was commercially important to local folks.

During the Civil War, the Wayside Home, a rest and convalescent facility for Confederate soldiers operated by local, civic-minded ladies, was established at Millen.[5] Today, a marker at the Olde Freight Depot Museum in Millen commemorates the Wayside Home, which, during the hectic year of 1864, served thousands of Confederate soldiers in transit. According to accounts by Sherman's troops who came through Millen, Confederate forces also warehoused supplies and, briefly, held Union officer POWs at the junction.[6] Despite its significance for the area's economy, however, for the vast majority of those who passed through the small town, Millen remained a point of departure or transit rather than a destination.

---

[4] Ibid., 102; "Millen" *The New Georgia Encyclopedia,* http://www.georgiaency-clopedia.org/nge/Article.jsp?id=h-2929 (accessed 7 November 2010). Some debate exists concerning exactly for whom the town was named, but the consensus supports Superintendent Millen (See article in "Diamond Jubilee Issue," *The Millen News,* 2 October 1980).

[5] Hillhouse, *Burke County,* 118–19; E. Merton Coulter, *The Confederate States of America, 1861–1865,* A History of the South, 10 vols. (Baton Rouge: Lousiana State University Press, 1950) 7:417; John Levi Underwood, *The Women of the Confederacy* (New York and Washington: Neale Publishing, 1905) 108–09.

[6] Henry Hitchcock, *Marching With Sherman: Passages from the Letters and Campaign Diaries of Henry Hitchcock, Major and Assistant Adjutant General of Volunteers, November 1864– May 1865,* ed. M.A. DeWolfe Howe (New Haven: Yale University Press, 1927) 130.

Five miles north of Millen on the Augusta and Savannah Railroad that connected Millen with Augusta, and just east of Magnolia Springs, was the community of Lawton. It featured a store, houses, and a nearby academy, and at least one resident doctor who attended to the health of the community; but, more importantly, it had a railroad station.[7] It was the proximity of the railroad running just to the east of Magnolia Springs that eventually attracted the notice of Confederate officials who were looking for a new prison site in 1864. In 1860, though, the members of this small community could hardly imagine the storm that was headed their way.

At the outbreak of the Civil War, a portion of Millen and all of Magnolia Springs were located in what was Burke County. Established by the revolutionary Georgia legislature in 1777, the region that encompassed Burke County was an important entranceway into the Georgia backcountry for those crossing the Savannah River from South Carolina. In addition, antebellum Burke County was located in an area that was developed into one of Georgia's most productive agricultural regions, with a well-established plantation economy centered around the cultivation of cotton. The terrain of Burke County consisted of a gently rolling landscape with cleared fields interspersed with large stands of native Southern yellow pine on high ground, while hardwood forests predominated in the low areas along the county's creeks and rivers.

Although small towns and villages were sprinkled around the county, they were not manufacturing centers but served rather as supply and distribution centers for the agrarian economy of the area. When one realizes that Waynesboro, the county seat, had a population of only 307 in 1860, one can readily sense the rural nature of antebellum Burke County.[8] Millen in 1860 was much smaller.

---

[7] Donald E. Perkins, "Old Lawtonville," *Jenkins County 1905–2005 Centennial History: The Millen News Centennial Edition* (24 August 2005) 55–58.

[8] Hillhouse, *Burke County*, 53; Adiel Sherwood, *A Gazateer of Georgia; Containing a Particular Description of the State; Its Resources, Counties, Towns, Villages, and Whatever is Usual in Statistical Works*, 4th ed. (Macon GA: S. Boykin, 1860; repr., Atlanta: Cherokee Publishing, 1970) 35–36; 35–36. A little more than a decade earlier, the town was recorded as having a courthouse, a jail, two churches, one academy, a market house, and miscellaneous buildings. Therefore, it had grown little in the intervening decade. See

The population of the county in the same year, however, was 17,165, of whom 12,052 were slaves.[9] In the state of Georgia, only Chatham County listed more slaves in 1860.[10] Therefore, the vast majority of the population lived on farms and engaged in agrarian pursuits. The census of 1860 listed Burke County as having more farms of 1,000 acres or more than any other Georgia county. Burke County was also at the top of the list in the number of farms of 500 to 999 acres in size.[11]

Burke County agriculture benefited from the existence of fertile land and good rainfall, and the aforementioned navigable streams and the two major railways that traversed its territory connected its planters and their produce with markets in Macon, Augusta, and Savannah. The key crop was cotton, and the kingdom started early in Burke County when Eli Whitney and a business partner established several cotton gins there in 1794 and 1795, attempting to realize commercial success from this revolutionary invention.[12] According to the 1860 census, Burke County was number one in Georgia in terms of the number of acres in improved land and the cash value of farms, and number three in the number of ginned cotton bales.[13] In addition to cotton, corn and sweet potatoes were major crops, and large numbers of livestock—cattle, swine, sheep, and goats—were also raised.[14] The agrarian nature of the county in the antebellum period intertwined two classes of people— those who owned the land and those who worked it. Many in both groups—both slave owners and slaves—were to find themselves caught up in the Camp Lawton story, and all were to find their lives profoundly altered by the coming conflict.

George White, *Statistics of the State of Georgia* (Savannah GA: W. Thorne Williams, 1849) 126–130.

[9] Hillhouse, *Burke County*, 90.

[10] US Bureau of the Census, Eighth Census of the United States, Agriculture of the United States in 1860, Compiled from Original Returns of the Eighth Census, under the Direction of the Secretary of the Interior, by Joseph C.G. Kennedy, Superintendent of the Census (Washington DC: Government Printing Office, 1864) 2:226–27.

[11] Ibid., 196.

[12] Hillhouse, *Burke County*, 162.

[13] US Bureau of the Census, Eighth Census, 2:22–29.

[14] Hillhouse, *Burke County*, 88.

What little industry that existed in 1860 was closely related to the agrarian economy. Flour and meal were produced by water-powered gristmills scattered across the county and generally located on ponds where streams had been dammed to provide sufficient flow to operate the milling machinery. These mills would attract the attention of Sherman's forces as they traversed the county in 1864. Also, the timber industry was just beginning to exploit the huge stands of virgin timber in the piney woods. In fact, a sawmill was operating downstream from Magnolia Springs before 1858.[15]

Given the plantation economy of the region, it is not surprising that white Burke County residents responded enthusiastically to the calls for secession from the Union during the winter of 1860–61. Their three elected representatives to the Georgia Secession Convention in Milledgeville in January 1861 voted unanimously to secede.[16] Moreover, many young white men in the county willingly voted with their feet by joining hastily organized volunteer companies that offered their services to the nascent Confederacy and headed to the front. By the end of the year, five such contingents of troops had left the county, and more units were created as the war progressed.[17] Also, women's auxiliaries formed to support their local boys as well as the overall war effort by sewing flags and uniforms, "moulding candles, knitting socks and scarfs, making bandages, writing letters to the front, [and] gathering and sending special foods."[18] Ultimately, the "Burke Ladies Volunteer Association" coordinated such efforts through a Central Committee working with local committees in each of the county's militia districts.

---

[15] Donald E. Perkins, *History of the Perkins Family of Perkins, Georgia* (Atlanta: Privately printed, 1979) 185, and Hillhouse, *Burke County*, 111. Given the close proximity of the mill to the springs, one wonders what role, if any, it played in the construction of Camp Lawton.

[16] Ibid., 115; the three representatives—Col. Edmund Byne Gresham, Elisha Anderson Allen, and Dr. William B. Jones—were all large landholders who possessed large numbers of slaves.

[17] Ibid., 116; the military groups and units that they joined in 1861 were the Burke Sharpshooters (Co. D, 2nd Georgia Vol. Inf.), Burke Guards (Company A, 3rd Georgia), Poythress Volunteers (Company E, Cobb's Legion), Alexander Greys (Company A, 3rd Georgia Volunteer Infantry) and the Miller Volunteers (Georgia State Troops).

[18] Ibid, 117–18.

These efforts were to complement the work of the previously mentioned Wayside Home at Millen. Ironically, while the local men found themselves for the most part stationed and fighting on the periphery of the Confederacy, the men who were to guard and administer the prison north of Millen were to come from other parts of the state and other states.

Beyond the initial excitement and enthusiasm, however, ahead lay years of hard work and privation as those who were left behind would not only worry about their young men who had gone "to see the elephant" but also find themselves having to manage their farms and the primary labor source without them. What the slave community—that primary labor force—thought about all of this, we do not know.

If Millen Junction was the hub that connected Savannah, Augusta, and Macon, it also was part of a much wider transportation web. The state of Georgia was a critical component of the Confederate war effort. With a population of one million, the largest state east of the Mississippi River was considered "the bread basket of the Confederacy." In 1860, Georgia ranked fourth in the country in the production of cotton, with 702,000 bales worth more than $25 million produced. In the same year more than 30 million bushels of corn, worth almost $25 million, were grown in Georgia.[19] This produce could be marketed beyond local confines because in 1860 Georgia had the best-developed railroad network in the Deep South.[20] Passengers, agricultural produce, mail, and other cargo were carried on the 1,200 miles of track within the state. Enhancing the capability of Georgia's pre-Civil War railway system was the fact that all of the tracks were built on the same gauge (5-feet wide).[21]

Not only Atlanta, but also Macon, Augusta, Columbus, and Savannah were significant hubs for this rail network, and the state's railway lines connected to those of Tennessee, South Carolina, and Alabama. During the Civil War, Georgia's railway network was vital to

---

[19] T. Conn Bryan, *Confederate Georgia* (Athens: University of Georgia Press, 1953) 118.

[20] Robert C. Black, Jr., *The Railroads of the Confederacy* (Reprint, Wilmington NC: Broadfoot Publishing, 1987) 10.

[21] John F. Marszalek, *Sherman's March to the Sea* (Abilene TX: McWhiney Foundation Press, 2005) 50.

the Confederacy's attempts to utilize interior lines of transportation in order to overcome a numerically superior enemy. A famous example of this was General Robert E. Lee's transfer of General James Longstreet's Corps from the Army of Northern Virginia to General Braxton Bragg's Army of Tennessee in September 1863 to counter Union General William Rosecrans's campaign into North Georgia. The result was a rarity as Confederate forces achieved localized superior mass and won a significant victory at the Battle of Chickamauga. Throughout the war, Confederate soldiers could be seen transiting through Millen Junction.

The Confederate rail system was crucial in the South's efforts to feed and supply its troops, as well. As the conflict lengthened into a war of attrition, local sources of supply for Confederate forces in the field became increasingly problematic. In the heavy, virtually non-stop 1864 campaigns in Virginia, for example, local and regional food supply sources for General Robert E. Lee's Army of Northern Virginia dried up. Concurrently, Sherman's spring and summer campaigns of 1864, along with the attendant railroad damage, had removed North Georgia from the Confederate larder. In spite of this dire logistical situation, the railroads running from Augusta and Savannah across the Carolinas into Virginia allowed the relatively untouched and remote east Georgia hinterland to serve as an alternative source of supply for Lee's army, which was besieged around Richmond and Petersburg.[22] By this time, the Union naval blockade had cut off Southern cotton from its foreign markets. Because of this, and the fact that the Confederate government was encouraging farmers to grow corn and wheat for the war effort, food

---

[22] Douglas Southall Freeman, *R.E. Lee: A Biography*, 4 vols. (New York: Charles Scribner's Sons, 1963) 3:450–52. As Freeman points out, "Lee was almost entirely dependent on the railway to feed his army" (451); see also L.B. Northrop's response to the dispatch from Winder to Cooper, 24 September 1864, United States, War Department, *The War of the Rebellion: A Compilation of the Official Records of the Union and Confederate Armies*, series 2, vol. 7 (Washington DC: Government Printing Office, 1880–1901) 499–500, in which Northrop explains the importance of Georgia to the supply of both the Army of Tennessee as well as the forces in Virginia. See, also, Hitchcock, *Marching With Sherman*, 127, 135; and Robert C. Black, III, *The Railroads of the Confederacy* (Reprint, Wilmington NC: Broadfoot Publishing, 1987) 197–98.

supplies that originated in Georgia were being shipped to the front.[23] The result of this was reported by Brevet Major George Ward Nichols, aide-de-camp to General Sherman, who wrote, as he moved with the Federal host from Atlanta to Savannah, "We daily traverse immense corn fields, each of which covers from one hundred to one thousand acres. These fields were once devoted to the cultivation of cotton, and it is surprising to see how the planters have carried out the wishes or orders of the Rebel Government...."[24]

As late as the summer of 1864, East Central Georgia remained productive, continued to be relatively removed from, and untouched by, combat operations, and contained an over-burdened and deteriorating, but still operative railway system. As the war progressed, these realities would be decisive as the Confederate government looked for places to house Union POWs, and as the Union government sought ways to bring the awful conflict to a close. Soon, the confluence of these two factors would bring an enormous Confederate prison camp to Magnolia Springs, and it would place Millen and the region in which it lay in the path of a resolute Union army determined to deny the use of the railroad, its junction, and the productive resources of the region to the enemy. Thus, the forces of history were moving, and the momentum was toward East Central Georgia. Events were to transpire that would briefly bring Magnolia Springs, Lawton, Millen, and Burke County, to the

---

[23] In 1862, the Georgia General Assembly had made it illegal for a farmer to plant more than three acres of cotton per farm hand. A fine of $500 for each acre planted above the maximum was to be levied (Bryan, *Confederate Georgia*, 121); moreover, by 1864, Georgia Governor Joseph E. Brown was campaigning against the conversion of grain into spirits (corn into whiskey) by cracking down on illegal production and by revoking the authority for many legal distillers. See Joseph E. Parks, *Joseph E. Brown of Georgia* (Baton Rouge: Louisiana State University Press, 1977) 267. Another factor in the need to produce more food crops was the problem of the destitute population in the state—the disabled, widows, orphans, and other poor. See Bryan, *Confederate Georgia,* 118–22.

[24] George Ward Nichols, *The Story of the Great March from the Diary of a Staff Officer*, 26th ed. (New York: Harper & Brothers, 1866) 81. Something of the hunger of the reading public for Civil War accounts, particularly relating to Sherman's march, can be gauged by the fact that Nichols's account had gone through 26 editions by 1866! Also, Black, *The Railroads of the Confederacy*, 197, discusses the shift from cotton to corn and Lee's need for foodstuffs from the interior.

forefront of the struggle. Ultimately, those who had not gone to war would find the conflict coming to them.

2

An Emerging Tragedy

The story of the treatment of POWs by both sides is a particularly dark chapter in the history of the American Civil War. It is a tale replete with poor planning, inadequate infrastructure, illness and death, mutual recriminations, and lingering bitterness. Tragically, many captured soldiers who had survived deadly battlefields were to find themselves in situations that rendered mortality in other, less "heroic" ways. In fact, the death rates at Civil War POW camps were higher than the corresponding combat death rates. The fragmentary nature of Civil War casualty statistics renders questionable any solid conclusions; however, comparing what data does exist indicates that soldiers who were killed in action or who died of wounds from combat did so at the following rates: Union, 7 percent; Confederate, 9 percent. As far as the proportion of deaths among soldiers who were captured, statistics reveal that Union POWs died at a rate of 15.5 percent, while 12.1 percent of Confederate captives failed to survive their imprisonment.[1]

At the beginning of the conflict, very few on either side expected the war to be of the scale and duration that eventually materialized. Despite the experience of the American Revolution, the War of 1812, and the Mexican War, little foresight was initially given to the issue of POWs in

---

[1] Digital History, "Civil War: Casualties and Costs of the Civil War," http://www.digitalhistory.uh.edu/historyonline/us20.cfm (accessed 7 November 2010); James M. McPherson, *Ordeal By Fire: The Civil War and Reconstruction* (New York: Alfred A. Knopf, 1982) 451f; however, Alfred Jay Bollet, MD, *Civil War Medicine — Challenges and Triumphs* (Tucson AZ: Galen Press, 2002) provides slightly different statistics: "... about 10% of all the deaths among Civil War soldiers occurred in military prisons" (377). He argues that 18 percent (or 23,000 out of 127,000) of Union POWs and 12 percent (or 26,000 out of 220,000) of Confederate POWs died in military prisons, statistics that also support the basic argument.

the Civil War.[2] The war would last for four years and become by far the costliest conflict in American history in human terms. The scale of numbers of those killed, wounded, missing and captured was epic and unprecedented in American history and formed a sobering reality that quickly revealed itself as the Union and Confederate forces got down to business. As soon as combat operations were initiated, casualties were incurred. The issue of how to handle POWs emerged rather early in the Civil War. The first Battle of Bull Run (Manassas), for example, resulted in both military and civilian prisoners. The question now was what to do with the POWs on both sides.

In the twentieth and twenty-first centuries the general method in dealing with POWs has been to intern them for the duration of the conflict, after which they are repatriated. However, for Civil War combatants the historical context for the handling of POWs derived primarily from the Revolutionary War (1775–83), the War of 1812 (1812–15), and the Mexican War (1846–48). None of these conflicts adequately prepared the two sides for the scale of what was to come; yet, collectively, these earlier wars established patterns and principles in handling POWs that were going to be followed in the aftermath of the bombardment of Fort Sumter. During the earlier conflicts, the practice of paroling and exchanging captured soldiers was standard procedure. The idea was that a captured soldier would be "paroled"; that is, he would be released on a formal promise not to bear arms again until he had been "exchanged." Once exchanged, a paroled soldier could re-enter the ranks. The specifics of the parole and exchange process were delineated in a cartel signed by the contending parties. Ironically, the War of 1812 cartel agreed upon by Great Britain and the United States in 1814 had been negotiated on the American side by General William H. Winder (1775–1824), the father of General John H. Winder (1800–1865), who was to play a major role in the history of Civil War prisons. In early 1862, when cartel negotiations between the Union and the Confederate governments began, both sides agreed that the Winder cartel of 1814

---

[2] Charles W. Sanders Jr., *While in the Hands of the Enemy* (Baton Rouge: Louisiana University Press, 2005) 7–24, devotes a full chapter to an enlightening discussion of the pre-Civil War American experience with POWs.

would be the model for any agreement, and when the resulting Dix-Hill Cartel was finally agreed upon on 22 July 1862, its provisions were quite similar to Winder's original War of 1812 instrument.[3]

The creation of a POW cartel during the Civil War was initially complicated by two factors, not the least of which was Lincoln's early concern that any such negotiations would imply recognition of the Confederacy, which the Union was not willing to countenance because it viewed the conflict as a rebellion. Secondly, since the manpower pools of the two sides were unequal, the ability of the less populous Confederacy to "recycle" its captured soldiers into combat once exchanged would serve to prolong the South's ability to continue to fight; whereas, such re-treading would not assist the Northern war effort to the same extent.

The Dix-Hill Cartel provided for an equal exchange of prisoners by each side according to a formula that swapped a private for a private, a non-commissioned officer for a non-commissioned officer or two privates, and so forth. Surplus POWs would be released and paroled until they could be formally exchanged in the next round. Initially, the cartel worked well; POWs were routinely paroled and exchanged, and both Northern and Southern prisons served essentially as temporary holding pens. But, early in 1863, as a result of Union General Benjamin Butler's retaliatory actions against citizens in New Orleans, the issuance of the Emancipation Proclamation, and the recruitment of black soldiers by the North, Confederate President Jefferson Davis issued draconian policies that were seconded by the Confederate Congress. Black soldiers were to be turned over to their respective states for prosecution under their laws, and white officers of black regiments as well as all Union officers captured in states included in the Emancipation Proclamation also would be turned over to the states for prosecution as slave insurrectionists which was a capital crime. In response, Union Secretary of War Edwin Stanton suspended exchanges of all Confederate officers so they could be kept as a pool of hostages to prevent Davis's orders

---

[3] Arch Frederic Blakey, *General John H. Winder, C.S.A.* (Gainesville: University of Florida Press, 1990) 153–54; also, see 217–18 for a copy of the Dix-Hill cartel. Both Blakey and William Best Hesseltine, (*Civil War Prisons: A Study in War Psychology* [New York: Frederick Ungar Publishing, 1964]) detail the creation and operation of the cartel.

from being carried out. Lengthy and acrimonious disputes, including the discovery by Union forces of paroled but not exchanged Confederate prisoners from Vicksburg and Port Hudson among those captured in the later battles around Chattanooga (Chickamauga, Missionary Ridge, and Lookout Mountain), resulted in the formal end of the exchange system in December 1863.[4]

The subsequent heavy campaigns in both the western and eastern theaters in the first half of 1864 added thousands to the numbers of POWs on both sides who languished in hastily prepared prison camps. Southern overtures to renew the exchange system were rebuffed by Union General Ulysses Grant. He held firm against a renewal of the exchanges:

> It is hard on our men in Southern prisons not to exchange them, but it is humanity to those left in the ranks to fight our battles. Every man we hold, whether released on parole or otherwise, becomes an active soldier against us either directly or indirectly. If we commence a system of exchange which liberates all prisoners taken, we will have to fight on until the whole South is exterminated.[5]

Thus, the end of the exchange system brought on a crisis in POW numbers, both North and South. Thousands of captured Union and Confederate soldiers were being held with no imminent prospect of parole or exchange; therefore, both sides had to make provisions for long-term confinement.

In large measure the origins of Camp Lawton stemmed from the intersection of the career of Brigadier General John H. Winder, C.S.A., with the operation of Camp Sumter, the infamous Confederate prison more commonly known as Andersonville. The two came together on 17 June 1864, when General Winder arrived by train to take command of

---

[4] General Orders, No. 111, 24 December 1862, United States, War Department, *The War of the Rebellion: A Compilation of the Official Records of the Union and Confederate Armies*, series 2, vol. 5 (Washington DC: Government Printing Office, 1880–1901) 795–97; Stanton to Lincoln, 5 December 1863, *Official Record*, series 2, vol. 6, 647–49.

[5] Grant to Butler, 18 August 1864, *Official Record*, series 2, vol. 7, 606–07.

both Camp Sumter and Camp Oglethorpe, a prison for Union officer POWs located in Macon, Georgia.[6]

General Winder was sixty-four years old that day and had spent almost his entire life in the US Army since he entered West Point in August 1814.[7] Winder was from a prominent Baltimore family, the son of General William Henry Winder (1775–1824) a well-known Baltimore attorney, whose brief military career during the War of 1812 was blackened by his failure, at the Battle of Bladensburg in 1814, to prevent the capture of Washington, DC, by the British. When he arrived at Camp Sumter, John H. Winder had spent more than thirty-six years as an Army officer and almost three years in the Confederate service. Prior to the Civil War, Winder had served in a variety of assignments. He had been an assistant instructor in tactics at West Point, seen service in the Seminole Wars in Florida, been brevetted major and lieutenant colonel for his "gallant and meritorious conduct" during the Mexican War, and served as the lieutenant governor of the city of Vera Cruz in the war's aftermath. His Army career had included postings in Florida, Arkansas, New York, Maine, South Carolina and North Carolina (where he had met his second wife); and in the process he had climbed the ladder of administrative positions for career officers, serving as assistant commissary, assistant adjutant, assistant quartermaster, company commander, and post commander. All in all, it was a solid if not distinguished career. However, promotions were slow in the peacetime army, and when the secession crisis led to war in early 1861, John Winder—at the age of sixty-one—held only the brevet rank of lieutenant colonel and the permanent rank of major.

According to his biographer Arch Fredric Blakey, Winder's career prior to the Civil War was driven by a desire to restore the Winder family reputation that had been damaged by the Bladensburg disaster. Throughout his life, John Winder felt a personal obligation to assuage the family's besmirched reputation through the honor of his conduct and

---

[6] General Orders, No. 45, 17 June 1864, *Official Records*, series 2, vol. 7, 377.

[7] The documentary record concerning Winder's life is sparse; however, Blakey, *Winder*, has mined the available material and skillfully constructed the only book-length account, from which this biographical sketch has been derived.

service. The result was a tension between his naturally impulsive and energetic nature and his determination to be absolutely correct and honorable in his career decisions. Therefore, he never took anyone lightly whom he believed was impugning his reputation or attacking his competency. He was quick to sense challenges to his personal rectitude and just as quick to defend himself, verbally or in writing. The result was that he developed a reputation as a difficult personality, and many considered him a martinet.

Winder had natural sympathies with the South. Most of his military career had been spent below the Mason-Dixon Line. In addition, Blakey points out that "[h]is family had owned slaves for two hundred years, and he twice married into slaveholding families.... Winder ... regarded slavery as part of the natural order ..."[8] Therefore, like many of his contemporaries in the military during the secession crisis of 1860–61, he was faced with a difficult decision. Resignation from the US Army for service in the Confederate Army held the potential of a commission as a general (although his age militated against a field command) and would align him in support of his long-adopted home state of North Carolina. Yet, virtually all of his adult life had been spent in the service of the United States. Like a number of his Army colleagues, he struggled over the best course of action to take, but he eventually resigned his US Army commission early in 1861 and offered his services to the Confederacy. He was ultimately rewarded with a commission as a brigadier general.

Winder had come to Camp Sumter in June of 1864 from Richmond, Virginia, where he had had a brief tenure as inspector general of the camps in the Richmond area and then a controversial career as provost marshal and commander of the Military Department of Henrico, the military district that enclosed the Confederate capital. As such, he was responsible not only for maintaining law and order but also for keeping track of those who came and went within the district. In addition, he found himself trying to manage the almost unmanageable problem of thousands of Union POWs who had been brought in and around the city as a result of the constant campaigns against Richmond in the eastern theatre of the war. Finally, he was in charge of "prisons for Confederate

---

[8] Blakely, *Winder*, 42.

offenders and deserters from the enemy."[9] Like a many-headed hydra, Confederate military prisons—Libby, Belle Isle, Castle Thunder, Scott's, among others (fourteen in total)—had sprouted all over the city. None of them had been expressly designed for the purpose for which they were now being used, but the one-time commercial buildings had been adapted and pressed into service anyway.[10]

Winder had a thankless job, one that grated on the individualist and states' rights sensitivities of many in the Confederate capitol. To staff his office, Winder employed a number of individuals from his home state of Maryland. This further sullied his reputation to some who accused him of surrounding himself with a group of Baltimore "Plug Uglies." The Plug Uglies were, in fact, a well-known gang or political club that operated in that city. Associated with riots and political violence, their notorious reputation and sobriquet were used to disparage Baltimorians under Winder's command. It was a criticism that was to follow Winder to the end.[11]

For three years Richmond had been the focus of Union armies attempting its capture and of Confederate forces trying to safeguard its defense. Their needs and those of the civilian population drained whatever local resources might have been available for Union POWs, and General Winder had found himself unable to keep up in terms of providing that beleaguered group with adequate shelter, food, and medical attention.

During the fall of 1863, at the suggestion of General Robert E. Lee, Confederate authorities decided to develop prison facilities in the interior of the Confederacy.[12] On 24 November 1863, Captain William Sidney Winder, General Winder's third son, and a member of his father's

---

[9] Anderson to Bragg, 6 June 1864, *Official Records*, series 2, vol. 7, 205–07, succinctly describes the duties of Winder's office in Richmond.

[10] For a complete list of Confederate military prisons, see Blakey, *Winder*, 213.

[11] Ibid., 51; Tracy Matthew Melton, *Hanging Harry Gambrill: The Violent Case of Baltimore's Plug Uglies, 1854–1860* (Baltimore: Maryland Historical Society, 2005).

[12] Lee to Seddon, 28 October 1863, *Official Records*, series 2, vol. 6, 438–39. Lee made the suggestion, and Secretary of War Seddon concurred (Seddon to Lee, 31 October 1863, *Official Records*, series 2, vol. 6, 455–56).

staff, was directed to select a prison site in Georgia.[13] He did so, and thus was born Camp Sumter. The plan, as Adjutant and Inspector General Cooper explained to Georgia General Howell Cobb, was "to establish a cantonment at Andersonville, in your state, for the safekeeping of the Federal prisoners now in this city [Richmond], numbering from 10,000 to 12,000...."[14] Confederate leaders hoped this would accomplish the two-fold purpose of housing Union POWs in areas with better access to food supplies and locating them more remotely from the fighting to forestall attempts to liberate them. In late February and early March 1864, Union cavalry raids by General Judson Kilpatrick and Colonel Ulric Dahlgren attempted to free the POWs in Richmond. The raids ultimately failed but proved to Confederate authorities that their concerns regarding the security of prisoners were well founded. As the prison population was shifted into the interior of the Confederacy, General Winder found himself in the unenviable position of being far removed from Camp Sumter, now the institution of his greatest responsibility.

That there were problems on the ground is evidenced by a report to Winder from Major Thomas Turner who had been sent by the general to inspect Camp Sumter. Turner reported that "[g]reat confusion and serious difficulties have existed in regard to rank among the officers, quarrels and contentions as to who ranks and commands, all tending to disturb the good order, discipline, and proper conduct of the post and prison."[15] Although Turner praised Captain Henry Wirz as a notable exception to the administrative problems, he urged the appointment of an officer of sufficient rank to establish control of the situation. In Richmond, Assistant Adjutant General R.H. Chilton realized that the problem was even broader than the local command issue at Camp Sumter, and he made a recommendation to Cooper:

> General Winder controls directly all prisoners arriving here, at Danville, and at Andersonville, Ga., and now at Macon, Ga., but has no

---

[13] Pegram to Winder, 24 November 1863, *Official Records*, series 2, vol. 6, 558. Winder's travails in building, staffing, equipping, and operating the camp in its initial stages are well summarized in Sanders, *While in the Hands of the Enemy*, 197–201.

[14] Cooper to Cobb, 7 February 1864, *Official Records*, series 2, vol. 6, 925.

[15] Turner to Winder, 25 May 1864, *Official Records*, series 2, vol. 7, 167–69.

general control over the subject…. With the multiplicity of duties performed by General Winder, it could not be expected that he could give that strict personal supervision to duties which of themselves are sufficient to occupy the best energies of a man of intelligence, energy, and industry, and no one can examine the records and character of service relating to the department of prisoners without being convinced of the absolute necessity for a commissary-general of prisoners.[16]

Earlier, Commandant of Georgia Reserve Troops General Cobb had urged that Camp Sumter be given a commander at the rank of brigadier general.[17] President Davis concurred and informed Cobb that Winder would be sent to the camp.[18] Chilton's recommendation to create a Confederate commissary general of prisoners would eventually be followed, but the immediate result of the conjunction of these suggestions and reports was that Winder was ordered to move his command to Camp Sumter and to "proceed with the least practicable delay."[19] As Union POWs had been shifted farther into the interior of the Confederacy, this would place General Winder at the location of his greatest responsibility.

When Winder arrived at Camp Sumter on 17 June 1864, he was thrust into an emerging tragedy. He had been instrumental in the creation of the prison and had been its absentee manager, so to speak, since it had opened in February of that year, but he had never been there. General Winder's new command was located just northeast of Americus, Georgia, but Adjutant General Cooper had instructed him that the Union officers' prison in Macon (Camp Oglethorpe) was also under his charge. Although it was known officially as Camp Sumter, it is more popularly known as "Andersonville," and Union prisoners at the time usually called it that, too. Ironically, given what eventually transpired, Camp Sumter had been constructed to allow the removal of thousands of Union POWs from the Richmond area, thus alleviating the intolerable overcrowding, supply problems, and security issues engendered by the

---

[16] Chilton to Cooper, 26 May 1864, *Official Records*, series 2, vol. 7, 172–73.

[17] Cobb to Cooper, 5 May 1864, *Official Records*, series 2, vol. 7, 119–20.

[18] Davis to Cobb and Browne, 3 June 1864, *Official Records*, series 2, vol. 7, 192.

[19] Withers to Winder, 3 June 1864, *Official Records*, series 1, vol. 39, 634.

presence of so many POWs in the Confederate capital. Opened in February 1864, well before it had been completed, camp facilities never caught up with the need. It was originally a 16-acre compound comprised of a pine log stockade straddling a low valley through which ran a tributary ("Stockade Branch") of Sweetwater Creek, in turn a tributary of the Flint River. A short distance from the stockade was Anderson Station, a stop on the Southwestern Railroad line and the derivation of the prison's popular name.

In retrospect, the choice of General Winder to command this post was a good one. He was conscientious, energetic for his age, and the most experienced man in the Confederacy in administering POWs. That he could be fractious was well known, but much of that reputation had developed because he was a strong advocate for his command. He also might have had an exaggerated sense of honor and a willingness to defend it, but in that he was not alone. The Civil War was populated with many such individuals, and the pace, stress, and overlapping administrative responsibilities of the conflict led to numerous turf wars and personality clashes. Resignations, backbiting, and publications of correspondence relating to personal controversies were the order of the day. These were especially prevalent and problematic within the Confederacy. In fact, well-known Civil War historian Bell Irwin Wiley devoted one of the chapters ("Failures That Were Fatal") of *The Road to Appomattox* to the issue of disharmony among Southern leaders. In the chaos of war, the POW camps needed a leader who was persistent and who would badger his superiors to get what was needed.[20] Winder was that man.[21]

His first inspection of the prison revealed a horrifying situation. He found 24,000 prisoners in the stockade—double the number earlier projected by Cooper—guarded by a force that on paper numbered 2,867, but which in reality totaled only 1,462 present for duty. Provisions were

---

[20] Bell Irwin Wiley, *The Road to Appomattox* (New York: Athenuem, 1971); See Blakey's assessment of Winder (*Winder*, 202–15).

[21] Although Winder has been generally castigated in POW accounts, two recent studies of his performance as an administrator have argued persuasively that, given the tasks he was assigned and the lack of support he faced, he did as well as could have been expected. See Sanders, *While in the Hands of the Enemy*, and Blakey, *Winder*.

inadequate, and measles and whooping cough were "prevailing in command." The vast majority of the guards were ill-trained, poorly led, and poorly supplied reserve troops, many of whom were unarmed. Within the next three days, Winder sent a stream of dispatches to various authorities—General Cobb, General Bragg, and Adjutant and Inspector General Cooper—apprising them of the conditions at Camp Sumter, asking for more guards and provisions, and urging the establishment of another prison.[22]

In the meantime, Winder took local action to improve the discipline of the guard units, ordering "measures to bring in every man not with his regiment," and issuing General Orders Number 48 which specified the expectations of the new commander as regarding the garrison and its officers.[23] Not only were the numbers of guards insufficient for the task at hand but also the quality of the garrison units was poor and would continue to be a point of concern for Winder. Occasionally Winder even found it necessary to detain temporarily Confederate field units that had been detailed to guard the prison trains in order to secure enough guards for the camp.[24] Winder inherited a staff, some members of whom would eventually follow him to Camp Lawton. When Winder arrived at Camp Sumter, the Camp Commandant was Lieutenant Colonel Alexander W. Persons of the 55th Georgia Volunteer Infantry; however, Winder also brought some aides with him from Richmond and requested others.

As spring turned to summer, conditions at Camp Sumter worsened. The heat was innervating to many Northern soldiers, the water supply fetid, the food inadequate in quantity and poor in quality, and occasional rains created septic quagmires. Both prisoners and guards suffered. And then there was the overcrowding. The POW population at Camp Sumter peaked at nearly 33,000 in August 1864, at which point an average of nearly 100 men a day were dying.[25] Ultimately, almost 13,000 POWs

---

[22] Winder to Bragg, 18 June 1864, *Official Records*, series 2, vol. 7, 378; Winder to Bragg, 20 June 1864, *Official Records*, series 2, vol. 7, 286; Winder to Cooper, 21 June 1864, *Official Records*, series 2, vol. 7, 392.

[23] Winder to Cooper, 20 June 1864, *Official Records*, series 2, vol. 7, 386; W.S. Winder, General Orders No. 48, 21 June 1864, *Official Records*, series 2, vol. 7, 393.

[24] See, for instance, Winder to Cooper, 13 July 1864, *Official Records*, series 2, vol. 8, 463.

[25] Winder to Cooper, 13 August 1864, *Official Records*, series 2, vol. 7, 588–89.

perished at Camp Sumter. Of the more than 45,000 Union prisoners who were sent to the camp, 12,912 died, making a mortality rate of 28.7 percent.[26] The sheer number of deaths at Camp Sumter ensured that it would emerge from the war as the focal point of the controversy over the handling of POWs by both sides. Numerous histories of Camp Sumter have been written, and the purpose of this cursory discussion is not to recapitulate its story in any detail but rather to place it in the context of the origins of Camp Lawton.[27]

While General Winder and his staff attempted to manage an increasingly unmanageable situation, Winder continued to press his superiors with what he saw as the necessity of opening another prison to alleviate conditions at Camp Sumter. He referred to his new post as "a fearful responsibility."[28] The following dispatch sent by Winder to Adjutant and Inspector General Cooper one week (24 June 1864) after his arrival at Camp Sumter clearly reflects the tenor of his many communications to Richmond:

> GENERAL: The pressing necessities of this post and the great irregularity of the mails have induced me to send Lieutenant Davis with this letter, though I can very illy spare his services, as he is one of my most efficient assistants. The state of affairs at this post is in a critical condition. We have here largely over 24,000 prisoners of war, and 1205 very raw troops (Georgia Reserves), with the measles prevailing, badly armed worse disciplined to guard them; the prisoners rendered more desperate from

---

[26] This calculation (12,912 divided by 45,000 = 28.7 percent) derives from the statistics on the National Park Service website related to Camp Sumter, http://www.nps.gov/history?NR/twhp?wwwlps/lessons/11andersonville/11facts1.htm (accessed 18 September 2008). See, also, the estimate of monthly death rates by former Camp Sumter inmate Ezra Hoyt Ripple in *Dancing Along the Deadline: The Andersonville Memoir of a Prisoner of the Confederacy*, ed. Mark A. Snell (Novato CA: Presidio Press, 1996) 20.

[27] Among the better scholarly secondary accounts of Camp Sumter are Ovid Futch, *History of Andersonville Prison* (Gainesville: University of Florida Press, 1968) and William Marvel, *Andersonville: The Last Depot* (Chapel Hill: University of North Carolina Press, 1994). A fascinating investigation of some of the mysteries and details of the Camp Sumter experience can be found in Robert Scott Davis, *Ghosts and Shadows of Andersonville: Essays on the Secret Social Histories of America's Deadliest Prison* (Macon GA: Mercer University Press, 2006).

[28] Winder to Cooper, 22 June 1864, *Official Records*, series 2, vol. 7, 396.

the necessarily uncomfortable condition in which they are placed. With the present force a raid on the post would almost of necessity be successful, as the prisoners would occupy the attention of the troops. I do most conscientiously think the force should be largely re-enforced, and I respectfully ask that it be done with the least possible delay. There has been, and I am satisfied that there is now going on, a correspondence in the prisons with disaffected persons outside, and I have every reason to believe that just before my arrival an agent of General Sherman had been here tampering with the prisoners. From the information I have been able to collect since I have been here I am satisfied that there is apportion of the population around here who ought to be looked after, and who actively sympathize with the prisoners.

In order to enable me to watch and counteract this influence I respectfully ask that Capt. D.W. Vowles, with a detailed man by the name of Weatherford, on the police at Richmond, and two other well-selected detectives, be ordered to report to me immediately. It is difficult for those at a distance to realize the great responsibility of the command of this post and the great danger of a successful outbreak among the prisoners. Twenty-five thousand men, by the mere force of numbers, can accomplish a great deal. If successful, the result to the country would be much more disastrous than a defeat of the armies; it would result in the total ruin and devastation of this whole section of country. Every house would be burned, violence to women, destruction of crops, carrying off negroes, horses, mules, and wagons. It is almost impossible to estimate the extent of such a disaster. A little timely, prudent preparation will easily render it impossible. The rawness of the troops, the almost impossibility of getting a court-martial from the Department of South Carolina and Georgia, and other circumstances connected with the prisoners, render it very necessary that I should have the power to order courts-martial, and I respectfully request that such an arrangement be made. Let me again urge upon the attention of the Department the great danger hanging over this post and to the necessary steps to arrest it. Another prison should be immediately established, as recommended in my former letter, and that no more prisoners be sent to this post [Italics added]. The force is becoming too ponderous, and, indeed, it is not possible with my present means to extend the post fast enough to meet the demands.

Within the last four days we have discovered two extensive tunnels, reaching outside the stockade, showing great industry and determination on the part of the prisoners....

P.S.—We have just discovered a tunnel reaching 130 feet outside the stockade.[29]

Winder's concerns had already been corroborated by two reports on the prison as a result of a request by General Braxton Bragg (then military advisor to President Davis) to General Samuel Jones, Commander of the Department of South Carolina, Georgia, and Florida, on 15 June 1864. The first report had been written by Isaiah H. White, chief surgeon of Camp Sumter.[30] He stressed that conditions were overwhelming the medical staff and urged an increase in medical personnel. White's support was submitted to Captain W.H. Hammond, Assistant Adjutant General to General Jones. The other report was Hammond's own summary in which he had described the camp as "crowded, filthy, and insecure," with only twelve of the sixteen acres suitable for occupation by prisoners because of the marshy area alongside the stream.[31] He also urged that both the guard and medical staff be increased.

Camp Sumter was simply not working. Its capacity had been hugely exceeded; the guard force was poorly trained and numerically inadequate; the medical facilities were terribly insufficient; and supplies—food, clothing, etc.—were either non-existent or could not meet the growing demand. Further, given the ongoing impasse between the Federal and Confederate governments on the prisoner exchange issue and the continuing heavy campaigns of 1864, particularly in Georgia and Virginia, the need for additional facilities to house Union prisoners was obvious to Winder. He believed that the ability of the area around Camp Sumter to handle prisoners had been far exceeded and would not support the continuing flow of Union POWs. Therefore, an additional site or sites must be found. The question was, where?

---

[29] Winder to Cooper, 24 June 1864, *Official Records*, series 2, vol. 7, 410–11.
[30] Hammond to Bragg, 21 June 1864, *Official Records*, series 2, vol. 7, 386–87.
[31] White to Hammond, 20 June 1864, *Official Records*, series 2, vol. 7, 392–93.

From the time that he had arrived at Camp Sumter and determined the need for an additional prison or prisons, General Winder had been looking for specific sites. On 27 June 1864, Captain C.E. Dyke (Florida Light Artillery) was detailed to proceed to Cahaba and Union Springs, Alabama, to "examine thoroughly into the merits of the places for the establishment of a military prison."[32] Captain Dyke completed his mission and submitted his findings on 5 July 1864. Dyke, in fact, visited Union Springs and Silver Run but not Cahaba. Both locations were along the Mobile and Girard Railroad whose terminus was Union Springs. He found Union Springs problematic in terms of providing sufficient water and timber, but it was located in an area of significant food supplies and with railroad access. He found Silver Run to be more suitable as it had railroad access—with the railroad in better condition from Columbus, Georgia, to Silver Springs than from Silver Springs to Union Springs— and it possessed sufficient water and timber resources as well. Dyke did not go to Cahaba, as Winder was apparently unimpressed with its potential as a site for a prison of the scale he intended to construct, and he orally informed the captain of this opinion.[33] Following up on Dyke's recommendation, therefore, Winder informed Cooper that Silver Run seemed to be the best place to establish a new prison and asked him for the authority to impress labor and teams to begin construction.[34] Justifying his recommendation, Winder telegraphed Cooper from Macon on 16 July:

> Cahaba not at all suited for a large prison—timber too distant. Cost will be enormous, Still worse, the time to build will be entirely too long for any useful purpose.... Silver Run is the most convenient place that I can hear of; the next place is Pulaski County, Georgia.

---

[32] Dyke to Winder (W.S.), 5 July 1864, *Official Records*, series 2, vol. 7, 441–44.

[33] Cahaba, a converted tobacco and corn shed, was already being used as a prison. It held as many as 5,000 Federal POWs, but the site was prone to flooding, quality drinking water was limited, and the grounds were relatively small. See Jesse Hawes, *Cahaba: A Story of Captive Boys in Blue* (New York: Burr Printing House, 1888).

[34] Winder to Cooper, 7 July 1864, *Official Records*, series 2, vol. 7, 446; Winder to Cooper, 13 July 1864, *Official Records*, series 1, vol. 7, 463.

However, Silver Run was not without problems, and he also informed Cooper that, "General Withers, commanding [Alabama] reserves, says that he cannot furnish guard."[35] In the meantime, Winder had also sent Major E. Griswold into Alabama to explore possible prison locations. Griswold traveled the Montgomery and Mobile Railroad, the Alabama and Tennessee River Railroad, and the Mississippi Railroad, ultimately recommending (on August 31) two sites within 25 to 30 miles of Selma.[36]

The plan to build another prison in Alabama was temporarily brought to an end by news of a Federal cavalry raid led by General Lovell H. Rousseau against the West Point and Montgomery Railroad. Rousseau's 2,500-man force destroyed more than thirty miles of track on 17–19 July, which cut the rails between Columbus and Silver Run.[37] This setback forced Winder to telegraph Cooper that it "… for the present, puts an end to the idea of a prison in Alabama."[38] In the meantime, W.H. Mitchell, President of the Mobile and Girard Railroad (the rail line servicing the Silver Run site), had written to Seddon urging that a site farther west in Alabama be considered so as not to interfere with food supplies being sent from the eastern part of the state to the main Confederate field armies.[39]

With Alabama at least temporarily out of the question, Winder's attention now shifted to potential sites for a new prison in Georgia. Moreover, Richmond authorities were frustrated by the seemingly endless problems involved in finding a suitable site for another prison as well as guards to staff it. Yet, everyone involved was extremely concerned because Sherman's advance on Atlanta and Rousseau's raid across Alabama revealed that even a relatively remote area of Southwest Georgia like Anderson Station was no longer far removed from the military front. Compounding this issue was the fact that things had gone

---

[35] Winder to Cooper, 16 July 1864, *Official Records*, series 2, vol. 7, 469.

[36] Griswold to Winder (with endorsements), 31 August 1864, *Official Records*, series 2, vol. 7, 706–08. By 14 September 1864, the fear of Federal raids and the strength of local opposition brought an end to these proposals.

[37] Futch, *Andersonville*, 82.

[38] Winder to Cooper, 19 July 1864, *Official Records*, series 2, vol. 7, 476.

[39] Mitchell to Seddon, 8 July 1864, *Official Records*, series 2, vol. 7, 448.

terribly awry at Camp Sumter, as reports by insiders and outside inspectors confirmed, and opening new facilities in other, more remote regions seemed the only answer. On 17 July 1864, Secretary of War Seddon asked Cooper to

> [i]nstruct Genral Winder to exercise his best judgment to procure safe prisons for the prisoners and to proceed to distribute and procure safe guards in the best manner and with the least delay forthwith. He must act on his own responsibility, as there is no time for consultation, nor knowledge to enable us to instruct.[40]

This was facilitated by Special Orders Number 175 (26 July 1864) by which Winder was appointed "to the command of the military prisons in the States of Georgia and Alabama."[41] In the same dispatch, Brigadier General W.M. Gardner was assigned command of the Confederate prisons in the other states east of the Mississippi River. The commands were equivalent; both commanders were to report directly to Cooper's office. With the Confederacy in extremis, Richmond authorities were finally attempting to make more efficient the cumbersome bureaucracy and vaguely delineated lines of responsibility that had administered the prisons to date. It was going to prove to be too little, too late. Two days after his appointment, Winder sent Captains D.W. Winder and W.S. Winder from Camp Sumter

> ...to proceed, as directed, to select a site for a new prison in the neighborhood therein designated. After selecting the site you will secure by rent the land, water privileges, timber, and such houses adjacent as may be thought advisable. You will use sound discretion in your selection, conferring with reliable men in the vicinity as to the health of the section, &c.[42]

---

[40] Winder to Cooper, 19 July 1864, *Official Records*, series 2, vol. 7, 476.

[41] Special Orders No. 175, 26 July 1864, *Official Records*, series 2, vol. 7, 501–02.

[42] Winder to D.W. Winder and W.S. Winder, 28 July 1864, *Official Records*, Series II, Vol. VII, 509.

3

The Solution:
The Construction of Camp Lawton

The site selection team for the new prison undoubtedly took the train from Anderson Station to Macon, transferred to the Georgia Central Railroad, steamed to Millen Junction, and then proceeded to Magnolia Springs by train or other conveyance to look at the potential site. Since the two captains were coming from Camp Sumter and traveling in what was normally the hottest part of a hot and humid South Georgia summer, Magnolia Springs with its refreshing shade trees and cool, gently flowing stream must have seemed like an oasis to them. Juxtaposed against the realities of Camp Sumter, Magnolia Springs as a potential prison site would have appeared to be an easy choice. In the meantime, General Winder wrote Adjutant and Inspector General Cooper informing him of his action in sending the team.

The first explicit mention of Millen as a potential site for the new prison is found in this dispatch of 30 July 1864, in which Winder told Cooper that he had "sent Captain Vowles and W.S. Winder to Millen, Georgia, to select location for a new prison."[1] However, Millen must have been considered as a potential site for some time because Winder's original orders to the search team called for them "to select a site for the new prison in the neighborhood therein designated."[2] We have no documentation that indicates how the Confederate authorities came to see the Millen area as a possible location. One can surmise, however, that in addition to the resources available—land, water, labor, food—the railroad with its connections to Macon, Savannah, and Augusta was a

---

[1] Winder to Cooper, 30 July 1864, *Official Records*, series 2, vol. 7, 514.

[2] Winder to Vowles and D.W. Winder, Special Orders No. 143, 28 July 1864, United States, War Department, *The War of the Rebellion: A Compilation of the Official Records of the Union and Confederate Armies*, series 2, vol. 7 (Washington DC: Government Printing Office, 1880–1901) 509.

crucial factor. POWs, guards, equipment, and supplies could be brought in and out by rail. Moreover, the surrounding area was remote from the fighting, at least at that time.

It is easy enough, however, to understand why Magnolia Springs, in particular, drew their attention. Captains Vowles and Winder were looking for a site that was secure, located near an operational railroad, provisioned with plenty of water and supplies of wood, and contained land that was available for lease. Magnolia Springs easily met those requirements and, on 4 August, General Cooper received a telegram from the search team: "We have made a selection for a new prison, five miles from this place [Millen], on the Augusta railroad."[3] General Winder was pleased with the choice, and when he eventually saw the site he commended the selection team to Cooper: "The location is an admirable one and I think does great credit to Capts W.S. Winder and Vowles for the selection."[4] The new location seemed at the time to be relatively safe from Federal cavalry raids; the propinquity of the railroad would allow for transport of men and supplies; a better supply of water afforded by the spring would solve the poor water situation prevailing at Camp Sumter; and easy access to free-standing timber would provide materials for the construction of a stockade. The land was available, and Confederate authorities leased it from its owner, Mrs. Caroline Elizabeth Jones.[5] In his dispatch of 30 July, Winder also asked Cooper to give the two officers the "authority to impress negroes and teams and wagons" so that construction could begin "as soon as possible."

The selection of the site must not have been much of a secret because a local medical doctor, C.R. Johnson from Waynesboro, the seat of Burke County, quickly responded to the news. Perhaps Dr. Johnson

---

[3] Vowles and Winder to Cooper, 4 August 1864, *Official Records*, series 2, vol. 7, 546.

[4] Winder to Cooper, 24 September 1864, *Official Records*, series 2, vol. 7, 869–70.

[5] Winder to Jones, 21 January 1865, *Official Records*, series 2, vol. 8, 111. In the *Official Records* she is referred to as "Mrs. C.M. Jones." In fact, her name was Caroline Elizabeth Jones, and she was the widow of Batt Jones who had died in 1862. She owned the land on which the prison was built and was one of the major slaveholders in Burke County. Both her and her husband's families were slaveholders. In 1860, Batt Jones was listed as owning 121 slaves, most of whom Caroline probably brought into the marriage. This makes Dr. Johnson's estimate of her ownership of about 150 slaves four years later plausible if not slightly exaggerated.

was one of the "reliable men" with whom General Winder asked the site selection team to confer. If he was, his opposition to the planned prison was quickly made manifest. On 10 August, Dr. Johnson wrote to Secretary of War Seddon:

> I have the honor to report to you the following facts: I am informed by Captain Winder of Richmond, Va., that he is authorized by you to locate a military prison in this section of the State, and has selected a location on the plantation of a widow lady of this county. There are many objections, in my judgment, why it would be an objectionable location. First. The health of the prisoners and the guard should be considered. The water to be inclosed in the stockade is the most unhealthy, rotten limestone, and no one in our country ever thought of drinking it, and there is no other water in five miles of the place. The water is from a spring (rotten limestone). Second. The interest of the government should be considered. This lady's plantation has about 150 negroes on it, and her crops are of vast importance to the Government and community. Her tithe alone last year was 1,300 bushels of corn, 2,500 pounds of bacon, &c. This plantation is within half a mile of the place anticipated for the prison. There are also several other plantations within a few miles of the place; at least 600 or 800 negroes in five miles of it. In my opinion it would be better for the Government to place the prison more remote from the large plantations and where the troops could get good water, when there are so many such places on all our lines of railroads. I have no doubt but Captain Winder has had false representations made to him by certain parties in the immediate vicinity of the spot he had selected, and entirely for pecuniary purposes—men who are not in the service of the country and never have been, and who care nothing for the interest of the Government or any one else, so they are putting money in their coffers. These facts can be substantiated by every prominent man in the county, and if Your Honor will hear from us on the subject I will send a petition of the inferior court of the county for a change of location for potent causes.[6]

Dr. Johnson's description of the quality of the water for drinking was manifestly incorrect. The water was plentiful and potable and was one of the best qualities about the prison mentioned in the inmate accounts. Whether Dr. Johnson represented that grand old American

---

[6] Johnson to Seddon, 10 August 1864, *Official Records*, series 2, vol. 7, 579.

tradition of not wanting a prison near him, whether he was concerned about the impact of the prison on the local slaves and agricultural production, or whether he was worried about the problem of escaped prisoners as well as the possibility that the prison would bring Federal forces into the area, or some combination of all these factors, will probably never be known, but his letter was not the only one of its type reaching authorities in Richmond. C.H. Stillwell of Thomson, Georgia, wrote to President Davis on 7 September. Although his letter was specifically addressed to the issues of POWs at Camp Sumter, his comments represented a strain of thought that was not often overtly expressed but that perhaps had an increasing number of silent adherents:

> Permit a poor man to say a word in these days of trouble and distress. Please read the sixth chapter of Second Kings. Follow the example of the King of Israel. Send the prisoners at Andersonville home on their parole. Send them home before the cold proves more destructive of their lives than the heat has been in the open and unshaded pen your officers provided for them.
>
> It will prove the greatest victory of the war and do our cause more good than any three victories our noble troops have gained.[7]

Interestingly, Jefferson Davis's private secretary, Burton N. Harrison, checked Stillwell's Bible reference and thought it was erroneous: "Refers to sixth chapter, Second Kings ... the chapter is twenty-eighth Chronicles." Actually, both men were correct. Both 2 Kings (chapter 6) and 2 Chronicles (chapter 28) contain accounts of letting prisoners go home. While Dr. Johnson seems to have been mainly concerned about the location, Stillwell dealt with the moral issue with which the POW problem confronted the Confederacy. During the fall of 1864 and the spring of 1865, more letters from Southern civilians protesting the conditions of the Confederate POW camps and their inmates arrived in

---

[7] Stillwell to Davis, 7 September 1864, and Endorsement by Harrison to Seddon, 14 September 1864, *Official Records*, series 2, vol. 7, 783.

Richmond.[8] As the war drew to its inexorable close, voices from the Southern populace as well as from within Confederate officialdom increasingly mentioned the need to resume the exchange of POWs, even if it were unilateral.

But there were official concerns about locating another military prison in Georgia, as well. Major General Howell Cobb, Commander of the Georgia Reserves, wrote Secretary of War Seddon from his headquarters in Macon on 12 August:

> Allow me to impress upon you the importance of preventing any more prison camps being established at this point. I need hardly call your attention to the various and important public interests at this place already too much exposed to raiding parties of the enemy. The force here is small and scarcely able to protect the place, and will become wholly so if any considerable portion has to be reserved, as heretofore, to guard prisoners. In the establishment of new prisons I beg to suggest the propriety of locating them in different States. On reason alone is sufficient to decide the matter, and that is that you are able thus to use the reserve force for a guard; but as this force can only be employed in the State in which it was raised, if you multiply the prisons in one state you lose the use of the reserves of other states, and will be compelled to obtain from the army in the field a prison guard. This consideration, in connection with security of the prison and the obtaining of supplies, should control the question of the location.
>
> I write these suggestions because I understand that General Winder proposes to send a portion of the prisoners from Andersonville to this place, and so proposes to put up another large prison at Millen, in this State.[9]

Therefore, Cobb opposed both sending additional POWs to Macon and the construction of a new prison near Millen. He argued that concentrating prisons in one state deprived the government of the use of reserves from other states as guards since they were detailed for use only

---

[8] See, for instance, letter from Sabina Dismukes containing an editorial, "The Prisoners at Florence," *Sumter Watchman* (SC), 12 October 1864, *Official Records*, series 2, vol. 7, 976–77.

[9] Cobb to Seddon, 12 August 1864, *Official Records*, series 2, vol. 7, 585–86.

within their own states, and the resulting gap in guards would have to be filled from regular army units that were desperately needed at the front.[10] Cobb was also concerned about the approach of Federal forces as they operated against Hood's defense of Atlanta, as well as the continuing issue of provisions. The Georgia Reserves commander, like most Confederate civil and military officials, was caught in the middle of competing demands—in his case, the needs of prison authorities for more camp guards versus those of Confederate forces in the field desperately seeking to augment their troop numbers to oppose Sherman's invasion of Georgia, both of whom were constantly pressuring Cobb for reinforcements.

Although the situation at Camp Sumter required his continued attention, General Winder pushed the construction of the new prison as quickly as possible. He and his staff, as well as the authorities in Richmond, were anxious to have the new prison completed. When heavy rains damaged the stockade at Camp Sumter in early August, Winder pleaded with Cooper: "I beg you to send every facility to the new stockade near Millen, Ga., to have it finished at once... One hundred and three died yesterday... Send me some company officers to help the new stockade."[11] On 14 August, casting his nets wide to secure the necessary labor to build the new prison, he ordered Lieutenant R.S. Hopkins to "visit such counties as have become the homes of planters from Florida and Georgia, with their slaves, and in which you have reason to believe you can hire negroes. I desire to avoid impressments, but the work must be hurried to completion."[12] Although reluctant to do so, Confederate authorities found themselves more and more frequently having to authorize impressments to secure needed services in the waning months

---

[10] Georgia reserve troops were, in fact, later employed out of state in the Confederate victory at Honey Hill, South Carolina, on 30 November 1864, and in other, ancillary operations. See Charles C. Jones, Jr., *The Siege of Savannah in December, 1864, and the Confederate Operations in Georgia and the Third Military District of South Carolina during General Sherman's March from Atlanta to the Sea* (Albany NY: Joel Munsell, 1874) 34–43.

[11] Winder to Cooper, 11 August 1864, *Official Records*, series 2, vol. 7, 583–84.

[12] Winder to Hopkins, 14 August 1864, *Official Records*, series 2, vol. 7, 593.

of the war as Southern morale declined and privation increased.[13] However, one other potential source of labor may not have been overlooked. According to Edmund Brannen in a 1955 article in *The Millen News*, some 300 Union POWs from Charleston assisted in the camp's construction along with the previously mentioned slave labor.[14]

In fact, POWs William Lightcap (Company E, Fifth Iowa Cavalry) and Thomas R. Aldrich (Company B 154th New York) reported that Confederate authorities requested volunteers to help build Camp Lawton from among the Union prisoners being temporarily held in Savannah. Lightcap's concluding comment—"Thank God there were but few among us of that kind"—indicates that some were receptive and echoed Aldrich's antipathy: "I could have gone out here but I swore that I would rot before I would lift a hand in any way to assist the Dumb Confederacy or anyone connected with it."[15] Lightcap's account is supported by documentary evidence that Winder asked for and was given fifty "mechanics" from among the Savannah POWs to help finish Camp Lawton.[16]

As Sherman's campaign against Atlanta progressed, supply problems and concern for the possibility of a Union raid that might liberate the prisoners at Camp Sumter increased. Secretary of War Seddon urged Winder to "[h]asten to the utmost the preparation of the other prisons," and asked, "How soon can they be prepared?"[17] Moreover, the Richmond authorities' interest in spurring construction of the new prison was strengthened by more negative official reports as to

---

[13] Allen D. Candler, ed., *The Confederate Records of the State of Georgia Compiled and Published under Authority of the Legislature,* 6 vols. (Atlanta: Chas. P. Byrd, State Printer, 1908) 2:313, 375.

[14] Edmund Brannen, "Magnolia Springs State Park—Jenkins County's Playground; Once Site of World's Largest Prison Camp," *The Millen News,* 24 September 1955, section C, 1.

[15] William Henry Lightcap, *The Horrors of Southern Prisons During the War of the Rebellion, from 1862 to 1865* (Platteville WI: Journal Job Rooms, 1902) 52; Thomas R. Aldrich, Unpublished Memoir (courtesy of Patricia Wilcox of Fairport, New York) 26.

[16] Edward C. Anderson Papers No. 3602, Southern Historical Collection, The Wilson Library, University of North Carolina at Chapel Hill, 6:121–28, 132–33 (cited in Arch Frederic Blakey, *General John H. Winder, C.S.A.* [Gainesville: University of Florida Press, 1990] 194).

[17] Seddon to Winder, 25 August 1864, *Official Records,* series 2, vol. 7, 678.

the situation at Camp Sumter.[18] As a stop-gap measure plans were drawn up to evacuate as many POWs as possible from Camp Sumter and Camp Oglethorpe and to send them to Charleston and Savannah, where they could be held temporarily until the new prison could accommodate them. Camp Lawton was indeed under construction, but not yet complete. In his 5 September order to Winder to begin the transfer of prisoners, Seddon encouraged the rapid completion of the new prison at Millen and asked, "Cannot part [of the prison] at once be prepared before completion of the whole prison grounds?"[19] This request must have reminded Winder of the fact that Camp Sumter had been occupied before its completion, with disastrous results. Winder responded:

> Prison very nearly complete and admirably adapted to the purpose. Large amount of property at the post; nineteen guns mounted in the batteries. Prisoners commenced to moving this morning. Instruct me what to do when prisoners are all gone.[20]

This dispatch can be a bit confusing at a first reading because Winder is discussing both Camp Sumter and Camp Lawton. The first two sentences refer to the construction of the new prison near Millen; the remainder of the dispatch references the situation at Camp Sumter. The dispatch also indicates that Camp Lawton was intended not just to supplement the facility at Camp Sumter but to replace it.

But completing the new prison and ensconcing the POWs there were not the only things on General Winder's plate. He also selected a staff for the upcoming task. Captain Wirz was left at Camp Sumter, retaining his position as commandant of the prison stockade, where he would remain until the war's end. Colonel George C. Gibbs replaced General Winder as post commandant (Camp Sumter). Winder, as

---

[18] Chandler to Chilton, 5 August 1864, *Official Records*, series 2, vol. 7, 546–50 and 551–53. For an enlightening discussion of the Chandler visit to Camp Sumter, his reports, and the retorts of Winder and his associates, see Charles W. Sanders, Jr., *While in the Hands of the Enemy: Military Prisons of The Civil War* (Baton Rouge: Louisiana State University Press, 2005) 230–31.

[19] Cooper to Winder, 5 September 1864, *Official Records*, series 2, vol. 7, 773.

[20] Winder to Cooper, 7 September 1864, *Official Records*, series 2, vol. 7, 783.

commanding general in charge of the military prisons in Georgia and Alabama, determined to move his headquarters to the new prison. His son, Captain William Sidney Winder, who had located the site, overseen the initial construction of Camp Sumter, and been its first commandant, followed his father to Camp Lawton as his assistant adjutant-general. In addition, Captain W. Shelby Reed, who was provost marshal at Camp Sumter, probably moved to Camp Lawton in the same capacity.

Dr. Isaiah H. White, chief surgeon at Camp Sumter, also moved with Winder to Camp Lawton. The medical staff at Camp Sumter in the summer of 1864 included 35 surgeons, as well as numbers of hospital stewards, ward masters, clerks, and other assistants.[21] It can be assumed that many of these were detailed to Camp Lawton as the former prison was emptied. The only other doctor at Camp Lawton besides White who is mentioned by name in POW accounts is a Dr. Herndon.[22] At any rate, White was authorized to make medical staff appointments in the locations where the Camp Sumter prisoners were sent.[23]

Other Camp Lawton staff included Colonel Henry Forno, who had commanded the guard at Camp Sumter and now would serve in the same position at the new prison. In addition, Captain D.W. Vowles, who had worked for General Winder during his Richmond days before coming to Camp Sumter in March 1864, and who had helped select the

---

[21] "Return of Officials, Officers, Agents, and Employees, Medical Department, Andersonville, Ga.," 4 August 1864, *Official Records*, series 2, vol. 7, 542–45.

[22] Return of Staff Officers [Andersonville], 31 July 1864, *Official Records*, series 2, vol. 7, 518–19; Robert Knox Sneden, *Eye of the Storm: A Civil War Odyssey*, ed. Charles F. Bryan, Jr., and Nelson D. Lankford (New York: The Free Press, 2000) 268–69, and *Images from the Storm: 300 Civil War Images by the Author of Eye of the Storm*, ed. Charles F. Bryan, Jr., James C. Kelly, and Nelson D. Lankford (New York: The Free Press, 2001) 228. Sneden mentions "Mrs. Shely Reed" at Camp Lawton, who was probably the wife of the above-mentioned Captain W. Shelby Reed, which would imply his presence at Camp Lawton. This Dr. Herndon was probably Dr. Brodie Herndon, Jr., who was assigned to Camp Sumter on 6 August 1864, as a surgeon under Dr. White and then must have gone to the new prison with most of the other staff. See Special Orders No. 185, 6 August 1864, Confederate States of America, War Department, *Special Orders, Adjutant and Inspector General's Office, Confederate States* (Richmond, 1864) 504. Sneden identifies Dr. Herndon as the surgeon for the guards (Robert Knox Sneden, Diary, 1 September 1864–May 1865, Virginia Historical Society, Mss 5:1 Sn 237:1 v.6, 153).

[23] Moore to White, 12 September 1864, *Official Records*, series 2, vol. 7, 817.

site of the new prison in July, was appointed commandant of Camp Lawton. Vowles, however, desired to return to field service and in October, he applied for a promotion, sending a request for a colonelship to Adjutant General Cooper along with the endorsements of Generals J.L. Kemper, Winder, and Harris and a Colonel Shields.[24] Ultimately, this did not materialize because not only was the specific assignment not available but also Winder was possibly growing concerned about Vowles's conduct. (See p. 144) Vowles stayed at the prison for its duration.

General Winder's nephew, Captain Richard B. Winder, the first quartermaster at Camp Sumter, was assigned the same position at Camp Lawton. Also accompanying General Winder to the new prison, in addition to those who were appointed to high staff positions, were functionaries such as Jackson Marshall, the general's clerk, who kept the official books. [25] Besides his family members, many of these individuals had been with General Winder for some time, some going back to his days in Richmond. No staff return seems to exist for Camp Lawton; therefore, the composition of most of the rest of the staff is conjecture, with a few names surfacing here and there in dispatches to and from the prison. One may assume, however, that many of the Camp Sumter staff were transferred to Camp Lawton, with the exception of those needed to administer the greatly reduced POW population at Camp Sumter.

The guard for Camp Lawton also came from Camp Sumter. At least a portion of the Florida Light Artillery was transferred to Camp Lawton. Captain Charles E. Dyke was its commander at Camp Sumter. Although he is not mentioned in any records of the Camp Lawton period, he probably served there, as well. Prior to Camp Lawton's construction, the infantry force detailed to guard Camp Sumter was composed of the First, Second, Third, and Fourth Georgia Reserves, two companies of the 55th

---

[24] Vowles to Cooper, 24 October 1864, National Archives and Records Administration, RG77, Letters Received by the Confederate Adjutant General and Inspector General, 1861–1865, Jan.–Dec. 1864.

[25] Samuel B. Davis, *Escape of a Confederate Officer from Prison: What he Saw at Andersonville, How he Was Sentenced to Death and Saved by the Interposition of President Abraham Lincoln* (Norfolk VA: Landmark, 1892) 40.

Georgia and a battalion of Georgia Militia.[26] General Winder was not happy with the performance of the reserve units and complained to both General Cobb and the Richmond authorities.[27] At times, Winder even "held on" to units that accompanied trainloads of POWs to Camp Sumter in order to bolster the guard force. However, Confederate soldiers were in such short supply in the face of the Union offensives in 1864 that his complaints and actions had little effect. Initially, the guards at Camp Lawton were made up of the First and Second Georgia Reserves; at least those are the units mentioned by Winder in his 15 October dispatch to Cooper from the prison:

> ...I have here two regiments—First and Second Georgia Reserves. They are the most unreliable and disorganized set I have ever seen. They plunder in every direction and are creating a very bitter feeling against the Government. It is impossible to prevent it or identify them, as the officers will not exercise any authority, and some of them even encourage it.
>
> If they could be substituted by the Second Regiment Georgia State Troops [militia], raised in this and the adjoining counties, it would be a great benefit to the country, the First and Second Reserves should be where there are other troops to control them.[28]

In fact, the Second Georgia State Troops were then in Augusta, and nothing indicates that such an exchange was ever made. In addition to the First and Second Georgia Reserves, at least part of the Third Georgia Reserves was at Camp Lawton. A muster roll for Company F of that regiment for September–October 1864, listed its location as Camp Lawton.[29] One POW diary account mentions guards belonging to the

---

[26] Winder to Cooper, 24 June 1864, *Official Records*, series 2, vol. 7, 410; Cobb to Cooper, 22 December 1864, *Official Records*, series 1, vol. 44, 977–78.

[27] Chandler to Chilton, 5 August 1864, *Official Records*, series 2, vol. 7, 548.

[28] Winder to Cooper, 15 October 1864, *Official Records,* series 2, vol. 7, 993.

[29] File of material from Doug Carter relating to the Third Georgia Reserves and his ancestor Jesse Taliaferro Carter, http://files.usgwarchives.net.ga/military/civlwar/rosterss/3rdreserve.txt, (accessed 5 October 2009).

53rd Georgia, although he probably meant the 55th Georgia, and the Fourth Georgia Reserves may have been there, as well.[30]

As for the prisoners themselves, there now began a tragic odyssey. Accompanied by their guards, over the next few weeks thousands of POWs from Camp Sumter rode the rails to Charleston and Savannah. Many of them eventually found themselves at the new prison north of Millen after it was completed. Ultimately, some even ended up back at Camp Sumter. The rail accommodations were poor. POWs were loaded into boxcars, unroofed cattle cars, or even flatbed cars; and guards accompanied each train.

As she traveled across the state in 1864, young Rebecca Latimer Felton witnessed such a POW shipment:

> On that trip we passed car-loads of Andersonville prisoners being moved to another camp as it was expected that Sherman would strike for Andersonville. The night was gloomy and the torch fires made a weird scene as our train rolled along beside flat cars on which those Federal prisoners were guarded, with torch lights illuminating the faces of those ragged, smoke begrimed, haggard, and miserably filthy men. I had a glimpse of war conditions that was new to me. Prison treatment of such men has always been a disgrace to Christianity and civilization. I had read of Camp Chase and Johnson Island [Union military prisons] and had been angered at the treatment accorded to our Confederate prisoners, but the sight of trainloads of Federal prisoners on the wild night in Southern Georgia, when I could look into their faces within a few feet of the train I became an eye witness to their enforced degradation, filth and utter destitution and the sight could never be forgotten.[31]

The overtaxed engines, cars, and poorly maintained rails meant that a trip from Camp Sumter to Savannah, Millen, or Charleston could take from two to four days, and the journey was not without its hazards. Among the trainloads leaving Camp Sumter that fall, one load of POWs

---

[30] Sneden, *Eye of the Storm*, 265.

[31] Rebecca Latimer Felton, *Country Life in Georgia in the Days of My Youth* (Atlanta: Index Printing Company, 1919) 85. Felton, who became the first female US senator in 1919, traveled across Georgia as a refugee trying to avoid Sherman's forces.

and their guards suffered deaths and injuries when the train derailed.[32] At times trains carrying POWs were shunted to sidings to permit higher priority traffic to pass. In the process of such low speed, stop-and-go transport, some prisoners escaped; some died; all suffered.

Most of the prisoners who were to be housed at Camp Lawton, upon its completion, were shipped by Winder to Savannah as a temporary expedient. Although a stockade already existed in the city, it was not adequate to handle the numbers involved. Camp Davidson was located in an orchard next to the US Marine Hospital, and it was used primarily for officers, many of whom had been transferred from Camp Oglethorpe in Macon. Therefore, another stockade for enlisted men was built adjacent to the city jail.[33] This stockade was on a bare, sandy spot of land and was surrounded by a wall of three-inch thick planks, twenty feet high. Sentry boxes were spaced at intervals around the walls, and the stockade had a deadline like Camp Sumter as well as a water-filled moat on three sides.[34] The prison commander was Lieutenant S.R. Davis. At one point approximately 10,000 Union POWs were held in the Savannah stockades.[35] Initially, POWs arriving in Savannah found their new accommodations a welcome respite from the horrors of Camp

---

[32] Anonymous, *A Voice from Rebel Prisons Giving an Account of Some of the Horrors of the Stockades at Andersonville, Milan and Other Prisons by a Returned Prisoner of War* (Boston: Rand & Avery, 1865) 13, says that "ten of the guard [were] killed;" Daniel G. Kelley says that "seven or eight men were killed" and that the accident occurred on 13 September (*What I Saw and Suffered in Rebel Prisons* [Buffalo: Thomas, Howard & Johnson, 1868] 64–65). J.E. Hodgkins, *The Civil War Diary of Lieut. J. E. Hodgkins: 19th Massachusetts Volunteers from August 11, 1862 to June 3, 1865*, trans. Kenneth C. Turino (Camden ME: Picton Press, 1994) 104, states that he was on that train and that seven men were killed and eighteen were injured in the derailment. Levi Whitaker, 13 September 1864, Diary transcription, Andersonville Diaries, Andersonville National Historic Site, 3:486, also mentions the wreck.

[33] Lennie R. Speer, *Portals to Hell: Military Prisons of the Civil War* (Mechanicsburg, PA: Stockpole Books, 1997) 269, gives a helpful synopsis of the prisons built in Savannah.

[34] Sneden, *Images from the Storm*, 220–22, and *Eye of the Storm*, 258–59, include several illustrations of the prison.

[35] Speer, *Portals to Hell*, 269.

Sumter. Sergeant Francis J. Hosmer (4th Vermont) described his new surroundings as "fairly wholesome" and found the rations improved.[36]

The POWs from Camp Sumter hoped that their arrival in Savannah presaged an exchange. Rumors of prison exchanges were rife in the fall of 1864, and, as Union POWs were being shifted from camp to camp, prisoners eagerly sought out any chance to board a train for possible freedom. Those not selected for transport often resorted to the tactic of "flanking" to get on the trains. Henry Davidson described a successful episode of this type in Savannah:

> The next morning another train load was ordered to be in readiness, this time we were informed, for Millen. The detachments were taken out in the order of their entering [the prison], and, as we were among the very latest of the arrivals, our detachment was not included in the order. Notwithstanding which, Beach and myself, desirous of seeing as much of the Confederacy as possible, by a little strategy, succeeded in joining the departing column, just as it reached the gates, and though Lieut. Davis discovered the trick, he confined his wrath to a "terrible cussin," ...[37]

Unfortunately, for Davidson and his comrades, the Savannah sojourn would prove to be but a way station on the road to Camp Lawton, which was hurriedly being completed. Some of them would ultimately end up back at Camp Sumter before the war ended.

The transfer of Union POWs to Charleston and Savannah caused a strong reaction among their respective local authorities, as their presence in both cities greatly strained local resources. Both General Lafayette McLaws, commander of the Savannah military district, and General Samuel Jones, commander of the Department of South Carolina, Georgia, and Florida (headquartered in Charleston), remonstrated about the situation, arguing that keeping the prisoners at those sites seriously undercut their resources and degraded their ability to counter any Union offensive actions against their commands. Illness was also a concern. However, both Secretary of War Seddon and Adjutant and Inspector

---

[36] Francis J. Hosmer, *A Glimpse of Andersonville and Other Writings* (Springfield MA: Loring and Axtell, 1896) 42.

[37] Henry Davidson, *Fourteen Months in Southern Prisons* (Milwaukee: Daily Wisconsin Printing House, 1865) 326.

General Cooper informed their subordinates that General Winder had orders to ship the POWs to their locales and, moreover, to expect more, although it was a temporary, emergency action.[38] In the meantime, Seddon and Cooper were anxiously awaiting word that Camp Lawton was completed and ready for occupancy.

In order to see for himself the progress of construction of the new prison, Winder left Camp Sumter and arrived at Camp Lawton on Saturday, 17 September. He telegraphed Cooper the next day that he would probably stay the rest of the week and that he anticipated that he would need to spend most of his time henceforth at the new post. Anticipating that the stockade would be completed within a week, he asked Cooper if he should bring to Camp Lawton the prisoners from Savannah as well as from Andersonville.[39] Apparently, however, the realities of the situation were more revealing as the new week progressed, and three days later he informed Cooper that work on the camp had been "much delayed for want of labor" and that the work "will be brought to a standstill if funds are not furnished."[40] He asked Cooper for $250,000.

Interestingly, even though Camp Lawton was incomplete, Union General Sherman was already aware of its existence. On 22 September, he wrote to both his Confederate counterpart, General John Bell Hood, as well as to the head of the US Sanitary Commission in Saint Louis, Missouri, James E. Yeatman, indicating his knowledge of Union POWs being transported from Camp Sumter "to Savannah, Charleston, and Millen."[41]

A week after he first arrived at Camp Lawton, Winder informed Cooper that he was still there and would "remain and press forward the stockade." He told Cooper that he believed the prison would be ready to

---

[38] Jones to Seddon, 5 September 1864, *Official Records*, series 2, vol. 7, 773; McLaws to Stringfellow (with endorsement by Jones), 8 September 1864, *Official Records*, series 2, vol. 7, 788–89; Cooper to Jones, 5 September 1864, *Official Records*, series 2, vol. 7, 773; and Seddon to Jones, 9 September 1864, *Official Records*, series 2, vol. 7, 795.

[39] Winder to Cooper, 18 September 1864, *Official Records*, series 2, vol. 7, 841.

[40] Winder to Cooper, 21 September 1864, *Official Records*, series 2, vol. 7, 854.

[41] Sherman to Hood, 22 September 1864, *Official Records*, series 2, vol. 7, 857; Sherman to Yeatman, 22 September 1864, *Official Records*, series 2, vol. 7, 858.

receive POWs by "Wednesday next" (8 September), at which point he proposed to move the prisoners from Savannah to the new prison. He also said that he had brought eleven artillery pieces from Camp Sumter and intended to "remove my headquarters to this place."[42] On 26 September, Winder sent Cooper a plan of the stockade and another timetable: "[I]t will be inclosed this week."[43] Construction of the prison did not advance as rapidly as anticipated because on 8 October it was still not completed. Winder had, in the meantime, returned to Camp Sumter to complete the arrangements to move his headquarters to Camp Lawton. As he told Cooper,

> I have the honor to report that the work at Camp Lawton is being pushed forward as fast as the want of transportation will allow…. These delays have obstructed the removal of prisoners. There are now about 2,000 yet to be moved, and about 3,000 to remain, being too sick to travel.
>
> I shall remove to Camp Lawton on Monday, the 10th instant. I shall push things forward as soon as possible.[44]

Other than scattered intermediate reports on the progress of the construction, the official records contain few details of how the camp was built. According to Major Theodore Moreno's account, he oversaw the construction of Camp Lawton. Moreno had been a civil engineer before the war, and after enlisting he was eventually assigned to the Confederate Engineer Corps. In a memoir he wrote after the war, he recalled, "From Columbus I was ordered in haste to build a new stockade for the Yankee prisoners at Camp Lawton, near Millen, Ga."[45] A letter in the Georgia Department of Archives indicates that Washington Daniel and William Warnock were the civilian overseers of the work, but

---

[42] Winder to Cooper, 24 September 1864, *Official Records*, series 2, vol. 7, 869–70.

[43] Winder to Cooper, 26 September 1864, *Official Records*, series 2, vol. 7, 881.

[44] Winder to Cooper, 8 October 1864, *Official Records*, series 2, vol. 7, 955–56.

[45] Theodore Moreno, "A Brief History of My Military Career," *Confederate Reminiscences and Letters, 1861–1865* (Atlanta: Georgia Division, United Daughters of the Confederacy, 2001) 9:87–90. Moreno, descended from an old Hispanic Florida family, was an experienced engineer who also responsible for the construction of fortifications at Camp Sumter, earthworks around Tallahassee, and river defenses downstream from Columbus.

there is no corroboration of this claim.[46] On 8 August, Secretary of War Seddon responded to Winder's request for the power to impress labor to build the new camp, and told Cooper: "If the requisite labor, transportation, materials cannot be obtained on reasonable terms by hire or purchase, impressments must be resorted to. The law then should be carefully observed."[47] However, authorization to impress labor and materials must not have reached Winder in a timely fashion because as late as 13 August, he was repeating his request to Cooper.[48] The 4 June 1924, issue of *The True Citizen* (Waynesboro), contained an article by Julia Garlick ("Reminiscences of Federal Prison at Lawtonville") in which she mentioned the use of slave labor and implied the use of impressment: "Every farmer was supposed to send an able slave to help build the wall, and 500 were engaged in building the Fort."[49] As indicated earlier, a force of 300 Union POWs from Charleston may also have been conscripted to help construct the stockade.

Since there are so few authenticated details of how the camp was built, the researcher has to "reverse engineer" the story from extant remains, study of the site, the example of similar camps, and contemporary descriptions of the prison. The new prison site was similar to that of Camp Sumter in that it was located with nearby railroad access, and the camp would be built in a shallow valley through which ran a stream. The earliest visual depiction of the prison is found in the *Official Records*. It is the map submitted by General Winder to Cooper showing him a plan of the camp.[50] Winder's plan, which depicts no

---

[46] W.R. Crites to Ruth Blair, 15 September 1922, Georgia Department of Archives, cited in Billy Townsend, "Camp Lawton: Magnolia Springs State Park" (Atlanta: Recreation and Programming Section, Parks and Historic Sites Division, Georgia Department of Natural Resources, July 1975) 3.

[47] Seddon to Adjutant General, 8 August 1864, *Official Records*, series 2, vol. 7, 565.

[48] Winder to Cooper, 13 August 1864, *Official Records*, series 2, vol. 7, 589.

[49] Julia Garlick, "Reminiscences of Federal Prison at Lawtonville," *The True Citizen* (Waynesboro), 4 June 1924, 10.

[50] Winder to Cooper, 26 September 1864, *Official Records*, series 2, vol. 7, 881–82. Sneden's representations of Camp Lawton show the stockade as being slightly larger in size—44 acres to 42 acres—and as rectangular rather than square with walls of 1,500 x 2,000 feet. (making a perimeter of 7,000 feet; however, several POW accounts describe the stockade as being nearly square.

ancillary facilities, shows a stockade much like Camp Sumter, only significantly larger and more nearly square in shape. Whereas Camp Sumter's log walls ultimately enclosed an area of 26½ acres, the interior of Camp Lawton contained approximately 42 acres. The stockade was slightly more than a quarter of a mile square, 1,398 feet by 1,329 feet.

According to Winder's plan of the stockade, then, the circuit of the wall was slightly more than one mile in length (5,454 feet). Assuming an average log diameter of 18 inches, it would have taken 3,636 logs to complete the walls, not counting the gate structure. Again, assuming an average log diameter of 18 inches, as well as a log length of 20 feet, the amount of wood used in the construction of the stockade walls would have totaled 1,588,932 board feet of timber. This extraordinary number does not take into account Camp Lawton's considerable ancillary facilities—hospital buildings, administrative structures, quarters—but it does indicate the size of the undertaking.[51] Considering the fact that the prison was built with human and animal labor, its construction was a significant feat in the fall of 1864. It involved the cutting and transportation of timber, digging the latrine ditch, preparing the foundation of the stockade, building brick ovens, constructing defensive earthworks, and building the necessary housing and administrative structures for the camp.

The stream that ran through the center of the camp derived from two sources—a large spring, part of a local artesian spring system that the locals called Magnolia Springs, as well as a branch into which the spring connected. The flow of water was significant, with a quantity and current that both much exceeded Camp Sumter's ironically named Sweetwater Creek. As the stream coursed through the stockade from the direction of the spring, it made an angle of approximately forty-five degrees as it doglegged to the right.

Winder's drawing shows both the spring and this feature, which are visible at the site today, though the spring area is eroded and the stream

---

[51] Calculations based on a chart in Hiram Hallock, Philip Steele, and Richard Selin, "Comparing Lumber Yields from Board-Foot and Cubically Scaled Logs" (Research Paper FPL 324, Forest Products Laboratory, Forest Service, US Department of Agriculture, Madison WI, 1979) 13, http://www.fpl.fs.fed.us/documnts/fplrp/fplrp234.pdf, (accessed 7 November 2010).

was modified during the CCC era so that it is considerably wider today than it was during the Civil War. The ground rose on either side of the flat bottom through which the stream flowed. The low ridges on each side were from 200 to 220 feet above sea level, while the streambed was fifty to sixty feet lower. Sneden reported that the stream was "about twelve feet wide and in some places four feet deep."[52]

Given the measurements and geographic reference points on Winder's map, it is not difficult to establish the general location of the stockade on a modern map. Billy Townsend, of the Georgia Historic Preservation Division, did just that in his 1975 report on Camp Lawton.[53] He took Winder's plan, adjusted the scale and superimposed it on a 1940 map of Magnolia Springs State Park. Although only archaeology can determine the precise location of the camp's features, Townsend's helpful exercise provides a reasonably close approximation of the stockade's placement.

Also, according to Winder's map and its legend, the lower half of the stream was dammed at the dogleg, and the water was turned into an artificial channel that had been dug for sinks. This channel was "planked and sides boarded up," thus creating a sluice effect that washed the sewage downstream.[54] An entry in John Wool Bartleson's (81st Illinois) diary provided a more detailed description of the sluice: "... [B]ut this spring branch was boarded up with a wooden bottom and rail and made sanitary, and adequate for carrying away filth."[55] Therefore, the upper part of the stream was set aside for drinking, washing, and bathing; that

---

[52] Sneden, *Eye of the Storm*, 261.

[53] Townsend, "Camp Lawton," 27.

[54] John L. Ransom, *Andersonville Diary: Escape, and List of Dead with Name, Company, Regiment, Date of Death and Number of Grave in Cemetery* (Philadelphia: Douglas Brothers, 1883) 164. Several modern authorities have questioned Ransom's veracity. Although he was a POW, the issues are whether there was a diary or not and how much imagination was used to construct his narrative. Therefore, one should probably use him only when corroborated by other sources. See, for example, William Marvel, "Johnny Ransom's Imagination," *Civil War History* 39 (September 1995): 181–89.; Ann Fabian, *The Unvarnished Truth: Personal Narratives in Nineteenth Century America* (Berkeley: University of California Press, 2002) 121–22; and Gerald Cole, *Civil War Eyewitnesses: An Annotated Bibliography of Books and Articles 1986–1996* (Columbia: University of South Carolina Press, 2000) 78.

[55] Marvin V. Leyman, *Bartlesons of Grand Chain* (Tulsa OK: True Image Printing, 1995) 133.

water then flushed through the ditch that served as a camp latrine. Today, there is an artificial channel at this very site. It may very likely be the remains of the latrine ditch. Interestingly, none of Sneden's drawings show a separate latrine ditch.

Another feature visible on Winder's plan is a "deadline." The deadline was a device used in many prisons, North and South, to keep prisoners away from the walls. According to Winder's plan, the deadline at Camp Lawton was marked thirty feet inside the stockade walls. At Camp Sumter the deadline was a low fence constructed of posts across which lay pine scantlings. This feature is visible in the famous photographs taken of the camp in August of 1864 by Andrew Jackson Riddle.[56] We may assume that the deadline at Camp Lawton was similarly constructed, although not all of the known contemporary illustrations of the interior of Camp Lawton show it as a fence. For example, the illustration of the camp that was published in the 28 January 1865, issue of *Frank Leslie's Illustrated Newspaper* shows the deadline as a narrow ditch *inside* the perimeter of the wall across which at regular intervals were placed square flat platforms upon which stood armed guards.[57] However, one contemporary observer, Brigadier General John H. Geary, one of Sherman's generals who visited Camp Lawton after it had been evacuated in the face of the Federal advance toward Millen, described the deadline, running thirty feet from the inside of the stockade walls as depicted in Winder's plan, as "a fence of light scantling, supported on short posts."[58] Since Camp Sumter, having a deadline comprised of a low fence made of pine scantlings, was the model for Camp Lawton, and since the depiction in *Frank Leslie's Illustrated Newspaper* is unlikely, given the fact that armed guards could police the deadline from their "pigeon roosts" along the outside of the

---

[56] Ovid Futch, *History of Andersonville Prison* (Gainesville: University of Florida Press, 1968) 66–67; see William Marvel, *Andersonville: The Last Depot* (Chapel Hill: University of North Carolina Press, 1994) 182–87, for a detailed account of photographer Riddle's visit to Camp Sumter.

[57] "Sherman's Campaign—the Prison Pen at Millen," *Frank Leslie's Illustrated Newspaper*, vol. 19, no. 2.

[58] Geary, 6 January 1865, *Official Records*, series 1, vol. 44, 274; Geary commanded the Second Division, Twentieth Corps.

stockade wall, we can assume that Geary's description is correct. This is supported by Sneden's drawings of Camp Lawton showing a deadline much like the one at Camp Sumter.[59]

In addition, Winder's map shows a "gatehouse" along the center of one of the prison's walls. It was thirty feet square and projected out from the prison wall. The size of the gatehouse allowed the movement of wagons and units of prisoners in and out of the prison in a secure manner. One entered the prison via the gatehouse with the opening of the outer gate, which was then closed. Then the inner gate would be opened, and one could enter within the prison compound itself. The reverse procedure was used to exit the prison. This also was similar to the design that was used at Camp Sumter, although that camp had two such gates.[60]

Winder's map also shows a grid of streets within the camp running at right angles to one another. The streets were to range from fourteen to twenty feet in width and divide the interior of the camp into thirty-two "divisions," each of which could contain as many as 1,000 or even 1,250 federal POWs. Each division was to measure 315 by 140 feet and contain ten subdivisions that measured sixty-three by twenty feet each. The stream, of course, cut through the center of the camp, interrupting the regularity of this plan. One should consider Winder's plan as a drawing of what was intended, not as representative in every detail of that which was ultimately built. For instance, contemporary drawings and prisoners' accounts show the interior of the stockade as not so neatly organized, with the POWs' huts clustered across the stream to the northwest and the "streets" running in an irregular pattern. The stream was bridged, and a sutler's cabin "about 12 x 20 feet" in size was located near it on the northern bank of the stream.[61]

---

[59] Sneden, *Images of the Storm*, 224 and 228, shows six ovens; on page 269, he shows five. Sneden, *Eye of the Storm*, 269 shows five.

[60] Futch, *Andersonville*, 5, 66.

[61] Sneden, Diary, VHS, vol. 6, 113. During the Civil War a "sutler" was a purveyor of goods for soldiers. They could be found traveling with the troops, selling goods in encampments, and sometimes operating in prisons. According to Sneden, the sutler closed up shop on 10 November because few POWs had any money.

Camp Lawton was located in a pine forest; therefore, the stockade walls were constructed of locally harvested pine logs. The logs were placed vertically, side by side, and planted in a trench. John McElroy (16th Illinois Cavalry), who spent time as a POW in both Camp Sumter and Camp Lawton, wrote that the "principle difference was that the upright logs were in their rough state [at Camp Lawton], whereas they were hewed at Andersonville ..."[62] One account indicates that the walls were made secure "by iron bolts all around the enclosure," and it would have made sense to strengthen the log walls through the use of such bracing.[63] To date, no such archaeological evidence has surfaced. Contemporary illustrations of the camp also show the tops of the logs sharpened to a rough point. Some drawings of the prison show the walls as constructed of unhewn logs; others show the logs as hewn. Most written descriptions of the stockade, including McElroy's comments, indicate that the walls were made of unhewn logs. Given the haste of construction, this was probably the case. Interestingly, Townsend reports that during dragline operations in the lake below the spring some years ago two large timbers were pulled from the water. Located 1,400 feet from the center of the mouth of the spring, one of the timbers was "hewn rectangular with a flat pointed end."[64] If these timbers were contemporary with the prison, they may have been parts of the stockade wall, timbers from the bridge that crossed the stream within the stockade or timbers that lined the latrine ditches.

To allow guards to keep an eye on the inmates of the prison, sentry boxes or guard shacks were placed at regular intervals along the outside of each wall. These guard stations, sometimes called "pigeon roosts," were placed along the tops of the wall so that guards could look into the camp. Chaplain George S. Bradley (22nd Wisconsin) described the pigeon roosts when he visited the prison as his unit camped nearby on 3 December: "Around this log enclosure, were forty sentry boxes, entered

---

[62] John McElroy, *Andersonville: A Story of Rebel Military Prisons, Fifteen Months a Guest of the So-called Confederacy. A Private Soldier's Experience in Richmond, Andersonville, Savannah, Millen, Blackshear and Florence* (Toledo OH: D.R. Locke, 1879) 455.

[63] Julia Garlick, "Reminiscences of Federal Prison at Lawtonville," *The True Citizen* (Waynesboro), 7 June 1924, 1.

[64] Townsend, "Camp Lawton," 29.

from the outside by means of ladders."[65] Bradley actually climbed up into one of the sentry posts and surveyed the scene from that vantage point. He also noted that the POWs' huts were located on the northwest side of the stream. General Geary estimated the height of the stockade wall as "from twelve to fifteen feet above the ground."[66]

The similarity of the new prison to Camp Sumter caused POW John McElroy's friend Andrews to exclaim as they entered the new prison, "My God, Mc, this looks like Andersonville all over again."[67] Indeed, as one examines Winder's plan, it is obvious that Camp Lawton was designed with Camp Sumter in mind, both to replicate those things that had worked and to correct those that had gone wrong. The size of the new camp was designed to prevent the terrible overcrowding that was a feature of Camp Sumter. In fact, Winder estimated the new prison had the capacity to hold 32,000 (at 1,000 per division) or even as many as 40,000 POWs (at 1,250 per division).[68] Also, the water supply was far superior to that of Camp Sumter, and the channeling of the water once it entered the stockade was well thought out. In other words, Winder believed that he had built the prison that Camp Sumter should have been. Of course, given the purpose and available resources, the stockade design made the most sense. Fortunately, however, the stockade was never filled to Winder's estimate of its capacity, and this fact probably accounts for the more favorable POW comments about conditions at Camp Lawton.

Plans were made for building brick ovens within the stockade for the prisoners' use, but transportation problems prevented their timely completion. In a progress report on the camp's construction to Adjutant General Cooper on 8 October, General Winder complained about the situation:

> The work is and has been inclosed [sic] for the last week and ready to receive prisoners, but the baking and cooking arrangements have not yet

---

[65] George S. Bradley, *The Star Corps or Notes of an Army Chaplain During Sherman's Famous "March to the Sea"* (Milwaukee WI: Jermain & Brightman, 1865) 203.

[66] Geary, *Official Records*, series 1, vol. 44, 274.

[67] McElroy, *Andersonville: A Story of Rebel Military Prisons*, 453.

[68] Winder to Cooper, 26 September 1864, *Official Records*, series 2, vol. 7, 881–82.

been completed, as I stated, for want of transportation. At Macon three cars were being loaded with brick for Camp Lawton when the railroad company had them unloaded, and the cars turned over, as I understand, to cotton speculators to transport cotton. If the transportation is furnished, the arrangements will soon be made.[69]

The ovens were eventually completed because the previously cited *Harper's Weekly* and *Frank Leslie's Illustrated Newspaper* illustrations as well as the Sneden drawings show them on the northwest side of the stream where the prisoners' huts were located. Also, several POW accounts mention the brick ovens. As bricks were brought in to construct the ovens, POWs tried to pilfer them for use in their huts. Sneden indicated in his journal that when moved across the stream on 20 October, they were still being built:

> The foundation for several brick ovens had been started in the camp for our use, and as fast as the bricks were dumped for their completion, they would be appropriated by the prisoners at night for making side walls to their shanties, so a guard composed of the camp police had to be set over the brick piles, and the stocks, and buck and gag, [were] the penalty for using them.[70]

Archaeological confirmation of both the brick ovens and POW pilferage was found during the spring 2010 excavations. Historic brick was found in situ with mortar fragments, and bricks were discovered in at least one shebang site.

When completed, the ovens were equipped with kettles for boiling. Sneden's drawings of the ovens vary. In several versions he shows six ovens in the stockade; in another he shows five.[71] However, in his diary he stated that, "ten ovens have been built" and gave their measurements as "about 10 x 6 feet" with 20 foot high chimneys.[72] His illustrations also

---

[69] Winder to Cooper, 8 October 1864, *Official Records*, series 2, vol. 7, 955.

[70] Sneden, *Images from the Storm*, 226, and *Eye of the Storm*, 261. Recent archaeological investigations have found evidence of just this use of bricks by POWs in their shebangs.

[71] Two illustrations (p. 224 and 228) show six ovens, and one illustration (p. 226) shows five (Sneden, *Images from the Storm*). One illustration (p. 269) in *Eye of the Storm* also shows six ovens.

[72] Sneden, Diary, VHS, vol. 6, 116. The chimney height also represents good design in that the smoke would be carried over the stockade walls.

vary in the details of the ovens themselves. Depending on the drawing, he shows the kettles located on opposite sides of a central oven or positioned on one side of the oven.[73] A contemporary newspaper account in a Northern newspaper, derived from a correspondent who saw the camp while he was with Sherman's forces, describes the latter configuration for the kettles.[74] Chaplain Bradley also reported, "Through the middle of this mass of huts, was a row of bake ovens, each having two good sized arch kettles set for heating water."[75]

Ancillary facilities were constructed outside the stockade. These facilities included fortifications, log huts for the guards and quarters for their officers, log hospital buildings for the guards, a tent hospital for the prisoners, and administrative buildings. Except for the fortifications, the only visual record of these support facilities that exists is found in Sneden's drawings. According to him, the two hospital areas were located downstream from the stockade on the southern bank of the stream.[76] Inmate Henry Davidson (Battery A, 1st Ohio Volunteer Light Artillery) also remembered an area set aside for the sick inside the stockade:

> A hospital for receiving the sick was established in the southwest corner of the area, but no shelter was provided, no blankets given to those who occupied it, and medicines were not used there. The only advantage to the sick man, in this arrangement, was that he would be certain to be found by the surgeons, who were examining with reference to the special exchange [an exchange of invalid POWs arranged in early November 1864]. From this hospital, those who were deemed unfit to stay in the

---

[73] Ibid., 227.

[74] See, for example, "Our Grand March," 149th Regiment, New York Volunteer Infantry, Civil War Newspaper Clippings," http://www.dmna.stae.ny.us/historic/reghist/civil/infantry/149thInfCWN.htm (accessed 7 August 2008).

[75] Bradley, *The Star Corps*, 203; Sergeant Henry W. Tisdale reported in his 17 October 1864 diary entry that there were "ten brick ovens, and ten large iron kettles ... set in position on the west side ..." "Civil War Diary of Sergeant Henry W. Tisdale, Co. I, Thirty-fifth Massachusetts Volunteers, 1862–1865," transcript. Margaret Tisdale, 1926, http://www.civilwardiary.net/ (accessed 3 June 2010).

[76] Sneden, Diary, VHS, vol. 6, 149. Sneden described the "rebel hospital" as comprising "20 or more log cabins more or less filled with sick." Having the hospitals located downstream from the prison was a design flaw.

stockade were transferred to a hospital outside the pen, where they remained, until forwarded to the exchange point.[77]

The guards' camp was on the ridge near the large fort that overlooked the stockade from the south. Administrative buildings— General Winder's office, Quartermaster Captain Richard Winder's office, Prison Commandant Captain D.W. Vowles's headquarters, Guard Commander Col. Henry Forno's headquarters, and Chief Surgeon Isaiah White's office—were located along the ridge to the east of the large fort.[78] A pentagonal earthen fort, whose impressive remains can be seen today, overlooked the stockade from the ridge to the south. It was constructed by digging a ditch around the intended perimeter of the fortification, then using the extracted dirt to make a wall on the inside of the ditch. Artillery ramps stood at the corners of the fort, which would indicate placements for five guns. These were mounted in the fort and perhaps commanded by Captain Charles E. Dyke. The tops of the walls may have been surmounted with head logs and the gun ports may have been framed and floored with timbers as was typical of Civil War practice, but contemporary illustrations of the earthworks do not allow firm conclusions to be drawn. Winder initially had eleven guns of Dyke's Florida Light Artillery sent to Camp Lawton.[79] Where the other six guns were placed is not clear, although some accounts mention two other earthen fortifications on the site, the remains of at least one of which is visible.

Sneden's drawings of Camp Lawton show seven guns mounted in the fort; however, his drawings of the fort do not agree in all particulars with the remains on the site.[80] For example, Sneden depicts the fort as irregularly shaped with an entrance facing away from the stockade, while the extant remains are, as previously mentioned, pentagonal in configuration with an entrance (or sally port) facing the stockade. Nor do Sneden's drawings of the camp show any other major fortifications than

---

[77] Davidson, *Fourteen Months in Southern Prisons*, 332.

[78] Sneden, *Eye of the Storm*, 269; Davidson (*Fourteen Months in Southern Prisons*, 328) mentions eight artillery pieces. Sneden, Diary, VHS, vol. 6, 112, described Winder's headquarters as occupying "a yellow frame house."

[79] Winder to Cooper, 24 September 1864, *Official Records*, series 2, vol. 7, 869.

[80] Sneden, *Eye of the Storm*, 269.

the earthen fort, yet the remains of one and possibly two other earthworks exist on the site. (See Appendix.) The fort would have contained a magazine, and Sneden's illustrations show one. In addition, he depicts at least two log buildings within the fort. Beyond the walls of the fort, the area was cleared for open fields of fire. According to Sneden's paintings, trees near the fort were felled away from it to create an abbattis, a pre-barbed wire defensive device that created defensive entanglements by facing a potential attacker with tree branches and brush. In addition, rifle pits (trenches) were dug along the ridge. When one walks around the area outside of the earthen fort today, faint depressions can be seen that may or may not be the impressions left of the rifle pits. The result was a rather formidable barrier to an attacking force. Sitting as it did on top of the ridge overlooking the stockade, the fort also provided a vantage point from which the guards could easily see into it, particularly the far side of the stockade across the stream where the POWs were located. This location would also allow artillery to sweep along the interior walls if necessary. The fort also commanded the gatehouse leading into the stockade.

Approximately one hundred yards to the southwest of the fort and facing south, the Confederates constructed a redan to protect the fort from an assault from the rear. The remains of this outerwork are still visible and quite impressive. Perhaps one or more of the other artillery pieces were mounted in the redan. The Townsend report also mentions the remains of a third earthwork across US 25 southwest of the stockade location.[81] Indeed, the remains of what appear to be an earthwork, although badly damaged, can be seen from the highway. This fortification would be in the general area of the Confederate hospital and some quarters as shown on the Sneden drawings.[82] Additionally, Sneden mentioned "another smaller fort ... in our rear, but no artillery in it."[83] By

---

[81] Townsend, "Camp Lawton," 7.

[82] Sneden, *Eye of the Storm*, 269.

[83] Sneden, Diary, VHS, vol. 6, 114. Existing surveys of the area to the north of the prison site have not revealed evidence of the smaller fort. However, Highway 25 was built across the prison site, and it may well have obliterated any such evidence. It is also possible a survey of the privately held property near the park may uncover remnants of the earthwork.

"rear" one can assume that he meant on the opposite side of the stockade from the gate that would be to the north. This fortification system served two purposes—as a deterrent to a mass POW escape attempt and as a defense against attempted raids on the camp.

Camp Lawton had telegraphic communication with the outside world. Millen had a telegraph office that connected with the Savannah, Macon, and Augusta offices. The lines ran along the railroad beds, and a telegraph line was patched into the camp from the railroad that ran from Millen to Augusta.[84] Thus, Winder at his headquarters at Camp Lawton—and he was initially in charge of all Confederate prisons in Georgia and Alabama before ultimately becoming commissary-general of all Confederate prisons east of the Mississippi River—could communicate rapidly with both those who were responsible to him as well as those to whom he was responsible, as long as the lines were not broken.

Beyond the wartime destruction, environmental and human modifications of the Magnolia Springs area since the Camp Lawton period have hidden, obscured, or destroyed many original features of the prison and its support facilities. For example, during the construction of the state park by the CCC in the 1930s, the stream was dammed, parts of the valley floor may have been graded, and a number of new structures were erected. Ultimately, many of the specifics will remain elusive until a comprehensive archaeological survey of the site is conducted. Until then, one of the best overall descriptions of the prison is one found in the memoirs of Lucius D. Barber (Company D, 15th Illinois):

> Our camp here is much more pleasant that it was at Andersonville or
> Sumter. It consists of an inclosure of about forty acres, surrounded by a

---

[84] Evidence for a telegraph operation at Camp Lawton is found in a dispatch from Winder to Cooper, 25 November 1864, *Official Records*, series 2, vol. 7, 1160, in which Winder mentions, as the camp is evacuated, that his telegraph operator will be leaving for his new post with his battery. The telegraph office in Millen is mentioned in the *Daily Chronicle and Sentinel* (Augusta), 25 November 1864, 1, as well as in several accounts by Sherman's soldiers. See, for example, Charles J. Brockman, Jr., "The John Van Duser Diary of Sherman's March from Atlanta to Hilton Head," *Georgia Historical Quarterly* 53 (1969): 220–39.

single line of stockades. A splendid stream of pure water runs through the center. The ground is well adapted for a camp. It slopes gently from the east and west toward the stream. Below, at one side of the stockade, is a privy built over the stream, and all filth is thus carried away. At the upper portion of the stream we get water for cooking purposes, and a little below we do our washing. There are at present nine thousand prisoners here, all camped on the west side of the stream.[85]

---

[85] Lucius W. Barber, *Army Memoirs of Lucius W. Barber, Company "D," 15th Illinois Volunteer Infantry. May 24, 1861, to Sept. 30, 1865* (Chicago: J.M.W. Jones Stationery and Printing Co., 1894) 177–78. The camp was not built on a north-south axis, rather on a northwest-southeast axis. Therefore, some accounts speak of the north side of the stream, while others describe it as the west side of the stream. Sgt. Thomas Hyatt (118th Pennsylvania) also praised the prison grounds, especially when compared to Camp Sumter. See Survivors' Association, *History of the 118th Pennsylvania Volunteers, Corn Exchange Regiment, from Their First Engagement at Antietam to Appomattox* (Philadelphia: J.L. Smith, 1905) 630.

4

The Reality:
Life's Necessities at Camp Lawton

What we know about how Camp Lawton operated during its brief existence comes mainly from two sources. The first source is the very limited number of surviving official records relating to the prison, deriving mainly from Confederate correspondence, and the second source stems from the accounts of POWs who were incarcerated there and those of Union soldiers who marched past it.[1] Besides the body of published POW accounts mentioning Camp Lawton, the research for this book has unearthed several unpublished accounts by inmates of the prison. In addition, several unpublished diaries by Sherman's soldiers who saw the camp during the March to the Sea exist and throw new light on its history. Moreover, since the Winders, Forno, Vowles, and White had come from Camp Sumter, one can infer that in an operational sense things were similar at Camp Lawton. Therefore, any history of the prison must necessarily be a synthesis of these sources.

But these sources fit into a broader context, as well. The Civil War holds an unending fascination for the reading public, with the result that

---

[1] The materials in the *Official Records* and the National Archives are fragmentary. Much of what remains are communications between General Winder and Richmond officials, a large portion of that dealing with administrative matters deriving from Winder's position as head of the military prisons east of the Mississippi River. Written records relating specifically to Camp Lawton from Vowles, Forno, White, and the "lesser" Winders are almost non-existent and, of course, oral directives did not survive. Letters and memoirs by prison guards and administrative sub-alterns are lacking. For most on the Confederate side, service at Camp Lawton was a brief episode in their Civil War careers and, given the public outcry in the North following the war and the demands for punishment of those involved in the prisons, was not something with which to "pad one's resume" in the postwar period. Therefore, the bulk of what is known about the day-to-day activities at Camp Lawton derives from the POW accounts written by those who did have a reason to remember and to publicize their experiences there. See Arch Frederic Blakey, *General John H. Winder, C.S.A.* (Gainesville: University of Florida Press, 1990) 206.

it is the most written-about period in American history. From its beginning the conflict spawned a huge literature, one of the most popular genres of which was the POW narrative. Civil War soldiers were great letter and journal writers and that fact, plus the intrinsically fascinating subject of the war, as well as the enormous volume of records generated by the respective governments, provided ample materials for books and articles on the subject. Well before the war ended, prison narratives were appearing, first in newspapers and journals of the day and then in books rushed to print to meet the demands of an eager public. Civil War prison historian William Best Hesseltine estimated, for example, that "[d]uring the years 1862–66 fifty-four books and articles were published giving the experiences of prisoners in the South", and the stream of publications on this subject has continued to flow to this day.[2] Previously unknown materials relating to Civil War prisons occasionally surface in unexpected places despite generations of scholars who have assiduously searched for them, and the case of Camp Lawton is no different. The Sneden collection is a case in point. Although there are examples of Confederate POW accounts, the vast majority of Civil War POW narratives were written by Union veterans of Southern prison camps.[3] The large Northern reading public was both fascinated and outraged by the stories they read. Moreover, the depictions of horrible conditions and brutal treatment in these accounts seemed to confirm the Northern public's beliefs about Confederate military prisons and the moral superiority of the Union cause. Many expected the horror stories and would accept nothing less. These early accounts contributed to the superheated atmosphere surrounding the trial, conviction, and execution of Major Henry Wirz, Confederate commandant of the stockade at Camp Sumter, and the call for punishment of others responsible for the conditions in the Southern prisons.

Typically, the Civil War POW narrative summarized the subject's military service up to the time of capture, then detailed his experiences in journal form to the time of release or escape. Although Andersonville

---

[2] William Best Hesseltine, *Civil War Prisons: A Study in War Psychology* (New York: Frederick Ungar Publishing, 1964) 247–48.

[3] Ibid., 256.

is featured prominently in many of the POW narratives, stories related to Camp Lawton and other Confederate prisons are common as well. Many Union POWs, particularly late in the war, were transferred from camp to camp in an effort to keep them from falling into the hands of advancing Union forces. Therefore, POW narratives often include mention of several camps.

As with all source material one has to approach each account with critical judgment and evaluate each on its own merits. Hesseltine reminds us that Civil War POW accounts were not written in a vacuum. The motivations of their authors varied. Some simply wanted to take advantage of the economic opportunity opened by the intense public interest in the POW experience. Others wrote, in part, to support the efforts at the end of the war to ensure the punishment of those responsible for conditions in Confederate prisons, the Wirz trial being a case in point. Still others recounted their trials to foster efforts by groups such as the "National Union Ex-Prisoners of War Association" and the "Andersonville Survivors Association" to raise money for memorials and to secure government pensions and settlements for ex-POWs. Of course, some who wrote these kinds of memoirs simply did so as old men sharing the travails of their youth with their readers. Further, Hesseltine implies that their "uniformity of testimony" should in itself make us wary and points out that some of it derives from significant instances of borrowing among the POW accounts.[4]

With these considerations in mind, then, what do the sources tell us about life at Camp Lawton? One thing is for certain; the first prisoners to enter the stockade were not "fresh fish." This was the moniker given by Civil War POWs to prisoners who had just been captured and were

---

[4] Ibid., 250–54. The National Association of Union Ex-Prisoners of War held reunions, and members could purchase and often wore ribbons and devices that represented the organization. If a former POW had been incarcerated in more than one Confederate prison, he could place a name bar for each prison on a ribbon worn on his clothing. The device that symbolized the organization included the image of a stylized stockade within which was a POW being attacked by a dog. The perimeter of the device featured a series of sharpened stakes illustrating the top of a stockade wall. At each corner was an artillery piece aimed at the interior of the stockade. On the bottom edge of the device was a terse aphorism— "Death Before Dishonor."

entering the prison system for the first time. Rather, the initial Camp Lawton inmates were in prison parlance "dry cod," "salt fish," "pickled sardines," or "suckers"; that is, veterans of the prisons camps. Most had been in Camp Sumter; many had been held temporarily at Savannah (Camp Davidson); all had been shuttled around on the railroads. Sergeant James H. Dennison's odyssey as a Union POW was typical of those of many of his fellow prisoners. A member of Company K, 113th Illinois, he found himself at Camp Sumter within nine days of his capture following the Union reverse at Brice's Crossroads (10 June 1864). He remained there through that terrible summer from 19 June until 29 September, when he was transported to the stockade in Savannah. On 12 October, he again rode the rails to Camp Lawton where he was to stay until 21 November.[5]

Whatever their status, all POWs desperately hoped that the exchange system would be resumed before they might be "paroled" (shot dead by prison guards) or die of disease.[6] On arrival they were usually off-loaded on the railroad tracks east of the camp and marched under guard through the pine woods to the stockade. However, at least two diary accounts tell of being taken to the camp in wagons from the railroad.[7] Once at the prison gate, they were processed prior to being admitted to the stockade. They were counted; their names (and regiment,

---

[5] James H. Dennison, *Dennison's Andersonville Diary: The Diary of an Illinois Soldier in the Infamous Andersonville Prison Camp*, notes and transcript. Jack Klasey (Kankakee IL: Kankakee County Historical Society, 1987) 10.

[6] Lonnie R. Speer, *Portals to Hell: Military Prisons of the Civil War* (Mechanicsburg, PA: Stockpole Books, 1997) 315, 317. Speer's book has a glossary ("The Language of the Prison Camps," 313–22) containing numerous slang terms and their definitions that one often comes across in prison memoirs.

[7] John L. Ransom, *Andersonville Diary: Escape, and List of Dead with Name, Company, Regiment, Date of Death and Number of Grave in Cemetery* (Philadelphia: Douglas Brothers, 1883) 163; Anonymous, *A Voice from Rebel Prisons Giving an Account of Some of the Horrors of the Stockades at Andersonville, Milan and Other Prisons by a Returned Prisoner of War* (Boston: Rand & Avery, 1865) 14. Robert Knox Sneden (*Eye of the Storm: A Civil War Odyssey*, ed. Charles F. Bryan, Jr., and Nelson D. Lankford [New York: The Free Press, 2000] 260) remembered that, upon reaching the prison, his group was led through the gate into the stockade but had to spend the first night on the south side of the stream. The next day he and his comrades were allowed to cross over the stream to the POW encampment on the north side.

company, and state) were recorded; and they were organized into "hundreds" and "divisions." A division was composed of ten hundreds, and sergeants were appointed over each.[8] When Sergeant Dennison arrived at Camp Lawton, he and his fellow POWs spent the first night bivouacked outside the stockade. The next morning, as he described the process, "we are counted of[f] and are waiting to go in to our new home well it is a good place for a camp there is plenty of wood and water."[9]

Mentally and physically the POWs who found themselves in the newly constructed camp in the piney woods north of Millen were not in very good condition. Furthermore, the reality of Civil War prisons on both sides was that their very nature increased the chances of illness and death for inmates. The fact that more Civil War soldiers' deaths were caused by disease rather than combat is well known. When troops first congregated in training camps during the initial stages of the war, the death rate rose. The raising of armies on both sides brought together individuals and groups from widely separated geographical regions with varying histories of exposure to diseases. The addition of sanitation problems caused by the massive concentrations of troops made a recipe for the rapid spread of contagious ailments among the troops.[10] When troops were encamped for any extended period during the war (such as

---

[8] Lessel Long, *Twelve Months in Andersonville: On the March—In the Battle—In the Rebel Prison Pens, and at Last in God's Country* (Huntington IN: Thad and Mark Butler, 1886) 85. Lucius W. Barber (*Army Memoirs of Lucius W. Barber, Company "D," 15th Illinois Volunteer Infantry. May 24, 1861, to Sept. 30, 1865* [Chicago: J.M.W. Jones Stationery and Printing Co., 1894] 178), presents a more detailed, slightly different picture. According to him, the POWs were divided into divisions (1,000 men each), detachments (250 men each), messes (two of 100 each and one of 50 each), and then subdivided into smaller groups depending on the wishes of the prisoners. A Confederate sergeant was in charge of each division, while the detachments, messes, etc., were in the charge of Union NCOs.

[9] Dennison, *Andersonville Diary*, 74. Private George A. Hitchcock (21st Massachusetts) also remembered arriving at Camp Lawton in the evening and being bivouacked outside the stockade until the next morning. George A. Hitchcock, *From Ashby to Andersonville: The Civil War Diary and Reminiscences of George A. Hitchcock, Private, Company A, 21st Massachusetts Regiment, August 1862–January 1865*, ed. Ronald Watson (Campbell CA: Savas Publishing, 1997) 266.

[10] Alfred Jay Bollet, MD, *Civil War Medicine—Challenges and Triumphs* (Tucson AZ: Galen Press, 2002) has two chapters of pertinent material related to the impact of recruitment and imprisonment on the health of soldiers. See Chapter 10 ("Epidemic Diseases in Recruits") and Chapter 15 ("Prison Camps: the Most Appalling Story").

winter quarters, for example), the death rate increased. Poor hygiene and sanitation, plus the lack of understanding of disease processes and vectors, made Civil War encampments dangerous. Civil War prisons typically exacerbated these kinds of conditions by crowding POWs into limited confines and failing to provide adequate housing, food, sanitation, and medical services. The results included problems related to exposure, scurvy, chronic dysentery, diarrhea, gangrenous wounds, and contagious diseases. Vermin was omnipresent in the camps, even more so than in the field. Ezra Hoyt Ripple, a member of the 52nd Pennsylvania who was captured on 3 July 1864, in a failed assault on Fort Johnson on James Island in Charleston harbor, recounted a "skirmish" between vermin types:

> We came into Charleston from the sand hills of Morris Island full of fleas, but the first night in prison was the last we saw of them. The lice attacked them in overwhelming numbers, drove them off, and took possession of our bodies. From a very intimate and prolonged acquaintance with these plagues I much prefer the active, sprightly, vivacious though wicked flea.
>
> The other fellow is not so active or graceful in his movements but he is more persistent in his attacks and he gets there just the same, and if anything more so.[11]

POWs constantly combated lice, and even camp visitors could find themselves infested after a visit. Father William John Hamilton, one of the Catholic priests who ministered to prisoners at Camp Sumter and Camp Oglethorpe, had "to cleanse himself of vermin in his basement before he could enter his house."[12]

Another factor in understanding the mortality rate in Civil War prisons derives from the circumstances of the moment of capture. It was a traumatic event. Soldiers hoped to be victorious, but if defeated, they expected to remain with their unit as they withdrew. Capture by the

---

[11] Ezra Hoyt Ripple, *Dancing Along the Deadline: The Andersonville Memoir of a Prisoner of the Confederacy*, ed. Mark A. Snell (Novato CA: Presidio Press, 1996) 11–12.

[12] Robert Scott Davis, *Ghosts and Shadows of Andersonville: Essays on the Secret Social Histories of America's Deadliest Prison* (Macon GA: Mercer University Press, 2006) 132.

enemy was dreaded because, unless one's unit was captured en masse, it involved separation from comrades as well as possible abuse, the uncertainty of knowing what was going to happen, loss of control, and a sense of defeat and helplessness. The psychology of capture, therefore, involved shock that could lead to despair. But capture could involve physical injury, as well. Many soldiers became prisoners because they were wounded and could not escape. Thus, the combination of the psychological shock of capture, sometimes accompanied by physical trauma, and the subsequent poor conditions to which POWs on both sides were exposed, predisposed prisoners to illness and death. Of course, individuals were affected differently. Some were resilient psychologically and/or physically; some were not. Some POWs consciously developed strategies to ensure their best chance of survival. For example, George Shearer (17th Iowa) wrote in his diary while at Camp Lawton, "I find it necessary for one to keep up and be a prisoner to keep in good spirits—keep clean and exercise as much as possible—never give way to your fate."[13] Comradeship was a factor that statistically had a positive impact on a POW's survival in the camps.[14]

---

[13] Transcript of 17 November 1864, diary entry of George M. Shearer, provided digitally by the University of Iowa Libraries Special Collections Department, www.lib.uiowa.edu/spec-col/MSC/ToMSC100/MsC80/MsCo80_shearergeorgemarion.html (accessed 24 September 2008.

[14] Dora L. Costa, and Matthew E. Kahn, *Heroes & Cowards: The Social Face of War* (Princeton NJ: Princeton University Press, 2008). Chapter five, pages 120–59, focuses on the Civil War prison experience and analyzes a POW database of 2,972 men and 3,026 cases of captivity. Although disease, especially the triple diseases of scurvy, diarrhea, and dysentery, accounted for the greatest portion of Civil War POW deaths, Costa and Kahn have introduced intriguing new research on other factors relating to survivability in Confederate prison camps. Based on a POW subset of an extensive longitudinal database of 41,000 Federal POWs (35,000 whites and 6,000 blacks) and using multivariate statistical analytical techniques (A multivariate statistical analysis allows all other factors to be held constant while varying one explanatory factor at a time.), Costa and Kahn have identified a number of social factors—age, rank, possession of useful skills, and the degree of camp overcrowding—that correlate positively with POW rates of survival. Moreover, keeping each of those factors constant, they found that comradeship within the camps (which they refer to as social networks) "increased a soldier's survival possibility." The components of comradeship—acquaintance, friendship, family relationship, unit membership, race/ethnicity, and occupation—were all significant. Additionally, Costa and Kahn

Sergeant Daniel G. Kelley (Company K, 24th New York Cavalry) found out its importance while at Camp Lawton. He had a terrible case of scurvy, had lost the use of his legs, and had several large, running sores on his limbs:

> I was almost dead, and undoubtedly should have died, had it not been for the kindness of one of my comrades, Corporal George Riber, of Company C, 2d Regiment N.Y. Mounted Rifles, who drew our rations together, prepared them together, and during the three weeks that I was not able to leave our tent, took care of me with all the tenderness of a father or brother. God bless my faithful comrade; may he live a hundred years, and every day of his life be happy.[15]

Thaddeus L. Waters (Company G, 2nd Michigan Cavalry) also commented on the benefits of friendship in the prisons. He remembered watching as a new group came into Camp Lawton, "… and among them Charles Garnier, the Chicago Frenchman who had helped carry me out of the stockade at Andersonville to die. He was, as he expressed it, 'glad very much' to see me, and we chummed together till the latter part of the winter when he was sent to Vicksburg."[16]

The POWs who entered Camp Lawton came from several sources. Some were transported from Charleston and Savannah where they had been shipped from Camp Sumter until the new prison was completed. Another group of POWs who entered Camp Lawton was shipped directly from Camp Sumter. In his diary entry of 2 November, Dennison noted the arrival of 600 prisoners from yet another source—"Cahobey" [undoubtedly Cahaba].[17] Of those who were incarcerated at Camp

---

discovered that "ties between kin and ties between comrades of the same ethnicity were stronger than ties between other men of the same company." Of course, the fact that Civil War units, particularly on the company and regimental level, were normally recruited locally and in some cases had homogenous ethnic (not to mention racial) composition fostered the possibility of such social networks within the prisons. This finding of the importance of social networks squares with the anecdotal evidence coming from Camp Lawton.

[15] Daniel G. Kelley, *What I Saw and Suffered in Rebel Prisons* (Buffalo NY: Thomas Howard & Johnson, 1868) 78–79.

[16] Thaddeus L. Waters, *The Terrors of Rebel Prisons by an Old Andersonville Prisoner* (Newaygo MI: E.O. Shaw, 1891) 95.

[17] Dennison, *Andersonville Diary*, 81.

Lawton, therefore, most had been in the POW camps for extended periods of time, as many had been transported originally from the prisons in and around Richmond to Camp Sumter and then to Charleston or Savannah before they ultimately reached Camp Lawton. The real "fresh fish" were those who had been recently captured in the heavy campaigns in North Georgia and Virginia in the spring and summer of 1864. As Camp Lawton came on line in the fall of 1864, the number of prisoners at Camp Sumter was greatly reduced. Indeed, following the transfers, Winder reported to Seddon on 19 November 1864, that there were only 1,500 POWs left at Camp Sumter.[18]

Each time POWs were transported from one prison to another, opportunities for escape materialized. Private William B. Smith (14th Illinois) mentioned a successful one that occurred on the evening of 9 November, as he was being taken from Camp Sumter to Camp Lawton. According to his account, the prison train was on a siding in Macon.

> Just before the train pulled out that evening, a little after sundown, I was sitting near the car door by Henry Cowan, of Company A. He had on an old Confederate suit of gray, and, his faith in the exchange matter being on the wane, he very slyly dropped out of the car among the guards, and I soon lost sight of him in the fading twilight.[19]

That was the last Smith saw of Cowan until one day, 25 years later, he ran into him in a store in Springfield, Illinois, and Cowan recounted how he had successfully made his way from Macon to Union lines near Atlanta.

The noise, confusion, and disorganization associated with the arrival of a trainload of POWs could, according to Martin O'Hara (Company F, 16th Iowa), open opportunities for escape. He told of a POW dressed in grey who, as newly arrived prisoners were being organized into hundreds, surreptitiously joined the end of a line of

---

[18] Winder to Seddon, 19 November 1864, United States, War Department, *The War of the Rebellion: A Compilation of the Official Records of the Union and Confederate Armies*, series 2, vol. 7 (Washington DC: Government Printing Office, 1880–1901) 1,145.

[19] William B. Smith, *On Wheels: and How I Came There: The True Story of a 15-Year-Old Yankee and Prisoner in the American Civil War*, ed. Stacy M. Haponik (College Station TX: Virtualbookworm.com, 2002) 144.

guards going to the spring for water. Once at the spring "…. he walked leisurely into the woods."[20]

The journey to Camp Lawton was not a pleasant experience either for guards or prisoners. The POW-laden rail cars departing Camp Sumter traversed a section of Georgia whose landscape was alien and perhaps even exotic to most of their human cargo. The rail lines connecting Camp Sumter, Macon, Savannah, and Camp Lawton passed across a gently undulating terrain that featured vast stands of piney woods covering sandy, low-lying ridges alternating with shallow valleys cut by lazy streams and rivers and bordered by stands of hardwoods. Across much of this coastal plain region commercial lumbering did not get underway until after the war; therefore, large stretches of the primeval, open forest remained intact. The closer one traveled to the rivers or to the coast, the more likely one was to find swamps and marshes inhabited by such primordial, frightening creatures as venomous snakes and alligators, as well as trees draped with Spanish moss.

Whether passing through a remote, thinly settled district of scattered, isolated farmsteads or a carefully cultivated, well-populated plantation district, the prisoners could not help but notice the absence of the male population of military service age. Women, children, old men, and slaves constituted the remaining inhabitants. As the well-worn cars clattered and creaked along the rails, the war-weary countryside was made even more forlorn by the onset of fall—the season of decline matching the condition of the POWs. For some of them, the coming winter—the season of death—would presage their own fate. Given the state of the Confederate war effort in late 1864, the prospect was probably not much less bleak for the guards huddled on top of the rattling cars as they took their uncomfortable duty shifts.[21]

At least one POW reached the Lawton station but never made it to the stockade. In an 1882 article in *The National Tribune*, the pseudonymous "Free Lance," quoted from his diary when he recalled a tragic

---

[20] Martin O'Hara, *Reminiscences of Andersonville and Other Rebel Prisons: A Story of Suffering and Death* (Lyons IA: J.C. Hopkins, Printer, Advertiser Office, 1880) 40.

[21] Francis Marion Blaloch, "Account of Francis Marion Blaloch," ANHS, cited in Charles W. Sanders, Jr., *While in the Hands of the Enemy: Military Prisons of the Civil War* (Baton Rouge: Louisiana State University Press, 2005) 252.

incident involving a messmate as they were transported to Camp Lawton from Camp Sumter. When they reached the Lawton station on the morning of 4 November, his comrade "made a misstep and broke his neck" when he fell "between the car and the platform."[22]

As indicated earlier, problems with accessing sufficient funds, materials, transportation, and labor combined to slow the completion of the stockade. Extant records do not allow us to pinpoint the date when the first POWs arrived at Camp Lawton, but Sergeant Dennison's diary stated that the first contingents left Savannah for Camp Lawton on 10 October. He left on the twelfth.[23] This would seem to tie in to General Winder's 15 October dispatch to Adjutant and Inspector General Cooper that he was at Camp Lawton, the stockade was complete, and the POWs from Savannah (except for the very sick) were at the new prison.[24] They were all veteran prisoners and, finding the inside of the stockade littered with the sawn-off limbs and tops of trees that had been dressed to make the walls of the pen, immediately began gathering these materials to construct their "shebangs."[25] In addition, according to the testimony of POW diarists and the illustrations of Sneden, several large logs were left within the compound that the prisoners quickly appropriated to build fires.

Once the materials were gathered, the POWs surveyed their new environment and established a place to build their shebangs. Especially for veterans of Camp Sumter, this was a critical task. Lessel Long described the process used by his messmates:

> We commenced at once to fix up so as to make ourselves as comfortable as possible. We dug out a place about eight feet square and one and a half feet deep. By this means we could keep warmer than if we built our tent on top of the ground. We gathered up a good quantity of pine leaves, placing them in the bottom of our tent. This formed our bed and was much better than any we had before. We then took some sticks,

---

[22] Free Lance (pseud.), "Southern Prison Life," *The National Tribune*, 9 September 1882, 2.

[23] Dennison, *Andersonville Diary*, 74.

[24] Winder to Cooper, 15 October 1864, *Official Records*, series 2, vol. 7, 993.

[25] The term "shebang" was the most common name given by POWs to their homebuilt huts. The origin of the term is obscure but may have Celtic or French linguistic origins.

sticking one end in the ground near the side of the pit, coming together over the center, same as a rafter on a building, tying the ends together. Then we took other sticks and laying them on these they answered as lath of sheeting. Now we were ready to put on the roof. We gathered up the long leafed pine and thatched it over and closed up the ends in the same way. When completed it made a warm place to stay in. Our roof turned the rain very well. In this place we spent most of our time while at Millen.[26]

John Wool Bartleson described the shebang he and his messmates built: "We dug a hole five by six and one half feet into the ground, building a sod chimney and fireplace, built it up a little, secured some poles, pine boughs, covering all up with sod, just leaving a little entrance through which we could slide in and climb out."[27] Dennison mentioned that he was allowed to go outside the stockade to gather boughs that he used to improve what he called his "shantey." He wrote in his diary on 31 October, "[W]ell I have got a good place to liv in the best I have had since I have ben a prisoner."[28] Lucius Barber was a latecomer to Camp Lawton, only arriving there on 13 November. By that time all of the available wood in the camp had been used up. He was allowed to gather wood outside the stockade, but there was a caveat. As Barber described it, "Went out today [17 November] for the first time…. Only thirty can go out at a time. Forty squads go out in a day. If one man fails to come back with the rest, the division to which he belongs does not go out again until he is brought back."[29]

Chaplain Bradley recounted what he saw when he visited the evacuated prison in December:

---

[26] Long, *Twelve Months in Andersonville*, 87.

[27] John Wool Bartleson, "Memoirs of John Wool Bartleson as Transcribed and Edited by Tweed Ross." *Eye on Kansas: An Online Magazine about What Makes Kansas Our Home.* Chapter two: part three "Freedom and Home!" http://eyeonkansas.org/ncentral/riley/bartleson_biography/0802chaptertwo-partthree.html (accessed 15 July 2010. Bartleson may have had the distinction of being the last survivor of Camp Sumter (as well as Camp Lawton). He passed away on 19 April 1944 at the age of 97. See Barbara Stahura, *Sons of Union Veterans of the Civil War*, ed. Gary Gibson (Paducah KY: Turner Publishing, 1996) 52.

[28] Dennison, *Andersonville Diary*, 79.

[29] Barber, *Military Memoirs*, 179.

The huts were built in all manner of shapes, some had walls of logs, with a covering of timber, and over these a good layer of sand. Some had walls of turf, again others were cut into the ground perhaps two feet and then covered, sometimes with pine slabs, sometimes with sand, and some were simply thatched with pine boughs, while others were bare sheds.[30]

In his own inimical, colloquial style, Riley Beach (Company B, 113th Illinois) remembered helping his messmates build their shebang: "We got some logs rove clap-boards built a Shanty, 10 feet wide 18 ft, long 4 ft, at eaves 6 ft high in the centre. It was called the big Shanty. In one respect it was like Solomons Temple, no sound of hammer, not any nail in it."[31] In other words, the shebangs at Camp Lawton took whatever form ingenuity, available materials and the number of messmates allowed.

Once their "home" location was established, the next item on the POW agenda was food. This is the one topic that permeates all POW accounts. John Ransom, for instance, was conscious of this and apologized for his constant references to food in his Camp Lawton prison diary.[32] According to the diaries, the food at Camp Lawton included various quantities and combinations of corn meal, molasses, rice, peas, corn, sweet potatoes, and beef. Except for beef, the components of the diet were similar to the Camp Sumter regimen. Initially, rations were good. Dennison reported, "we get meal one pint   beans one pint bacon 3 oz salt one half spoonful per day."[33] Many veteran POWs found the rations at Camp Lawton to be an improvement over what they had been used to. Beef was a particularly welcome addition. McElroy's comments were typical:

> The rations issued to us were somewhat better than those of Andersonville, as the meal was finer and better, though it was absurdedly insufficient in quantity, and we received no salt. On several occasions

---

[30] George S. Bradley, *The Star Corps or Notes of an Army Chaplain During Sherman's Famous "March to the Sea"* (Milwaukee WI: Jermain & Brightman, 1865) 203.

[31] Riley V. Beach, "Recollections and Extracts from the Diaries of Army Life of the Rev. Riley V. Beach of Co. 'B' 113 Ills. Inft, Vols.," (Typescript copy courtesy of Terry McCarty, Georgetown, Texas) 39.

[32] Ransom, *Andersonville Diary*, 164, 166.

[33] Dennison, *Andersonville Diary*, 74–75.

fresh beef was dealt out to us, and each time the excitement created among those who had not tasted fresh meat for weeks and months was wonderful. On the first occasion the meat was simply the heads of cattle killed for the use of the guards. Several wagon loads of these were brought in and distributed. We broke them up so that every man got a piece of the bone, which as boiled and reboiled, as long as a single bubble of grease would rise to the surface of the water; every vestige of meat was gnawed and scraped from the surface and then the bone was charred until it crumbled, when it was eaten. No one who has not experienced it can imagine the inordinate hunger for animal food of those who have eaten little else than corn bread for so long.[34]

James Conway (1st Massachusetts Heavy Artillery) also remembered this: "We used to pick up old bones and burn them black and eat them." He was also the unique reporter that the prisoners were given cowhides to eat.[35] Lucius Barber recollected the cow heads' incident and stated that his mess made soup of them which were rather "ripe."[36] Another Camp Lawton veteran recalled being so famished when he arrived from Camp Sumter that he ate his first ration of three ounces of beef raw.[37] According to Corporal Thomas Aldrich (154th New York), at one point he "picked up old beef bones and broke them up and

---

[34] John McElroy, *Andersonville: A Story of Rebel Military Prisons, Fifteen months a Guest of the so-called Confederacy. A Private Soldier's Experience in Richmond, Andersonville, Savannah, Millen, Blackshear and Florence* (Toledo OH: D.R. Locke, 1879) 458–459.

[35] Testimony of James Conway, United States House of Representatives, 40th Congress, 3rd Session, *Report No. 45: Report on the Treatment of Prisoners of War by the Rebel Authorities During the War of the Rebellion to Which Are Appended the Testimony Taken by the Committee and the Official Documents and Statistics, etc.* (Washington DC: Government Printing Office, 1869) 922. Commonly referred to as the "Shanks Report," subsequent citations will be referred to as such.

[36] Barber, *Army Memoirs*, 179.

[37] Anonymous, *A Voice from Rebel Prisons*, 5. Actually, the eating of raw meat could have had a beneficial effect on those who had scurvy as medical literature in the late nineteenth and early twentieth centuries began to document. However, raw meat consumption could also bring other problems with it. See Kenneth J. Carpenter, *The History of Scurvy and Vitamin C* (Cambridge: Cambridge University Press, 1988) 135, 146; and Leonard G. Wilson, "The Clinical Definition of Scurvy and the Discovery of Vitamin C," *Journal of the History of Medicine and Allied Sciences* 30, no. 1: 40–60.

stewed them in a little water, and drank the broth, and would scrape the inside of the bones and chew them for a little nourishment."[38]

The initial improvement in both quantity and quality of rations at Camp Lawton did not last, though. By 15 October, only three days after his arrival, Dennison was reporting a diminution in the rations: ["W]e get small rations now."[39] Aldrich remembered: "The rations got very thin here, and I suffered from hunger more than I ever had before. In fact, I thought that I should starve."[40] However, virtually all POWs who arrived at Camp Lawton, whether early or late in its existence, commented favorably on the rations they received compared to those at Camp Sumter. Barber, one of the latecomers, commented in his diary, "We get double the amount of beef that we did at Camp Sumter, and of a great deal better quality.[41] The next day, however, he reported he got no rations. The decline in the rations may have been the result of Sherman's campaign for Atlanta and, then, his March to the Sea, which ultimately interdicted rail transport. In fact, Sneden reported that Captain Vowles told the POWs that any ration shortages were because "the Yankees have destroyed the railroad."[42] At the same time, what trains were available were in high demand for transporting troops, refugees, supplies for the Army of Northern Virginia, and Union prisoners for the exchanges of the sick. One must add, however, that the degree to which an inmate's messmates obtained a sufficient share of rations and then distributed the food equitably among their colleagues could affect the sufficiency of rations.

The rations were brought into the stockade by mule teams pulling wagons driven by blacks.[43] The division sergeants received ration allotments for those for whom they were responsible. These, in turn, were disbursed from the division level, sent down to the detachments,

---

[38] Thomas R. Aldrich, Unpublished Memoir (courtesy of Patricia Wilcox of Fairport, New York) 27.

[39] Dennison, *Andersonville Diary*, 75.

[40] Aldrich, Unpublished Memoir, 27.

[41] Barber, *War Memoirs*, 178.

[42] Sneden, *Eye of the Storm*, 262.

[43] Robert Knox Sneden, Diary, 1 September 1864–May 1865, VHS, Mss5:1 Sn 237:1 vol. 6, 114.

and eventually reached the individual messes. This process, plus a bit of personal resourcefulness, allowed William Smith to secure an additional, much appreciated "treat" for his messmates:

> I was near the gate our first day there when rations, consisting of meal and fresh beef, were brought in..... [T]he meat was issued that day at the gate to division sergeants, who called for men to carry the meat to the different quarters. Being close to the wagon, I took a small hind quarter that would weigh, perhaps, seventy-five or eighty pounds to carry to our division. It was quite a distance to where we were located, and I hardly expected to carry the meat so far, but I thought that while it was in my possession I could secure a good chunk of tallow [fat]. Failing to get any while I had it on my shoulder, after I had gone a little distance I fell down, managing to fall with the meat under me; and, while struggling to get up with it, succeeded in pulling off a full half pound of tallow, which I stuck in between my blouse and shirt, having left the former open for that purpose before starting.

Finding himself unable to lift the hindquarter from the dirt, Smith was reprimanded by the division sergeant for dropping it and then dismissed to return to his mess. When Smith distributed the purloined tallow to each of his messmates, they "... lauded my achievement as much as if I had been some great general who had gained an important victory."[44]

Among the hazards of POW cuisines were the insects that came with the rations. In describing their sojourn at Camp Lawton, William Lightcap and Henry Davidson remembered the "bean bugs" that emerged when peas were put into hot water for cooking. Their respective messmates were always careful to separate the insects from their food. Years later, though, this habit caused Lightcap some embarrassment:

> About five years after the close of the war I was boarding with a private family in Galesville, Ill. One day after I had finished my dinner, I had occasion to return to the dining room for something and there stood

---

[44] Smith, *On Wheels*, 145; only one POW, Sgt. Tisdale (17 October 1864, "Diary"), recalls the Confederates issuing iron kettles to each hundred (ten 2-gallon kettles) for drawing rations.

the lady of the house examining the crumbs by the side of my plate that she had seen me place there. I was so embarrassed and humiliated that I hardly knew what to do. I did not realize when I picked them out of the food and placed them there that I was doing so, but when I saw her looking at them I knew I had for it was a fixed habit of mine. I said, "Please don't examine them, there's nothing but clean food." I explained all to her satisfaction, told her the cause and that I could not help it.... tried hard to break myself of that habit from sad experience more than thirty-six years ago, still I sometimes catch myself doing the same thing.[45]

However, it must be added that not all Camp Lawton POWs made an effort to remove the bugs from their rations. Henry Harmon saw the insects as additional protein: "We thought that if travelers in the African deserts could eat roasted locusts, why not starving Yanks do the same with Confederate bugs?"[46]

Another problem was how to cook what food was available. The brick ovens and their accompanying kettles were not initially installed when the camp was first occupied; moreover, when they were completed, several prisoner accounts indicate that they were not used for cooking but rather for sleeping and shelter, as well as for a source of building supplies. In fact, recent archaeological finds have included what appears to be a shebang site with bricks, presumably purloined from the brick piles used to build the ovens. However, the POWs were not necessarily without cooking resources. Lightcap told of POWs picking up sheet iron roofing squares in Macon from a collapsed building that had burned near the railroad tracks. According to Lightcap the metal squares were about two feet by two feet, and several enterprising POWs were able to beat them into pans with a capacity of about two quarts. Later, when Lightcap reached Camp Lawton, he and the members of his mess secured such a pan in exchange for thirteen rations. This would allow the mess members to cook their rations in one pan and divide

---

[45] William Henry Lightcap, *The Horrors of Southern Prisons During the War of the Rebellion, from 1862 to 1865* (Platteville WI: Journal Job Rooms, 1902) 57; and Henry Davidson, *Fourteen Months in Southern Prisons* (Milwaukee: Daily Wisconsin Printing House, 1865) 331.

[46] Henry A. Harmon, "A Year in Six Rebel Prisons," Part 1, *The National Tribune*, 1 June 1893.

them equally.[47] This anecdote also reveals that rations became a kind of currency at Camp Lawton. In fact, Barber noted in his diary that "rice, bean soup, biscuits, pies and corn dodgers were made and sold on Market Street [the POWs name for the area in any prison where sellers congregated] at exorbitant prices."[48] POWs used wood for cooking and heating. As mentioned earlier, when the first prisoners entered the stockade, they found stumps, some logs, and the trimmings from the trees that had been felled to build the walls. This material was quickly taken both to build shebangs and to use as fuel. The use of wood fires for cooking and heating left a residue of soot on the exposed skin of the inmates. Since soap was not generally available, sand was used in its stead to clean the soot-darkened faces.[49]

Inmates who had the means supplemented their rations with food they obtained from other inmates or guards. Sergeant Kelley, for example, traded a gold watch-key for twenty-four sweet potatoes as he waited for transport to Savannah on 15 November, as a part of the exchange of sick POWs.[50] Some prisoners made candy from the molasses rations and sold it to their incarcerated comrades.[51] Also, a Confederate sutler, perhaps Philip Cashmyer, operated his business out of a small cabin next to the bridge that crossed the stream within the stockade.[52] George Hitchcock wrote in his diary: "For sale in abundance: roast chicken, boiled sweet potatoes, eggs, biscuits, butter, pumpkin and potato pies, rice and bean soups, soda cakes and molasses but our

---

[47] Lightcap, *Horrors of Southern Prisons*, 49, 55. Free Lance, "Southern Prison Life," also remembered POWs stealing tin to make pans, this time from the roof of a railway car (*The National Tribune*, 16 September 1882).

[48] Barber, *Army Memoirs*, 180.

[49] Sneden, *Eye of the Storm*, 264.

[50] Kelley, *What I Saw and Suffered*, 81.

[51] Ransom, *Andersonville Diary*, 159; Davidson, *Fourteen Months in Southern Prisons*, 331; John W. Urban, *Battlefield and Prison Pen, or Through the War and Thrice a Prisoner in Rebel Dungeons* (Philadelphia: Edgewood Publishing, 1882) 445.

[52] Sneden, *Eye of the Storm*, 269; Philip Cashmyer gave testimony after the war of his experiences in the Confederate prisons (Cashmyer to Chipman, 22 September 1865, *Official Records*, series 2, vol. 7, 764–66, and Cashmyer to Chipman, 12 October 1865, *Official Records*, series 2, vol. 7, 753–54).

experience is the same as the Ancient Mariner—'Food a everywhere, but not a morsel for us.'"[53]

Moreover, foraging within the prison could bring its rewards, as well. Lightcap remembered almost stepping on a large, black snake near a stump within the compound. The snake was promptly killed, skinned, and eaten. In addition, his messmates discovered a "gopher" and consumed it.[54] John Ransom mentioned a small alligator that was found in the stream and consumed by the protein-starved prisoners.[55] Alligators and snakes still reside at Magnolia Springs State Park. The "Do-Not-Feed-the-Alligators" sign next to the stream today is ironic given the fact that an alligator may have once fed human beings there. But not all of the other denizens of the stockade were edible. Engaging in a bit of prison hyperbole, Henry Harmon reported "immense" spiders that he called "tarantulas" and "musketos which might be mistaken for diminutive humming-birds."[56] One assumes that the November frosts ended some of these problems. Finally, P. Dempsey (12th Independent Battery, New York Light Artillery) remembered the discovery of another life form: "While in Millen we took a swim in the creek and it was so full of water snakes it nearly scared the life out of us as we never saw such things in the water before...."[57] Rather than snakes, Dempsey and his colleagues probably saw eels, as they are present in the stream today. In fact, Riley Beach mentioned one: "A fellow caught an Eel, in this creek, sold it for a dollar, the only Eel, I ever saw."[58]

---

[53] Hitchcock, *From Ashby to Andersonville*, 269.

[54] Lightcap, *Horrors of Southern Prisons*, 57. The color (black) and size (8 feet long) of the snake would indicate that it was probably an indigo snake (*Drymarchon couperi*), which is native to the area, although an endangered species today. However, one must keep in mind that snakes when measured often prove much shorter than their first impression would indicate. What is meant by the "gopher" is unclear. If a mammal, perhaps it was a chipmunk; however, locals in that part of Georgia refer to a large land tortoise that burrows in sandy soil as a gopher. It is also native to the area.

[55] Ransom, *Andersonville Diary*, 163.

[56] Harmon, "A Year in Six Rebel Prisons," 171. What Harmon called tarantulas were probably "wolf spiders," a large hairy spider common to the area, whereas tarantulas are not. His hummingbird-sized "musketos" existed only in a hyperbolic sense.

[57] P. Dempsey, Letter to Mrs. Van Deusen, n.d., MSC 17698, New York State Archives, New York State Education Department, Cultural Education Center, Albany, New York.

[58] Beach, "Diaries," 39.

POWs were not just assiduous in seeking out unusual food sources, they also diligently sought out any materials they could within the stockade. This was because they were not particularly well equipped upon entering the prison. Those who had been captured in battle were often without many of the accoutrements they normally would have had in camp. Units going into action typically left their knapsacks, blankets, cooking utensils, etc., with the unit baggage trains that were sent to the rear. Once captured, soldiers were stripped of their weapons and ammunition and reduced to their basic uniforms and whatever other items they might have been able to keep. J.C. Harriss (81st Illinois) recollected his capture experience on 11 June 1864, at Guntown, Mississippi: "When I was captured my blanket, watch, knife, haversack, & canteen were taken from me & the same way I [it?] was with the other boys & those who had money had it taken from them."[59] Even if the baggage trains were also captured, their cargoes became spoils of war. Moreover, the attrition of living in other stockades before they arrived at Camp Lawton had cost many useful items such as blankets and extra clothing. Obviously, bayonets and large knives were not allowed them; yet, these had often been used in the field for cooking, eating, and digging, and could have served the same purposes in the stockade. The Civil War soldier's ubiquitous tin cup and spoon were highly prized in the prison environment, and POWs tried very hard to keep them. Thomas Aldrich managed to keep his and, when he returned home after the war, he hung it up at the local post office room in Ellicottville, New York, where it remained for years.[60]

Veteran POWs were careful conservers of their few possessions. They included personal items that they had been able to preserve since capture, as well as useful things they had acquired since their incarceration. These consisted of essential items—cups, pipes, pocket knives, buttons, eating utensils (knives, forks, and spoons), coins, tokens,

---

[59] J.C. Harriss Civil War Letter Archive, POW Andersonville, Jordan Carroll Harriss, 81st Illinois Infantry, ca 110 letters, 1862–65, http://www.banksgrandretreat. com/PDF/Harriss%2081st%20Illinois.pdf (accessed 20 December, 2009).

[60] Anonymous, *A Voice from Rebel Prisons*, 5. The author calls the tin cup "invaluable." It could be used for digging, cooking, and as a container, beyond its designed use for drinking. Aldrich, Unpublished Memoir, 27. See also, McElroy, *Andersonville*, 102.

game pieces, blankets, extra clothing, etc.—and items that could be traded such as watches, money, brass buttons, medallions, etc. According to family lore, Private Sebastian Glamser (Company F, 37th Ohio) had preserved his lice comb, a very valuable implement within the stockade, and was able to secure additional food by bartering its use to others.[61] Examples of most of these items have been found within the bounds of the stockade by archaeologists. Most superfluous possessions were quickly discarded or exchanged. Interestingly, archaeologists have also recovered railroad spikes from the area inside the stockade, some with their heads removed. If these artifacts are, in fact, from the Camp Lawton era, they may have been used as tools. Because of their pointed ends they could have been used as wood chisels to split pieces of wood or even rough boards off of the logs lying in the compound. They could also have been used as tent stakes, hammers, or even digging implements to loosen the hard pan clay as they excavated areas for their shebangs. Given the fact that they were brought to Camp Lawton by rail, POWs could have easily picked up the spikes along the railroad bed. However, despite their presence among the archeological finds, POW diaries from the prison do not mention them.

Inmates at Camp Lawton attempted to secure needed implements through trade and thievery. Lacking that, some POWs were resourceful enough to make them out of available materials. For example, William Smith, the enterprising tallow thief, carried to Camp Lawton from Camp Sumter via Savannah a wooden plate and spoon he had fashioned from a small piece of one-inch-thick wood board one of his friends had brought into Camp Sumter from a work detail outside the stockade. These items, "...with my old jackknife, comprised my entire culinary outfit, which I zealously guarded all through my prison life."[62] Consequently, while

---

[61] Telephone interview with Nina J. Raeth, Glamser's great-grandaughter, 28 June 2011. Sebastian Glamser was a German immigrant who, like many of his compatriots, found himself embroiled in his adopted nation's unique conflict. Wounded in the head, he was captured on 22 June 1864 during the Atlanta campaign. His sojourn in the Confederate prison system included stops at Camp Sumter, Millen, Macon, Florence and Libby, and ended when he was exchanged in February of 1865. Civil War Records for Sebastian Glamser, transcribed by Nina J. Raeth, June 2010.

[62] Smith, *On Wheels*, 142.

searching for evidence of his captured brother Deloss, Sergeant Marcellus Darling (Company K, 154th New York) found numerous artifacts of such enterprise when he visited the abandoned camp as his unit bivouacked nearby: "I picked up many relics such as wooden and bone spoons, etc., but they were all lost on the march once the wagon overturned."[63]

Another issue with which the POWs had to contend was clothing. Generally speaking, clothing was rarely issued to inmates in Confederate prisons. Only one POW remembered any clothing being issued at Camp Lawton.[64] Prisoners entered the prison system with the clothes in which they had been captured, sometimes being much worse for wear. Once a person was incarcerated within the camps, his clothes simply began to wear out. One of the means employed of getting rid of vermin was to singe clothing over a fire.[65] In addition to getting rid of the nits, this also carbonized the cloth fibers and weakened the fabric, which led to further deterioration. Mended clothing was much in evidence, and Sergeant Henry Tisdale (35th Massachusetts) remembered that he "had fourteen different patches on my pants of almost as many colors."[66]

An additional, and potentially deadly, clothing problem faced the inmates at Camp Lawton—the arrival of cold weather. POWs sought additional clothing from any source. Blankets were highly prized. Within the camps POWs could trade with each other and sometimes were able to trade with the guards. Numerous accounts mention trading with the guards for Confederate gray clothing.[67] This also facilitated escape

---

[63] Marcellus Warren Darling, "Events and Comments of My Life," (unknown publisher, n.d.) 17; Darling, Letter of 16 December 1864, 1; courtesy of Mark H. Dunkelman, Providence, Rhode Island.

[64] Amos E. Yeakle, Diary (10 November 1864) Transcription, Andersonville Diaries, Andersonville National Historic Site (ANHS), mentions the issuing of "700 of Uncle Sam's uniforms to the prisoners."

[65] McElroy, *Andersonville*, 165.

[66] Henry W. Tisdale, 6 November 1864, "Civil War Diary of Sergeant Henry W. Tisdale, Co. I, Thirty-fifth Regiment Massachusetts Volunteers," transcript. Margaret H. Tisdale, http://www.civilwardiary.net (accessed 12 September 2008).

[67] J.B. Vaughter, *Prison Life in Dixie. Giving a Short History of the Inhuman and Barbarous Treatment of Our Soldiers by Rebel Authorities, by Sergeant Oates.* 3rd ed. (Chicago: Central Book Concern, 1881) 138.

attempts. For others, thievery was an option. A third source of clothing was more macabre. Lessel Long (13th Indiana) told of POWs going to the hospital grounds within the stockade and waiting for a prisoner who was near death to expire and then remove his clothing for their own use.[68]

Stories of Confederate guards shooting Union prisoners were a staple of post-war POW literature. Such shootings are well documented at Camp Sumter. Usually such events occurred when an inmate crossed the deadline and a guard responded to the transgression by shooting him. POWs were also shot during escape attempts along the railroad. Until completing the research for this study, the author had not seen an account of a POW being shot at Camp Lawton. In fact, this prison was often singled out as an example of a prison in which the shooting of prisoners was unknown. However, in the course of researching this history, several unpublished POW sources surfaced that mentioned such events. Corporal Thomas Aldrich reported in his manuscript memoir: "Once in awhile the Guards would shoot a poor fellow just to keep his hand in it, still there was not as much shooting as at Andersonville. One poor fellow was shot within 10 feet of my tent one night and he was not within 10 feet of the deadline."[69] Another POW, James Vance (Company M, 5th US Cavalry) wrote in his diary for 6 November: "2 men shot 1 killed. The first ones."[70] Sergeant Amos A. Yeakle wrote in his diary on the same day, "There was one shot dead by the guard, and one wounded for getting over the dead-line."[71] Jesse Alton (111th Illinois), who arrived at Camp Lawton on 12 October, wrote in his diary entry of that date, "I saw a prisoner shot dead for leaving the ranks to get some boards to make him a shanty."[72] Then, in a published account Alvin S. Graton (Company C, 21st Massachusetts) echoed Aldrich's comment that guards

---

[68] Long, *Twelve Months in Andersonville*, 101–02. Urban, in *Battlefield and Prison Pen*, also reported POWs getting clothes from the dead.

[69] Aldrich, Unpublished Memoir, 29.

[70] James Vance, 6 November 1864, "Andersonville Diary of James Vance," transcribed by Donald A. Huntslar (Collections of the Ohio Historical Society) 22.

[71] Amos A. Yeakle, Diary, 6 November 1864, ANHS.

[72] C.A. Frazer, "Marion County Prisoner of Rebels Kept Diary in Andersonville Prison," http://www.stkusers.com/lindas/jesse.html (accessed 24 August 2008).

shot at the POWs "but not so frequently as they did at Andersonville."[73] John Sammon's laconic comment was, "The usual number of deaths occurred at the deadline as at other prisons."[74] Except for the accounts by Vance and Yeakle, none of these statements are specifically corroborated. If, in fact, POWs were shot at Camp Lawton, it is surprising that some of the more rabid published POW authors failed to mention it, since such stories would have buttressed their depictions of the barbarities of Confederate prisons.[75] However, given the mention by Vance and Yeakle of what appears to be the same shooting incident on the same day, one may conclude that it happened here, as well. One might also conjecture that if POWs heard shots from the guards it is possible that they came from guards occasionally "clearing" their muskets of old charges.

POWs exhibited ingenuity, perseverance, adaptability, and enterprise in securing life's necessities in the situation in which they found themselves. Archaeologists have found numerous items documenting daily POW activities at Camp Lawton in the area north of the stream where the shebangs were located. One item is an artillery primer, perhaps brought in by a captured artilleryman and used to start a fire. Another interesting example of POW ingenuity in the face of scarcity is a homemade pipe. The smoker had taken a broken clay pipe stem and grafted it on to a crudely fashioned bowl made of lead, probably smelted from some minie balls. Other recovered artifacts support POW accounts of trade within the prison. Of course, under such circumstances barter was common, and POWs spoke in their memoirs of the particular interest the Confederate guards had in acquiring uniform buttons. Numbers of such items have been found on site. The discovery of foreign and domestic coins and tokens (sometimes used as currency)

---

[73] Alvis Graton, Testimony, "Shanks Report," 848–50.

[74] John H. Sammons, *Personal Recollections of the Civil War* (Greensburg IN: Montgomery & Son, n.d.) 48.

[75] Neither Urban, *Battlefield and Prison Pen*; Asa B. Isham, Henry M. Davidson, Henry B. Furness, *Prisoners of War and Military Prisons* (Cincinnati: Lyman & Cushing, 1890); nor John McElroy, *Andersonville: A Story of Rebel Military Prisons*, three of the most popular nineteenth-century POW accounts, mention a prisoner being shot at Millen.

reveals a money economy, as well. For instance, one coin, a large one-cent piece, was recovered that had been carefully cut in half.[76]

[76] For a preliminary description and discussion of the findings of the Spring 2010 archaeological dig at the site, see "Camp Lawton," Special First Edition. Georgia Southern University and Georgia Department of Natural Resources, 18 August 2010. Also, Kevin Chapman's recently completed master's thesis (James Kevin Chapman, "Comparison of Archeological Survey Techniques at Camp Lawton, a Civil War Prison Stockade [MA thesis, Georgia Southern University, 2012]) represents the first scholarly report on the archeological work at Magnolia Springs and discusses the recovered artifacts.

5

Voters, Recruiters, Galvanizers,
Escapees, Raiders, and Guards

The two major events that almost all of the POW diarists remembered as occurring at Camp Lawton were the mock presidential election held in November and the attempt by the authorities to recruit the POWs for Confederate service. However, neither effort worked to the advantage of their captors.

The presidential election of 1864 featured Lincoln, the Republican incumbent, running against one of his former generals, George B. McClellan on the Democratic ticket. McClellan, who according to Lincoln had contracted the "slows" and then been sacked by the president after his failure to follow up after the Battle of Antietam, campaigned on a platform calling for negotiations with the Confederacy and an end to the war. For Confederates who understood that the war of attrition would ultimately undo them, McClellan's candidacy brought renewed hope. For Northerners who were not sure the war or its aims were worth the cost, the Democratic campaign called for an end to the bloodshed. In fact, 1864 was the bloodiest year of the conflict; the blockade was tightening, and war weariness was evident in both the North and the South. At the time of the election and during the campaign, the two major Union offensives—Sherman's campaign in Georgia and Grant's advance in Virginia—had generated thousands of casualties, but many in the Northern public saw the war as no closer to a successful completion. Although Sherman had launched his campaign in north Georgia in the spring, as September opened he had not captured Atlanta nor had he destroyed the Confederate Army of Tennessee. True, Grant had pushed Lee back into a defensive position around Richmond and Petersburg, but he seemed unable to finish him off, and the casualty lists were getting longer and longer. For the Northern public, the "light at the end of the tunnel" seemed little brighter in the fall of 1864 than it had been in the previous spring, but the human cost had grown significantly. For Southerners, the exaltation of a quick, glorious victory in the spring of 1861 had long since disappeared in the reality of the grim struggle of attrition that the war had become. Even Lincoln, in one of his melancholic moods, wrote that he thought he might not win re-election.[1]

Given this environment, Confederate authorities at Camp Lawton thought it might be worthwhile to let the prisoners vote in a mock presidential election.[2] After all, would not the POWs blame Lincoln for their predicament and champion the return of McClellan, who had always been generally popular with the troops? If so, news that POWs had favored McClellan over Lincoln would make headlines in Northern and Southern newspapers, as well as demonstrate a disconcerting (at least to the North) political alignment between the captives and their captors. Several Camp Lawton POW accounts mention this election and its results. There was considerable electioneering, and both presidential candidates had their supporters in the camp. Private George A. Hitchcock (Co. A, 21st Massachusetts) witnessed the event, having only arrived from Camp Sumter four days before the mock election:

> Early in the day many stump speeches were made and vigorous campaigning done in behalf of both candidates.... Many of the old Potomac boys [veterans of the Army of Potomac under McClellan, who remained popular with his troops] vote for McClellan because they still remain loyal to him, yet believe in seeing the war pushed until the rebellion is overthrown [War Democrats]. Others in their weakness and misery are made to believe that our Government has hopelessly abandoned us.[3] P. Craham (Company D, 22 New York Cavalry) preserved

---

[1] "Memorandum Concerning His Probable Failure of Election," 25 August 1864, *The Collected Works of Abraham Lincoln*, 9 vols., ed. Roy P. Basler (New Brunswick NJ: Rutgers University Press, 1953–55) 7: 514–15. In the 1864 election, Lincoln actually ran under the banner of the "National Union" Party, representing an attempt to create a coalition of Republicans and War Democrats.

[2] Robert Knox Sneden, Diary, VHS, vol. 6, 122. Sneden remembered the idea of the vote as having originated within the stockade but then approved by prison authorities.

[3] George A. Hitchcock, *From Ashby to Andersonville: The Civil War Diary and Reminiscences of George A. Hitchcock, Private, Company A, 21st Massachusetts Regiment, August 1862–January 1865*, ed. Ronald Watson (Campbell CA: Savas Publishing, 1997) 268-269, and P. Craham, *The National Tribune*, 16 May 1907. Free Lance was among several Camp

some of the "campaign slogans": "Vote for Honest Abe the soldiers' friend," and "Vote for George B. McClellan, Little Mack the soul of honor."

Although reports of the results vary from source to source, several accounts agree that Lincoln received 3,014 votes to McClellan's 1,050.[4] Interestingly, Lincoln and McClellan's 1864 vote totals among the troops were 116,887 and 37,748, respectively, making for a similar ratio.[5] The staunchly Republican Hitchcock summarized his feelings in his diary: "I am highly satisfied with the result, and much chafing of the guard is indulged in over their disappointment."[6]

Lawton POWs who described the balloting as being done with beans—black for Lincoln and white for George B. McClellan ("Southern Prison Life," The National Tribune 16 September 1882).

[4] Willard W. Glazier, *The Capture, the Prison-Pen, and the Escape, Giving a Complete History of Prison Life in the South, Principally at Richmond, Danville, Macon, Savannah, Charleston, Columbia, Belle Isle, Millen, Salisbury, and Andersonville: Describing the Arrival of Prisoners, Plans of Escape, with Numerous and Varied Incidents and Anecdotes of Prison Life; Embracing, Also, the Adventures of Dr. Arthur's Escape from Columbia, South Carolina, Recapture, Subsequent Escape, Recapture, Trial as a Spy, and Final Escape from Sylvania, Georgia* (Hartford Ct: H.E. Goodwin, Publisher, 1869) 358; John W. Urban, *Battlefield and Prison Pen, or Through the War and Thrice a Prisoner in Rebel Dungeons* (Philadelphia: Edgewood Publishing, 1882) 449; Henry Davidson, *Fourteen Months in Southern Prisons* (Milwaukee: Daily Wisconsin Printing House, 1865) 334; Robert H. Kellogg, *Life and Death in Rebel Prisons: Giving a Complete history of the Inhuman and Barbarous Treatment of Our Brave Soldiers by Rebel Authorities, Inflicting Terrible Suffering and Frightful Mortality, Principally at Andersonville, GA., and Florence, SC., Describing Plans of Escape, Arrival of Prisoners with Numerous and Varied Incidents and Anecdotes of Prison Life* (Hartford, CT: Ls. Stebbins, 1865), 393. James H. Dennison (*Dennison's Andersonville Diary: The Diary of an Illinois Soldier in the Infamous Andersonville Prison Camp*, notes and transcript. Jack Klasey [Kankakee IL: Kankakee County Historical Society, 1987]) gives another, but close, figure—4,620 votes cast. Using the figures cited in the text, the ratios are, respectively, 1:2,870 and 1:3,097. These POWs, then, were slightly less likely to vote for Lincoln. This statistical difference, on which one should be cautious about coming to firm conclusions given the questionable accuracy of the data upon which it is based, might indicate that the Camp Lawton POWs were expressing some dissatisfaction with their situation. Henry W. Tisdale (20 November 1864, "Civil War Diary of Sergeant Henry W. Tisdale, Co. I, Thirty-fifth Regiment Massachusetts Volunteers," transcript. Margaret H. Tisdale, http://www.civilwardiary.net [accessed 12 September 2008]) stated that beans of different colors were used as ballots.

[5] Hitchcock, *From Ashby to Andersonville*, 269.

[6] Ronald C. White, *A. Lincoln: A Biography* (New York: Random House, 2009) 645.

Most Camp Lawton POW accounts mention the fact that the Confederates tried to enlist them in camp service. This scenario could take one of two forms. For example, inmates were needed to supplement the work of the guards—i.e., the burial detail. Also, administrative clerks, blacksmiths, carpenters, shoemakers, butchers, and machinists were in demand.[7] POWs who agreed to these kinds of work signed a parole, an example of which is found in Sneden's diary:

> I _____, a prisoner of war to the Confederate States of America, do pledge my parole as a man of honor, and as a military man, that I will not attempt to escape, nor pass beyond the prison limits, nor within 500 feet of the stockade, without permission of the authorities, or until regularly exchanged, under penalty of being shot without a court martial.[8]

Of course, Sneden's parole document was for a person who, like himself, no longer would live in the stockade. Sneden, who kept the death register for the camp, lived outside of the stockade on parole in a tent near the quarters of Dr. Isaiah White.[9] However, most of those on parole worked outside during the days but spent the nights within the prison. Therefore, the terms of their parole would be different from Sneden's. Some POWs refused such offers as a matter of principle, and tensions developed between those who "collaborated" and those who refused. Some POWs were happy for the chance to work outside of the stockade because, as Sergeant Henry Davidson (1st Ohio Light Artillery) put it, it was "something to relieve the terrible monotony of prison life."[10] Undoubtedly, it also gave them additional chances to collect news, to trade, to steal, or to escape. Davidson worked in the camp slaughterhouse processing thirty-five head of cattle per day. "The animals were small and very lean, averaging about, three hundred and fifty pounds each. This, after deducting rations for the officers and

---

[7] Francis J. Hosmer, "Memoir of Francis J. Hosmer" in *A Glimpse of Andersonville and Other Writings* (Springfield MA: Loring & Axtell, 1896) 43.

[8] Robert Knox Sneden, *Eye of the Storm: A Civil War Odyssey*, ed. Charles F. Bryan, Jr., and Nelson D. Lankford (New York: The Free Press, 2000) 267.

[9] Ibid., 267.

[10] Davidson, *Fourteen Months in Southern Prisons*, 336–37.

guards, left about, one-fourth of a pound per man per diem, including the bone, which in lean cattle bears a large proportion to the meat."[11]

Another POW who wangled a job outside the stockade at Camp Sumter was Second Lieutenant James Madison Page (Company A, 6th Michigan Cavalry). According to his account, as his group was being processed to go into the stockade, he met a friend of his who was already there and noticed that he looked "well and clean." Inquiring as to his situation, Page found that his friend was working on parole outside the stockade. Already a long-suffering veteran of Camp Sumter, Page told his friend: "Then you must get me out. I am at the end of my rope. I love my country but I love my own life a little more. I don't see how my death in prison will be of benefit to the Government."[12] His friend put in a good word for him with a Confederate Captain Asbury who was responsible for the shoe-making operation at the prison, and Page began a short career working as a cobbler at the workshop outside of the stockade. According to Page, the shoes they made were sold both to civilians and the military.

Sergeant Kelley, who was imprisoned at Camp Sumter, Savannah, and Camp Lawton, faced the issue of working for the Confederates at Savannah, when he was asked to sign an oath and work for the enemy for pay. In his memoirs published soon after the war, Kelley effectively described the dilemma facing him and others:

> The question which arose in the minds of thousands was: "Is it lawful for me to work for the Confederacy?"—and under ordinary circumstances the answer would invariably be: "No." Then another question: "Is it lawful for the United States to leave us here to perish with cold and hunger, when they have the power to redeem us?" Has not the government first broken the bond of mutual protection existing between us? And if that bond of mutual protection be first broken by the United States, does justice demand a fulfillment on our part, even unto death? No, it cannot." Thus reasoned thousands of prisoners, yet, out of utter detestation of the rebels and their cause, they remained in prison,

---

[11] Ibid., 337.

[12] James Madison Page, and M.J. Haley, *The True Story of Andersonville Prison: A Defense of Major Henry Wirz* (Washington: Neale Publishing, 1908) 164–68.

preferring to die than lift a hand, even indirectly, against the American flag.[13]

Kelley's comments aptly capture the conflicting feelings in the breasts of many POWs—their opposition to the Confederate cause, their desire to escape their trials of confinement, their loyalty to the Union, but their disappointment in their government's failure to exchange them.

By far, though, the most controversial effort at recruiting POWs was the Confederate attempt to enlist them for military service. The resulting antipathy of most Union POWs toward their comrades who accepted such recruiting offers is obvious, but it was controversial for both sides. Many Confederate officials, including General Hardee, expressed strong reservations about the practice.[14] Their feeling was that Union POWs who agreed to enlist did so with the idea, first, of getting out of prison, second, joining a Confederate unit, and third, deserting as soon as possible back to the Union cause. For the POWs, of course, this was a problematic plan, even if they did plan to escape, because formally enlisting in the Confederate military was in itself an act of desertion to the Union. In fact, some who did so found themselves in custody at war's end.[15]

Confederate recruiting officers felt their best chance of recruiting POWs was with foreigners, of whom there were many immigrants on both sides who had not yet qualified for citizenship, and soldiers whose terms of enlistment were up, particularly married men. Evidence of the German presence at Camp Lawton is illustrated by the recovery by archaeologists of a German game piece and a one-pfennig Austrian coin within the stockade area. Sneden remembered that a German POW who

---

[13] Daniel G. Kelley, *What I Saw and Suffered in Rebel Prisons* (Buffalo NY: Thomas Howard & Johnson, 1868) 74.

[14] Lt. Gen. Hardee, based on his experiences with galvanized troops in Savannah, recommended that, "all authority to organize similar commands be revoked" (Hardee to Cooper, 24 December 1864, United States, War Department, *The War of the Rebellion: A Compilation of the Official Records of the Union and Confederate Armies*, series 2, vol. 7 (Washington DC: Government Printing Office, 1880–1901) 1,268).

[15] See collection of documents related to the issue of the treatment of Union POWs who enlisted in the Confederate military (*Official Records*, series 2, vol. 7, 124–26).

had died at Camp Lawton left his "pencils and a few colors" to him.[16] Among the recruiters was Brigadier General Zebulon York who was authorized "to visit Federal prisoners and to recruit from them for his Brigade taking with him such Catholic Chaplains as he may select."[17] That last phrase is telling because the Irish were particularly targeted, as well as other Catholic immigrants. York was of Polish descent and had been severely wounded such that his left arm had to be amputated. Although he apparently never visited Camp Lawton to recruit his "Foreign Battalion," lesser officers operating under his authority did. This recruiting effort led to the most dramatic event in the history of the prison.

Lessel Long has left us an account of that visit; one that went terribly wrong (at least from the Confederate standpoint):

When the excitement of the election had died down, and after several days of weary monotony, orders came in to make out rolls of all those who were born outside of the United States and whose terms of service had expired.... [Many POWs, believing that an exchange was about to take place for those who met the above-mentioned terms, signed the rolls, falsely indicating a foreign birth.] The day following the completion of the rolls, an order came for all those whose names appeared thereon to "fall in." We did so almost as one man. We were on hands by hundreds and by thousands [divisions], and the few "native Americans" left were hardly large enough to have reorganized a lodge of "Know-nothings." We were marched outside the stockade and massed around a stump on which a rebel officer was standing for the purpose of making a speech to us. When all had marched out and silence had been restored, the officer began.... [He told them that the exchange system was broken, that their government had abandoned them, and that the Confederacy was on its way to independence in a few months.] "If you will now join with us,

---

[16] Sneden, *Eye of the Storm*, 264.

[17] Seddon to Adjutant General, 16 November 1864, National Archives, RG249, Records of the Commissary General of Prisons, General Records, Correspondences and Reports ..., 1862–67; and Jno. Blair Hoge to Maj. Garnett Andrews, 10 November 1864, *Official Records*, series 4, vol. 3, 821. For the Confederate preference for Irish and French POW recruits, see Seddon to Lee, 17 November 1864, *Official Records*, series 4, vol. 3, 825; and Hoge to Maj. Gen. D.H. Maury, 10 January 1865, *Official Records*, series 4, vol. 3, 1,011–12.

become our allies until the close of the war, you will receive the same rewards as other Confederate soldiers. You will be taken from the prison, clothed and fed, and when peace crowns our efforts, given a warrant for a good farm, a large bounty, -------"

At this point the sergeant of one of the Divisions, a man with stentorian lungs, sprang out of the ranks and shouted, "Attention, First Division!" The command was repeated down the line by the sergeants of the other Divisions. "First Division, about face," commanded the stout voiced sergeant. The same order followed to the other Divisions. "First Division, forward march," came next, and in an instant each man in all the thousands of prisoners turned on his heel and away the boys marched to the stockade, leaving the crest-fallen officer by himself on the stump.... [The Confederate guards followed the POWs into the stockade and began a search for contraband among the shebangs.] Among the prisoners was a young man named Lloyd, a member of the 61st Ohio Infantry.... Mounting a stump he began a fiery address [denouncing as lies the statements the prisoners had just heard] and predicted that before the spring came the "hell-born Confederacy and all the lousy moss-backs who support it, will be so deep in hell that nothing but a search warrant from the throne of great God of the Universe can discover it. The stars and stripes will wave in triumph over this whole Nation as sure as God reigns and judges in Israel."... A rebel officer came running up and demanded of one of the guards that he should shoot the Yankee son ------- ."

Before the order could be put into effect Lloyd was jerked from his position and his life saved.

Then ensued a scene that beggars description. Shouts were made to charge on the guards; take their guns and make an assault on the gates of the stockade. We hurriedly formed in line of battle and the rebel officers hurried behind the line of the guards. The guards were badly frightened, but held their ground, their muskets leveled to receive our assault. Captain Bows [sic, POWs knew Vowles variously as Vowels, Bows, Bowes, or Bowles], from an elevation outside the prison, had discovered the condition of affairs, loaded and shotted his cannon and stood ready to give the command to sweep the stockade with canister and grape. The long roll was sounded, and for a moment it looked as if the massacre was to begin. Cooler heads among the prisoners realized the desperate danger and lent themselves to an effort to dissolve the line from its menacing attitude. Slowly the boys deserted their line of battle and spread over the prison grounds. The guards by an indirect march, that they might keep their faces toward the prisoners cautiously withdrew. The agony was over, and all drew a sigh of relief.[18]

There is, however, a cautionary note to this fascinating tale. John McElroy (16th Illinois Cavalry) also reports this incident.[19] Long and McElroy's accounts are so similar that one wonders if this conjunction of facts and phrases results from the vivid memory of an actual event or from one borrowing from another. Such a dramatic and frightening event would have been seared into the memory of all those who witnessed it, but only one other POW account mentions it. Alvin Graton testified in the "Shanks Report" about an attempt at mass recruitment aimed at foreigners and married men whose enlistments had expired. His account seems to refer to the same incident reported by Long and McElroy but with much less detail (or perhaps embellishment).[20]

Although this attempt at mass recruitment failed miserably (if, in fact, it ever happened), some Federal soldiers did give in to Confederate efforts to enlist them. For example, Norwegian-born Knude Olson (Company A, 6th New Hampshire), who had originally enlisted as a substitute, was captured at Petersburg on 27 June 1864. Succumbing to the entreaties of a Confederate recruiting officer while at Camp Lawton, he took the oath and enlisted in the Tenth Tennessee (US).[21]

Union soldiers such as Olson who accepted blandishments to join the Confederate forces (and, conversely, Confederates who joined Union

---

[18] Lessel Long, *Twelve Months in Andersonville: On the March—In theBattle—In the Rebel Prison Pens, and at Last in God's Country* (Huntington IN: Thad and Mark Butler, 1886) 93. The Know-nothings were members of a nineteenth-century, anti-immigrant political movement.

[19] John McElroy, *Andersonville: A Story of Rebel Military Prisons, Fifteen Months a Guest of the So-called Confederacy. A Private Soldier's Experience in Richmond, Andersonville, Savannah, Millen, Blackshear and Florence* (Toledo OH: D.R. Locke, 1879) 467–69.

[20] Alvin Graton, Testimony, "Shanks Report," 848–50.

[21] "Norwegians in the Civil War: Knude Olson," Vesterheim Norwegian-American Museum, http://vesterheim.org/CivilWar/db/o/ols/index.html (accessed 25 November 2009). Olson was captured by Federal forces on 28 December 1864, at Egypt's Station, Mississippi. He was sent to Memphis and then to Alton Military Prison in Illinois. He was released after he took the oath of allegiance on 27 June 1865.

units) were said to have "galvanized." Many POWs heaped scorn upon such deserters. In the immediate aftermath of the war, John A. Cain (Second Massachusetts Cavalry) wrote a letter to Secretary of War Edwin Stanton that conveys the tenor of the feelings that he and some of his compatriots felt for those who had galvanized into Confederate service:

> Deeming it my duty to myself and my country, I here send you a partial list of Union prisoners who left the Stockade prison at Camp Lawton near Millen, Ga. On, or about the 1st of November last; and is supposed to have taken the "Oath of Allegience" to the late "confederate Government."
>
> Should this be of any service to you in bringing them to justice I shall consider myself amply compensated for my trouble,...[22]

However, not all Union POWs took the hard line against those who galvanized. Sergeant Oates explained the appeal of the Confederate recruiting offers that November at Camp Lawton:

> Winter was rapidly coming. Already its cold, driving rains and a few chilling frosts had reached our wretched abode.... Our own Government had refused to exchange us. There seemed to be no prospect of escape. The prospect of staying alive in there was about as hopeless. Is it strange that they found a few men who were willing to swear allegiance to the Confederacy—with the mental reservation that they would desert as soon as they could? As I look back across sixteen years at those events, my surprise is, that so few could be found who would go![23]

Following the war, a report by the House of Representatives tabulated the recruitment of Union POWs by Confederate authorities, and in the

---

[22] Cain to Stanton, 3 June 1865, "John Cain's Andersonville Testimony," http://2Mass.omnica.com/References/cains_andersonville.htm (accessed 10 May 2009). Cain wrote his letter from St. Johns College Hospital, where he was recuperating after being exchanged on 30 April 1865. The list he sent to Stanton included 134 names along with their respective units.

[23] J.B. Vaughter, *Prison Life in Dixie. Giving a Short History of the Inhuman and Barbarous Treatment of Our Soldiers by Rebel Authorities, by Sergeant Oates.* 3rd ed. (Chicago: Central Book Concern, 1881) 139–40.

case of Camp Lawton listed 118.[24] However, the sole official return for Camp Lawton, submitted by Captain Vowles on 8 November 1864, gives the number having "enlisted in Confederate service" as 349.[25] Union POW Sergeant Dennison's estimate in his diary entry for 11 November accords well with Vowles report: "[O]ne hundred Federal prisoners took the oath and went in to the Rebel ranks..." This number augmented the 200 whom he reported had already taken the oath on 28 October.[26] Sergeant Kendrick R. Howard (Company K, Fourth Vermont) echoed Dennison's comment in his diary, ["A] good many have gone out and joined the Rebel Army."[27]

Some, but not all of those who "galvanized," may have been "Raiders." The Raider element that had been quelled at Camp Sumter by the hanging of six of its ringleaders resurfaced at Camp Lawton. Their activities at the new prison led to a revival of the vigilante "Regulator" movement that had put an end to the Raider element at Camp Sumter. Ultimately finding themselves the target of the Regulators, many of the Raiders, according to McElroy, escaped by volunteering for Confederate service. As McElroy told the story:

> Our old antagonists—the Raiders—were present in strong force in Millen.... After things began to settle into shape at Millen, they seemed to believe that they were in such ascendancy as to numbers and organization that they could put into execution of vengeance against those of us who had been active participants in the execution of their confederates at Andersonville. [McElroy details the attempts of the Raiders to kill "Wat" Payne and Sergeant Goody (actually, William Goode), each of whom had played a role in the execution of the six Raider leaders at Camp Sumter.] ... [W]e determined to report the matter to the

[24] "Shanks Report," 750–51.

[25] Dispatch from Captain Vowles, 8 November 1864, *Official Records*, series 2, vol. 7, 1,113–14.

[26] Dennison, *Andersonville Diary*, 79, 82. See also "List of Prisoners of War Who Left the Stockade Prison at Camp Lawton Near Millen, Georgia; on or About the 10th of November Last [1864] and Are Supposed to Have Taken the Oath of Allegiance to the Late Confederate Government," National Archives, RG 249, Records of the Commissary General of Prisons, General Records, Correspondences and Reports ..., 1862–67, Box 1.

[27] Kendrick R. Howard, Diary, 8 October–28 October 1864, Miscellaneous File #696, Vermont Historical Society, Barre, Vermont.

Rebel Commandant, from whom we had reason to believe we could expect assistance. We were right. He sent in a squad of guards, arrested Dick Allen, Pete Donnelly, and several other ringleaders, took them out and put them in the stocks.... [T]hey staid there a day and night, and when released, joined the Rebel Army, entering the artillery company that manned the guns in the fort covering the prison.[28]

Knowing that the artillery post on the ridge to the south overlooking the prison was manned, at least in part, by such men must have been worrisome to those POWs who remained within the stockade.

Interestingly, P. Dempsey remembered things a bit differently:

[T]wo days after our arrival at Millen the man that hung the 6 men at Andersonville came in in one of the Detachments and he was quickly recognized by the crowd and they chased him up to the gate and he ran under the Dead line under the Protection of the Rebel Guards and they took him out of the prison and we never heard from him after[. T]hey called him Slim Jim.[29]

This would indicate that those who chased him were either Raider remnants or that the bulk of the prisoners, despite the Raiders' unsavory reputation, did not approve of Slim Jim's actions at Andersonville.[30]

---

[28] McElroy, *Andersonville*, 460–62; Ida Maude Walimaki was interviewed in *The Issaquah Press*, http://www.issaquahpress.comn/main.asp?SectionID=25&SubSectionID=32& ArticleID=20... (accessed 24 August 2008), about her two grandfathers, William Goode and George Tibbetts, who had been Union POWs during the Civil War. The article, "Ida Walimaki Recalls Her Grandfathers' Daring Exploits in the Civil War," by Joe Peterson, states that while at Camp Lawton, Goode was "discovered by the New York terrorists [the Raiders] and nearly beaten to death." Amos Yeakle (Diary, 4 November 1864, ANHS) mentions POWs taking an oath to the Confederacy and serving in the artillery unit at Camp Lawton. Free Lance, "Southern Prison Life," 9 September 1882, and Sneden, *Images from the Storm*, 228, indicate that the POWs organized a police force for the camp, and Free Lance repeated McElroy's story that the Raider leaders were placed in stocks, decided to galvanize, and ultimately helped man the prison's artillery.

[29] P. Dempsey, Letter to Mrs. Van Deusen, 27–28, and M.J. Umstead, 7 November 1864, Diary transcription, Andersonville diaries, ANHS, II, 378, also reported the "maltreatment of one of the regulators from Anderson prison."

[30] Robert Scott Davis, *Ghosts and Shadows of Andersonville: Essays on the Secret Social Histories of America's Deadliest Prison* (Macon GA: Mercer University Press, 2006) 103–28, devotes an entire chapter to a discussion of this mysterious character, also known as "Limber Jim," who was involved in the infamous hanging of the Raider leaders. Hitchcock

Not all prisoners saw the Regulators as much of an improvement over the Raiders whom they had deposed. William Hawkins (154th New York) maintained that they were little better than the Raiders, that they "became a tyrannical little oligarchy—entertaining complaints as they pleased, & trying the same without any form of law or rules of evidence." While at Camp Sumter, Hawkins remembered being the victim of "false complaint of theft & was not allowed to call a witness & was sentenced to help clean the streets &c one day."[31] Sneden, in fact, used the terms "Regulators" and "Police" interchangeably. Considering them "a hard and cruel set," he indicated that they not only enforced discipline through various corporal punishment devices—the buck and gag, flogging with "switches," the "cross"—but also divided the rations.[32]

Then, there were the inevitable escape attempts. In all wars prisoners try to escape their captors and, in fact, they are expected to make an effort to do so and are often trained for the purpose. Part of the "romance" of Civil War prison literature is the large number of prison escape accounts recounted by the authors. However, this is not a major feature of Camp Lawton stories. At least one of Sneden's camp illustrations includes dotted lines tracing the directions of escape tunnels, and excerpts from his journal tell of tunnels being planned and dug. His journal entries of 8 and 10 November 1864, tell of the measures taken by a group of "miners" of which he was a member and the countermeasures taken by the Confederate authorities.

> We worked hard at the tunnel in reliefs of ten men each, and struck the foundations of the stockade by daylight, when we stopped, all completely used up. We will have to dip three more feet to clear it. The night was windy and dark, which favored operations. A great quantity of tree roots had to be cut through, but we went around the stumps in all cases, which makes "the hole" very crooked. The earth and roots were carried down to a part of the enclosure not much frequented, and packed between two

---

says that the executioner of the Raiders was chased out of Camp Lawton by "some of the old gang" (*Ashby to Andersonville*, 268).

[31] William Hawkins, typescript of interview, c. 7–8 August 1880, 12, provided courtesy of Mark Dunkelmann.

[32] Sneden, Diary, VHS, vol. 6, 112.

large felled trees which still lay there about six feet apart. It was carried in the boxes with handles, used for policing the camp. [Before the tunnel was completed, the group was betrayed, and Sneden explains what happened] ... Duncan and Hughes [Confederate quartermasters] are sounding the space between the stockade and the deadline for it [the tunnel] with crowbars. In the meantime we are destroying the entrance, which is inside a log shanty, by first bracing sticks across the hole or well, three feet from the surface, stretching an old blanket over, with brush wood, and filling up level with sand. The whole shanty is then taken down, the occupants move off to some other part of the camp, and when the Rebels trace the tunnel to its former site, "nobody knows anything about it."[33]

Lessel Long detailed another account of an unsuccessful tunneling operation. The miners actually were able to burrow under the wall line, but when an attempt was made to break through to the surface beyond the stockade wall one night, the tunnel collapsed around the hapless POW who was left with only his head sticking out of the tunnel exit. He could neither climb out of the tunnel nor retreat within it. The guards discovered the wriggling POW, rescued the would-be escapee, and broke in the tunnel the next morning rendering it useless.[34]

Another, creative attempt to escape from Camp Lawton unraveled when a package arrived at the prison in the third week of October addressed to POW Joseph Adner. Suspicious, the prison authorities opened it, and Vowles reported to General Winder that it contained a "Conf. S. Uniform Jacket." Adner was interrogated and admitted that the jacket had been sent to him to facilitate his means of escape. He then implicated Savannah postmaster Solomon Cohen in the plot. When Winder accused Cohen of complicity, the postmaster responded to the Postmaster General denying involvement. Confederate House member Julian Hartridge defended Cohen's character, and prominent Georgia politician and former governor Herschel Johnson demanded to know the

---

[33] Sneden, *Eye of the Storm*, 261–63.
[34] Long, Twelve *Months in Andersonville*, 88–90.

truth. Unfortunately, as is the case with so many things related to Camp Lawton, the records do not tell the outcome of this controversy.[35]

Ultimately, though, the official report gives the number of escapees from Camp Lawton as only fourteen.[36] The reasons for the relative paucity both in the number of escape accounts and the numbers of escapees from Camp Lawton probably derive from the fact that the prison was short-lived and the POWs were living with the expectation of an imminent renewal of the exchange system. In the terrible and uncertain calculus of prisoner planning at that point in the war, waiting for an impending exchange with the prospect of a safe return home probably appeared to be a better option than making an escape into a hostile territory with unknown consequences.

Several accounts mentioned a set of stocks placed outside the walls near the gate. These were used to punish prisoners for serious infractions, such as tunneling and escape. Chaplain Bradley described the stocks as follows: "Near the entranceway was a small building, or rather the roof of one, set on posts, under which our soldiers were punished, I concluded, as stocks for the feet were lying near. I counted holes enough for seven persons, and they appeared to be well worn."[37] As previously mentioned, McElroy recollected that some of the Raider elements were put in the stocks.

Camp Lawton POWs eagerly sought news of the outside world. They wanted to know how the war was progressing but, more importantly to them, they hoped desperately for a renewal of the exchange of prisoners. Rumors of exchanges were rife, and the prison staff was complicit in stirring up such hopes. Many prisoners selected for transport to waiting trains eagerly boarded them because they believed that they had been selected for an exchange. Prisoners not selected for transport often attempted to "flank" their way into the railroad cars.

---

[35] Vowles to General Winder, 26 October 1864; Julian Hartridge to Seddon, 5 December 1864, National Archives, RG77, Letters Received by the Confederate Adjutant General and Inspector General, 1861–1865, Jan.–Dec. 1864, National Archives.

[36] House of Representatives, *Report No. 45*, 750–51.

[37] George S. Bradley, *The Star Corps or Notes of an Army Chaplain During Sherman's Famous "March to the Sea"* (Milwaukee WI: Jermain & Brightman, 1865) 203; Thomas R. Aldrich, Unpublished Memoir (courtesy of Patricia Wilcox of Fairport, New York) 29.

POW accounts are full of comments on how disappointed the prisoners were when they disembarked those trains only to find themselves marched to new prison compounds. The hopes of many POWs who had left Camp Sumter and Camp Davidson (Savannah) were deflated when they disembarked at Camp Lawton. Because of this, prisoners had lost faith in the official pronouncements of Confederate officials. When they had the chance, they probed their guards with questions. Newspapers provided another source of information. Paroled prisoners who worked outside of the camp smuggled newspapers into the stockade, which were read assiduously by the news-starved inmates.[38] Veteran POWs eagerly queried "fresh fish" as they entered the compound. Of particular interest were recently captured soldiers from Sherman's command. On November 15, Lucius Barber wrote in his diary that prisoners brought in from Sherman's command reported that the Union army was preparing to leave Atlanta for the coast and that Richmond had been captured.[39]

Obviously, the news that Grant had captured Richmond was erroneous, but the news relating to Sherman had more substance. Camp Lawton's POWs had no way of distinguishing fact from fiction. The paucity of hard news, thus, meant that "King Rumor" continued to reign at the prison as inmates attempted to discover what was going on beyond their walls. Ransom, for example, in his diary entry for 10 November, told of an unusual source of information and what he inferred from it:

> We are not far from the railroad track, and can listen to the cars going by. Very often Confederate troops occupy them and they give the old familiar rebel yell. Once in a while the Yanks get up enough steam to give a good hurrah back to them. Seems to be a good deal of transferring troops now in the South. I watch all the movements of the rebels and can

---

[38] Anonymous, *A Voice from Rebel Prisons Giving an Account of Some of the Horrors of the Stockades at Andersonville, Milan and Other Prisons by a Returned Prisoner of War* (Boston: Rand & Avery, 1865) 15; Urban, *Battlefield and Prison Pen*, 452.

[39] Lucius W. Barber, *Army Memoirs of Lucius W. Barber, Company "D," 15th Illinois Volunteer Infantry. May 24, 1861, to Sept. 30, 1865* (Chicago: J.M.W. Jones Stationery and Printing Co., 1894) 178–79.

draw conclusions, and am of the opinion that Mr. Confederacy is about whipped and will soon surrender. It certainly looks that way to me.[40]

Many rumors centered on the whereabouts of Sherman's forces, but Sherman's army was not the only thing advancing on Camp Lawton in November of 1864. The weather was changing.[41] POW veterans who had survived the innervating heat, merciless sun, and biting insects of the previous South Georgia summer at Camp Sumter were now going to face another challenge. As the fall progressed, the weather began to grow colder. Among newer entries in the catalog of complaints by Union POWs was the frequent mention of cold weather that led to considerable suffering among the prisoners, particularly at night. Beginning on 18 October and ending with his departure from Camp Lawton, James Dennison complained about the cold weather in fifteen separate daily diary entries. In three of those entries (23 October; 6, 12 November), he reported frost.[42] Sneden's meteorological reminiscences of that period were as follows: 17 November, "cold and some snow"; 18 November, "two inches of snow"; 22 November, "Snow is on the ground yet."[43] Adding to the discomfort and coupled with the lowering temperatures was the increasing precipitation of fall. Rain fell on 19 and 20 November, and continued the next morning. By that afternoon (21 November) freezing rain and snow pelted the countryside as the temperature plummeted. During the six-day period from 21 November to 26

---

[40] John L. Ransom, *Andersonville Diary: Escape, and List of Dead with Name, Company, Regiment, Date of Death and Number of Grave in Cemetery* (Philadelphia: Douglas Brothers, 1883) 165.

[41] Noah Andre Trudeau, *Southern Storm: Sherman's March to the Sea* (New York: HarperCollins, 2008). Trudeau, a recent chronicler of the March to the Sea, has made a study of the weather encountered by Sherman's troops from 15 November, when they left Atlanta, to 9 December, by which time they had invested Savannah. His analysis, based upon diary accounts of the March participants, dovetails well with the reports of Camp Lawton inmates. The synopsis of the weather is drawn from Trudeau's work. Cornelius C. Platter, who was marching with Sherman, noted that it "rained heavily" on November 21, that it was "very very cold" on 22 November (with snow and the ground frozen at camp), and that it was "still very cold" on 23 November. "Cornelius C. Platter Diary," Hargrett Library, Digital Library of Georgia, http//dlg.galileo.usg.edu/hargrett/platter/006.php (accessed 9 September 2009).

[42] Dennison, *Andersonville Diary*, 75, 78, 81, 82, 84.

[43] Sneden, Diary, VHS, vol. 6, 155, 156.

November, the East Central Georgia area experienced freezing or nearly freezing temperatures. W.F. Lyon (Company A, 9th Minnesota) remembered the suffering caused by the rain, wind, and low temperatures: "I think the most trying experience I ever had with the weather was during a rainy day in November [1864]. My clothes were wet through. There was no fire where I could warm myself; no way to escape the wind, and I couldn't exercise enough to keep warm."[44] Other POW accounts tell of inmates having to walk all night to avoid freezing to death.[45] Ezra Hoyt Ripple (52nd Pennsylvania), a prisoner at Camp Sumter, described an additional survival strategy adopted by POWs in reaction to the onset of cold weather: "[A]s the weather grew colder, we would hold our rations until nearly dark before we cooked them, and then eating our breakfast, dinner, and supper, as hot as we could bear it, would lie down at once and endeavor to sleep while the warmth of the food was in us."[46]

Ripple also detailed "spooning," a well-known cold weather sleeping technique employed not only by POWs but men in the field as well:

> We all had to lie the same way with the hand under our heads for a pillow, and the upper hand free for defensive purposes, against the common enemy [lice]. After a while our bodies would get so sore and tired that we would be obliged turn over, and from someone would come the order "spoon right" or "spoon left" and we would all change front to rear. We got so accustomed to this that we would change frequently while asleep or not thoroughly awake.[47]

One can imagine that the inmates of Camp Lawton followed similar prescriptions to deal with the cold nights. Sneden, in fact, reported in his diary entry of 10 November 1864, that the brick ovens built within the Camp Lawton stockade "have not been yet used for cooking rations for

---

[44] W.F. Lyon, *In and Out of Andersonville Prison* (Detroit IL: Geo. Harland Co., 1905) 81.

[45] J.E. Hodgkins, *The Civil War Diary of Lieut. J. E. Hodgkins: 19th Massachusetts Volunteers from August 11, 1862 to June 3, 1865*, trans. Kenneth C. Turino (Camden ME: Picton Press, 1994) 109.

[46] Ezra Hoyt Ripple in *Dancing Along the Deadline: The Andersonville Memoir of a Prisoner of the Confederacy*, ed. Mark A. Snell (Novato CA: Presidio Press, 1996) 68–69.

[47] Ibid., 69.

us as intended when built, and are filled by night by shivering prisoners who lie close together [spooning, no doubt] to keep warm."[48] One of the ovens was also the setting of a ghastly anecdote recounted by Private John Sammons (5th Indiana Cavalry): "While walking through the prison one day I passed an oven in which one of our prison boys had crept. He was lying there still alive, though the maggots were crawling out of his eyes and ears. This was the worst sight I had seen since I left Andersonville."[49]

Ripple's comments on the need to keep one hand free to deal with the lice were echoed by Henry A. Harmon:

> The weather was comfortable in the daytime, but the nights were cold. The "grayback" seemed to appreciate this fact, for they redoubled their excursions to creep into warm quarters. Their numbers increased in our clothing as the nights grew chilly, and we found it an impossibility to keep them down. Heretofore by careful search once a day we could, to a certain extent, keep their numbers reduced, but now our principal occupation was "skirmishing," otherwise they would have carried us bodily off.[50]

The snow and freezing rain that began falling on the afternoon of 21 November continued overnight and into the next day. From 22 November to 24 November, early morning temperatures were in the 20s, and the daily highs were no warmer than the low 40s. Both Sherman's oncoming troops and the inmates at Camp Lawton reported ice forming on the edges of ponds and streams. For some POWs the cooler temperatures, combined with the rain and snow, meant a death sentence. "We suffered most during the cold rains, for our clothing would get soaked with the ice cold water....You cannot understand the suffering

---

[48] Sneden, *Eye of the Storm*, 263; Aldrich (Unpublished Memoir, 29) actually uses the phrase "spoon fashion" to describe those who slept in the ovens.

[49] John H. Sammons, *Personal Recollections of the Civil War* (Greensburg IN: Montgomery & Son, n.d.) 48.

[50] Henry A. Harmon, "Memoirs of Henry A. Harmon," cited in Bill Giles, *"The World's Largest Prison": A Camp Lawton Compendium* (Magnolia Springs State Park GA: Café Press, 2004) 170. The term "grayback" was also used to describe Confederate paper currency as opposed to Union "greenbacks."

and terrible misery of this period by any description I can give you."[51] Scantily clad, ill-fed, and poorly housed, with weakened immune systems, POWs were susceptible to pneumonia and hypothermia. Some froze to death.[52]

As the weather turned colder, Free Lance wrote in his diary, "Boys, which do you like best roasting in Andersonville or freezing in Millen?"[53] Sergeant Dennison's diary entry for 24 October said it all: ["M]en dyes verry fast hear now on a count of the cold knights."[54]

The trauma of the Civil War prison experience caused many inmates to seek spiritual solace in an effort to cope with the difficult circumstances in which they found themselves. This could manifest itself in spontaneous revivals, visits by local ministers, and the reading of the Bible and other devotional literature. For example, Sergeant Boston Corbett (16th New York Cavalry), famous as the man who shot John Wilkes Booth and notorious for his eccentric religious beliefs, participated in religious services while at Camp Sumter.[55] At Camp Lawton, several POWs mentioned Bibles as prized possessions of their owners.[56] Sergeant Henry Tisdale (35th Massachusetts) wrote in his diary entry for 20 November: "Finished reading book of Job and commenced the book of Proverbs. Never has God's word been so full of good cheer and uplifting comfort as in these days of prison life."[57] Henry Harmon had a friend who had a copy of a devotional classic, *The Saints' Everlasting Rest* (c. 1650) by Richard Baxter, which the friend read

---

[51] Ripple, *Dancing Along the Deadline*, 70.

[52] Dennison, *Andersonville Diary*, 78-79, 81; Sneden, *Eye of the Storm*, 271; Aldrich, Unpublished Memoir, 29.

[53] Free Lance, "Southern Prison Life," 16 September 1882.

[54] Dennison, Andersonville Diary, 78.

[55] Davis (*Andersonville*, 26) gives a brief summary of Corbett's religious activities at Camp Sumter. See also the first-person account concerning Corbett in P. Dempsey, Letter to Mrs. Van Dusen, 16.

[56] Urban, *Battlefield and Prison Pen*, 455. Urban recalled a friend, William Dutton (Company A., First Pennsylvania Reserves) who read his Bible frequently.

[57] Tisdale, 6 November 1864, "Diary."

"incessantly."[58] The POWs at Camp Lawton were also ministered to by at least one local Catholic priest.[59]

However, other, more secular activities lightened the day-to-day activities in Camp Lawton. Several POWs told of recreational activities at the prison. In his diary entry for 2 November, John Ransom says, "Sort of prize fight going on now."[60] Henry Tisdale remembered an open space in the prison where ball games were played.[61] Chester Townsend Hart (Company E, 115th Illinois) also remembered "the men ... playing ball today."[62] One is left to wonder if this were baseball, a popular game among soldiers in the Civil War. Board games and cards and other games of chance were not unknown.[63] Sneden, for instance, mentioned "Honest John," Euchre," and "Seven Up" as being played at Camp Lawton.[64] POWs also undoubtedly engaged in what Mark Twain might have called "guying the guards"; that is, toying with their captors to amuse themselves.[65] William Smith told of verbally sparring with a guard soon after the mock election:

> It was just a few days after Mr. Lincoln was elected ... a fact which at the time we were not apprised of, though, I think, the Confederates were, and felt crusty over it.... One guard as if endeavoring to raise his drooping spirits and dampen mine, as I thought, broke out on that occasion with this jingle:
> "Davis on a white horse, Lincoln on a mule;
> Davis is the President, And Lincoln is a fool."
> Not knowing whether Lincoln had been reelected or not this sentimental poetry rather nonplused me for the instant, and the only

---

[58] Harmon, "A Year in Six Rebel Prisons," 171.

[59] Anonymous, *A Voice from Rebel Prisons*, 15; Yeakle, 4 November 1864, Diary, ANHS.

[60] Ransom, *Andersonville Diary*, 161; Yeakle, 6 November 1864, Diary; Chester Townsend Hart, Diary transcript, ANHS.

[61] Tisdale, 6 November 1864, "Diary," http://www.civilwardiary.net (accessed 12 September 2008).

[62] Hart, 17 November 1864, Diary transcript, ANHS.

[63] McElroy, *Andersonville*, 453, mentioned that he and his messmate Andrews had a chessboard. During the archeological explorations of the site in 2010, one game piece was uncovered within the stockade area.

[64] Sneden, Diary, VHS, vol. 6, 114.

[65] Taken from "Guying the Guides," a chapter in Mark Twain's *Innocents Abroad* (1869).

retort I could make was they would find out before a great while that Lincoln's mule could kick the hardest.[66]

The irregular events of life at Camp Lawton—the mock election, recruiting campaigns, escape attempts, acquisition of newspapers, exchanges, and recreational diversions—provided some relief from the repetitive, stultifying rituals of prison life. Besides the drawing of rations, the interminable daily roll call interposed a grim sense of regularity and tedium among the inmates.[67] In a sense, however, these experiences were shared with those on the other side of the stockade walls because POWs were not the only ones who suffered from the prison experience. As was the case with the administrative staff, the guard force at Camp Lawton was essentially a carry-over from that of Camp Sumter. Comprised mainly of units composed of those considered too old or too young for normal service in the field, prison guards were typically poorly trained and ill-equipped. General Winder believed, and he was not alone in this opinion, that they were often poorly led, as well. Winder and other regular officers viewed the reserves with professional disdain. He preferred to use regular field units as guards, but the necessities of war generally rendered those troops unavailable to him.

Guard duty in the camps was hard service because the prisons were typically understaffed. Rations and clothing were often scant. The type of service combined with the nature of the guards themselves resulted in low morale and homesickness. In one diary entry, Sneden gave a tally of dead Confederate guards at Camp Lawton as thirty-three (since 15 September), with 120 in the hospital.[68] Illness and malnourishment, therefore, affected both prisoners and their captors. Nor were POWs the only ones who had to endure the long, slow, rickety train rides to and from Camp Lawton. Guards accompanying the prisoners rode exposed to the same conditions as their charges, often riding on top of boxcars. If it were rainy and/or cold, the guards suffered, plus they had the

---

[66] William B. Smith, *On Wheels: and How I Came There: The True Story of a 15-Year-Old Yankee and Prisoner in the American Civil War*, ed. Stacy M. Haponik (College Station TX: Virtualbookworm.com, 2002) 146.

[67] Sneden, Diary, VHS, vol. 6, 113.

[68] Ibid., 153. In the same entry he listed 200 Union POWs in their hospital.

additional strain of required vigilance. Also, when they accompanied POWs to other sites, the guards were sometimes commandeered by local commanders who desperately needed them for other purposes. Guards were also exposed at times to the taunts of members of combat units who questioned whether their guard service was a dodge to remain out of the fight.[69]

Despite their mutually antagonistic positions, Confederate guards and Union POWs at Camp Lawton exhibited a wide range of attitudes toward one another. As is typical in wartime, many guards and prisoners demonized one another, and the diaries and post-war published accounts are full of such characterizations. Many of the stories recounted by Union POWs of their interactions with prison guards are of the "city mouse-country mouse" variety and focus on their perception of the ignorance of the typical Southerner as represented by the guards. Numerous accounts featured the prisoners outwitting their guards by flanking to join other groups, escaping, besting them in trades, smuggling contraband, stealing from them, and in general fooling them. Of course, this is an archetype in guard-prisoner literature across the ages, and there is a bit of the perverse humor of "Hogan's Heroes" in these tales. These stories also served to buttress their Northern readership's sense of the inferiority of their former foes and, therefore, augment their belief in the superiority of the Union cause.

However, in some cases both guards and prisoners came to see themselves as being caught in a bad situation, not of their making, that enjoined a kind of mutual empathy and comradeship. Sneden, for

---

[69] P. Dempsey remembered an incident at Danville, Virginia, in July 1864, when a fellow POW getting a drink of water from a stream "jolted against one of the Confederate Home Guards and knocked his gun in the water." The guard recovered his weapon and struck the prisoner in the side with the butt of his gun, at which point the prisoners retaliated "by giving him a good punch in the face and knocking him down." This dangerously escalating situation was defused when a Confederate combat veteran— Dempsey calls him one of Stonewall Jackson's men—"chastised the Home Guard by telling him that he would smash his face if he dared to hit the prisoner again." It turns out that his rescuer was a paroled POW whose experiences led him to sympathize more with the Union prisoner than his Confederate colleague. P. Dempsey, Letter to Mrs. Van Deusen, n.d, MSC 17698, New York State Archives, New York State Education Department, Cultural Education Center, Albany, New York, 7–8.

example, when facing what he thought was his possible execution at Camp Lawton, reported a conversation with a group of guards assigned to watch him:

> The guards were young fellows of the 53rd Georgia Reserves [probably the 55th] and were good natured and green at soldiering, for they sat on the tree on each side of me, and conversed freely on the situation, and cursed Winder for a drunken tyrant. It was now sundown, and the guards brought me some fried bacon, corn bread, and sweet potatoes.... [They] even volunteered to shoot over my head in case they would be detailed for my execution.... Several of the soldiers were fairly educated, and were "gentlemen's sons," others of the "poor whites" were ignorant as mules but not bad hearted in the main.[70]

The latter comment perhaps indicates that these "bottom-of-the-barrel" units were partly comprised of the sons of the wealthy whose families used their influence to avoid field service for them, if not reserve duty, as well as those who were not considered fit for regular service because of age or physical condition. Although the reserve units may have harbored those who were trying to avoid combat duty, many were there because they did not originally qualify for active duty but now had been called into service.

Others were driven by patriotism. One can also imagine that some of the young enrollees were eager lads whose worried families only allowed them to serve in reserve units since they were not to be taken out of state nor were such units expected to see combat. The reality, of course, is that each individual in the reserves had a unique set of circumstances leading to his enlistment. The records relating to the Georgia Reserve units, which composed the bulk of the prison guards in

---

[70] Sneden, *Eye of the Storm*, 265–66. The mention of a unit called the 53rd Georgia Reserves is problematic. There seems not to have been such a unit at Camp Lawton. The 53rd Georgia Volunteer Infantry existed, but it served with the Army of Northern Virginia for the duration except for detached duty under General Longstreet in the Western Theatre in 1863–64. However, a portion of the 55th Georgia Volunteer Infantry served as guards at Camp Sumter and may have been at Camp Lawton, as well. Perhaps Sneden was mistaken about the unit's nomenclature, or this might represent a transcription error from his diary. His depiction of the reserve unit as being made up of men from opposite sides of Southern society ("gentlemen's sons" and "poor whites"), however, rings true.

the Confederate prisons in the state, are fragmentary. What does exist provides an insight into the nature of the reserve units that guarded Camp Lawton. One of those units was Company A, 1st Georgia Reserves. In one of its muster rolls, dated 31 October 1864, its station was listed as Camp Lawton. When the unit was originally mustered into Confederate service, on 1 May 1864, its complement was seventy-three men, sixty-four of whose ages are given.[71] Of that sixty-four, forty-three were ages 17 or younger; nineteen were 45 or older; and only two were between the ages of 17 and 45. One of those was 23; the other was 34. Of the fifty-eight whose occupations are known, forty-seven were farmers. The company commander was Captain W.A. Wood. On the 31 October muster roll, under the "Recapitulation" section, there is a qualitative assessment of the unit's condition:

Discipline ... Tolerably good
Instruction ... Tolerably good
Military appearance ... Ordinary
Arms ... Good order
Accoutrements ... Bad quality ... not in good order
Clothing ... Indifferent

This "snapshot" of a guard unit reveals that, in fact, it was made up of older teenagers and men just over the normal service age and also reflects a degree of discipline, equipage, and dress that would have been considered, at best, mediocre in regular line units. These factors undoubtedly contributed to West Point-trained General Winder's frustration with the reserve units. In fact, such regiments were subjected to difficult service characterized by poor rations, lack of respect by officers and men of "regular" units, poor equipment and training, and a heavy workload. However, in actual field usage the Georgia Reserves belied their negative reputation and proved their worth in December 1864 when pressed into service in South Carolina defending the Augusta to Charleston railroad.

---

[71] Jane Benson, "Muster Roll of Company A," http://www.angelfire.com/tx/Randys Texas/casreserve1/page4.html (accessed 2 May 2010).

Although POW accounts from Camp Sumter routinely described Captain Wirz, General Winder, and others as monsters guilty of callousness and brutality toward their prisoners, most inmates' descriptions of Camp Lawton's administrators focused on Captain Vowles and were generally positive. According to Sneden, he was "a mild and lenient man."[72] McElroy also gave a positive evaluation of Vowles as commandant of the prison—"the best of his kind"—but he also added, "The only charge I have to make against Bowes [Vowles] is that he took money from well prisoners for giving them the first chance to go through the Sick Exchange."[73] Sergeant Kelley told of a "kind-hearted" officer of the guard (perhaps Vowles) who, on the cold night of November 15, while sick exchangees were waiting by the railroad for trains to take them to Savannah, "caused fires to be built, and those who could not walk, to be placed around them."[74]

Ransom described Vowles as "sociable and kindly disposed," as well as "kind hearted," and related that he even put up a kind of suggestion box in the stockade.[75] Herbert Taylor (1st New Hampshire Cavalry) also praised Vowles.[76] Henry Tisdale commented, "The officer in charge seems to be a gentleman as well as a soldier and as far as we can see does all he can for our welfare."[77] Free Lance was the most ebullient: "Captain Bowles [Vowles] is a splendid fellow, and is much respected by the prisoners," and he "appears to be a genuine gentleman and soldier."[78] Lucius Barber, however, held a dissenting opinion of Vowles, writing that "[h]e is a harsh commander."[79]

Because General Winder took such an active role in the administration of Camp Sumter, he often figured prominently in inmate memoirs stemming from that prison. However, despite his presence at Camp Lawton, the general is rarely mentioned in inmate accounts there.

---

[72] Sneden, *Eye of the Storm*, 261–62.

[73] McElroy, *Andersonville*, 206–07.

[74] Kelley, *What I Saw*, 81.

[75] Ransom, *Andersonville Diary*, 159, 161.

[76] Herbert Taylor, "Shanks Report," 826–30.

[77] Tisdale, 17 October 1864, "Diary."

[78] Free Lance, "Southern Prison Life," 16 September 1882.

[79] Barber, *Army Memoirs*, 179.

This probably stems from the fact that once General Winder had planned and overseen the completion of Camp Lawton, he let the prison staff run things while he concentrated on his broader administrative duties as Commissary General of Military Prisons in Georgia and Alabama.[80] The volume and content of his dispatches in the *Official Records*, as well his virtual absence from POW accounts, testify to this. Inmate letters, diaries, and published accounts relating to Camp Lawton and dealing with the Confederate prison staff tend rather to focus on Captain Vowles, Colonel Forno, the guards, and various doctors (especially Dr. Isaiah White).

One Union POW who did mention an interaction with General Winder at Camp Lawton was Sneden. He described a contentious encounter with the general that led to his threatened execution. Sneden had been escorted out of the stockade when he had volunteered to serve as a clerk at prison headquarters to the surgeon. He was marched through the gate and up the hill to the building that served as the general's headquarters.

> Winder was seated at a table covered with papers, while seven or eight officers stood around him. After several questions of how long I had been a prisoner? Whether I could write a Latin invoice of medicines? etc. I was accepted and a written parole given me to read over, which I must first take. [Sneden objected to the terms of the parole] … and as I told Winder that I did not recognize any "Confederate States of America" he sprang up with a volley of oaths, and said, "he'd damn show me," etc. I argued that I had a right to escape when opportunity offered, in fact, that "it was my business to run away, and their business to catch me." Winder was now infuriated and called on the provost marshal to read a document of some kind to me, which that individual proceeded to do after a delay to adjust his spectacles.

Sneden then listened as the provost marshal read to him a statement which ended with the phrase "shot to death by musketry" after which "Winder yelled with many oaths to 'take the prisoner away,' when two rebel guards entered and marched me off." Sneden spent a night under

---

[80] Davis, *Andersonville*, 28, mentions the fact that General Winder rarely even visited the stockade as the summer of 1864 turned to fall. He seems to have continued this practice at Camp Lawton.

guard fearing that he would be executed the next morning, but the Confederate surgeon, Dr. Isaiah White, apparently interceded to secure Sneden's services as a clerk.[81]

POW Daniel R. Ross (123rd New York) wrote a memoir in 1889 in which he reflected on his treatment by his captors:

> I never saw any actual cruelty deliberately planned and practiced except at Andersonville.... In happy contrast to this was the conduct of the great majority of the men that fought the battles of the Southern cause.... [Except for the guards at Andersonville] I never, during the time I was a prisoner in their hands nor during the many years since that I have lived among them, have heard an unkind word or seen an unkind act done by those that formed the "rank and file" of the Rebel army to their Yankee neighbors.[82]

Union POWs in the South were an attraction for the local populace. Whether in prison or in transport, local people would come out to "see the Yankees." Despite its location in a relatively remote area, visitors came to Camp Lawton out of curiosity. John Ransom remembered, "Many ladies come to see us; don't come through the gate but look at us through that loophole."[83] Free Lance also recounted the experience of a party of women who rode the train from Augusta to see the Union POWs at the prison. According to Free Lance their excursion came to an abrupt end when they peered into the contents of a passing military covered wagon and were shocked to discover that "it was filled with dead prisoners. Stark naked, piled up in a great heap, and being hauled to the graveyard."[84] Martin O'Hara remembered a similar episode with differing details:

---

[81] Sneden, *Eye of the Storm*, 264–68. Often, Sneden's accounts of his interactions with his captors place them at a considerable disadvantage in terms of manners, education, and moral standing. This is a common characteristic of POW literature, whether Union or Confederate.

[82] Cited in D. Reid Ross, *Lincoln's Veterans Win the War: The Hudson Valley's Ross Brothers and the Union's Fight for Emancipation* (Albany: State University of New York Press, 2008) 368.

[83] Ransom, *Andersonville Diary*, 162.

[84] Free Lance, "Southern Prison Life," 16 September 1882.

A party of ladies came to have a look at us…, one day. The gates [of the prison] were opened, and they stood looking in. One of the party, wishing to gratify her curiosity, stepped in far enough to look along the deadline. This would not do, she was quickly pulled back…. It would not do for her to see the dead lying at the gate.[85]

Assuming that the camp's death register is representative of the population within the stockade, camp visitors saw a population that came from twenty-three states, including from two Confederate states. The Confederate states were Tennessee and Virginia, and those POWs were members of loyal (Federal) units from those states—i.e., 2nd Virginia Cavalry and 7th Tennessee Cavalry, for example. Not represented in the death register were soldiers from California and Oregon, as one would expect, as well as men from Rhode Island, Missouri, Kansas, and Minnesota. Even after it was evacuated, the attraction remained as many of Sherman's soldiers, passing close to Camp Lawton, took the time to visit the depopulated compound.

Despite the paucity of official records deriving from Camp Lawton, those that did survive give us additional, fragmentary glimpses of the operation of the prison that POW accounts do not mention. As the war entered its final stages, the Confederate government increasingly found it more difficult to use its own currency to purchase items abroad or to engage in other transactions that required US currency. Refusing to recognize officially the growing gap between the real values of the two currencies, the Confederate government would not trade for US currency on any other terms than parity. In an attempt to secure such funds in an arena in which they could control the market, Richmond authorities turned to the prisons because captured Union soldiers often had US money on them when taken. Such money was usually taken from the soldiers for "safekeeping," and receipts were given. Accordingly, on 8 November, Captain R.B. Winder, Quartermaster of Confederate Military Prisons in Georgia and Alabama, who was stationed at Camp Lawton, received a request from Captain C. Morfit, Assistant Quartermaster in Richmond: "I have been appointed sole agent for the purchase of

---

[85] Martin O'Hara, *Reminiscences of Andersonville and Other Rebel Prisons: A Story of Suffering and Death* (Lyons IA: J.C. Hopkins, Printer, Advertiser Office, 1880) 46.

Northern currency. I want to buy $10,000 for the Government. Can I get it in your department[?] Please let me know what can be done."[86]

This request was not necessarily directed solely to Camp Lawton because Captain Winder had broader geographic responsibilities. Weeks later Morfit was still trying to raise US currency from the prisons after Camp Lawton was evacuated because he wrote Captain Winder on 24 December, encouraging him to make sure the POWS were carefully "searched when received at the prisons."[87] A major reason for the lack of success in securing US currency was that the Confederate government officially insisted on a dollar (US) for dollar (CS) exchange, which was simply not tenable in the real world of 1864 currency values.

Official records also show Captain R.B. Winder involved in another episode at Camp Lawton that reflected the deteriorating situation in the Confederacy in late 1864. As the Confederacy became increasingly short of manpower for its armed forces, authorities in Richmond scoured the military bureaucracy for persons who could possibly serve in the field. Accordingly, Captain Winder received a request from the Adjutant and Inspector General's Office to furnish a list of men between the ages of 18 and 45 who had been detailed to his service, along with an analysis of their ability for field service and a justification of their continued use in their current positions. Winder responded on November 8, listing his chief clerk, William Butler, and Milton Pickett, who ran a team of thirty mules and fifteen black laborers. It was normal practice for military personnel, who incurred disabilities not serious enough to warrant their discharge from field service, to be detailed to clerkships, logistical support, and so forth. This was apparently the case with William Butler because Winder had received a request that he be returned to his original regiment, the 15th Virginia. In his response to the Adjutant General, Winder maintained that he needed both men to be able to conduct the business required of him, not only at Camp Lawton but also across his broader geographic responsibilities. The state was also attempting to call

---

[86] Morfit to Winder, 8 November 1864, National Archives, RG 92, Letters Sent by Captain C. Morfit, Assistant Quartermaster at Richmond, chap. 9, vol. 232, 107.

[87] Morfit to Winder, 24 December 1864, National Archives, RG 92, Letters Sent by Captain Morfit, chap. 9, vol. 232, 127.

up all available men for military service in the late summer and fall of 1864, and Winder's request to keep P.H. Oliver in his employ was approved by Henry C. Wayne, the Adjutant and Inspector General of Georgia.[88]

Except for slaves, the most anonymous group of men associated with the prison was the guards. Surviving letters written home from Camp Lawton by guards are rare, but the ones that have surfaced shed light on their lives and concerns. The guards at Camp Lawton were consumed not only by their day-to-day round of duties, but like most soldiers, were also concerned about what was going on at home. Captain George A. Cunningham (Company K, 3rd Georgia Reserves) worried about his family as news of Sherman's March reached him. On 20 November, while at Camp Lawton, he wrote his wife Mollie, who lived at Thomaston in Upson County:

> [W]e hear very bad news from up that way that Sherman & 25,000 men are near Griffin & marching on [.] I do hope you will be safe, if you think not trust in your judgement about moveing anywhere you wish.... I am very uneasy about you.... I would hide a portion of my meat & corn out somewhere.... [I]f I can I will come in a short time but our Genl says he can't grant furloughs now.... May God in his mercy protect you & our little Family from all harm is my prayer night & day [.][89]

Captain Cunningham's fears for the safety of his family were shared by an enlisted guard, H.C. Harris (Company A, 1st Georgia Reserves). On 27 October, he wrote his children from Camp Lawton echoing the captain's anxiety about the home front: "I still am uneasy because I frequently hear that everything in the Country up there is being pressed

---

[88] R.G. Winder to Cooper, 8 November 1864, "List of Detailed Men Between the Ages of 18 and 45 Years in the Employment of R.B. Winder, Captain and Chief Quartermaster of C.S. Military Prisons in Georgia and Alabama," National Archives, RG 109, War Department Collection of Confederate Records, Letters Received by Adjutant and Inspector General's Office, October–December 1864, Letters W (2529–3242); H.C. Wayne, Adjutant General and Inspector General (State of Georgia), 13 October 1864, Georgia Department of Archives and History, Adjutant General's Letter Book, 1864, Number 27, 20.

[89] George A. Cunningham to Mollie Cunningham, 20 November 1864, Cunningham Family Papers, MS 2679, Hargrett Manuscripts, The University of Georgia Libraries, Athens, Georgia.

but they don't rite to me any more about it…. I am afraid that they don't tell me the worst that is going on up there." He also told them about his more mundane concerns that throw a light on the guards' food supplies:

> We have tolerable hard time here now provision is scarce we git meal a plenty we git one pound of beef to the man for one days rations every other day and the next day about one half pint or a little more of green syrup for a man and some peas that the weavels has eaten almost up.

He explained that to help pass the time he was smoking a pipe: "I am a great slave of that now   I only smoke onst a day and that is from the time that I git up untill I lay down and I think that I fatten on it for I weigh 150 pounds now." He bemoaned the fact that he had not gotten the jar of preserves and loaf bread that had been sent from home because he had been transferred from Camp Sumter: "It would have been a great treat to me at this time…."[90] Cunningham's and Harris's feelings must have been replicated in the minds of many of their fellow reservists at Camp Lawton as they found themselves locked in their duties at the prison while knowing their loved ones might be in the path of a resolute enemy host.

Another interesting anecdote relating to Camp Lawton is story of Major Archibald Bogle, an officer of the 1st North Carolina Colored Infantry. Severely wounded in the Union debacle at Olustee (Florida) on 20 February 1864, Bogle, along with a number of black soldiers, was captured and transferred to Tallahassee and then to Camp Sumter. White officers such as Bogle who served in black regiments (officially known as United States Colored Troops), were often singled out for harsh treatment by their captors. Wounded in the chest and suffering a broken leg, Bogle was refused even the meager medical treatment available at the prison. In addition, Bogle's rank was purposefully ignored. Camp Sumter was a prison for enlisted men; as an officer he should have been sent to the nearby officer's prison, Camp Oglethorpe in Macon. While black troops at Camp Sumter were typically employed as prison labor, white officers of the black regiments attracted even more animosity

---

[90] H.C. Harris Letter, 27 October 1864, digital scan from Collection of Ted Berger, Courtesy, Alexander Autographs, Inc., 860 Canal Street, Connecticut 06902.

because they were the very embodiment of abolitionism. The recruitment of blacks for service in the US Army was an especially galling development for the Confederacy because it underscored the fact that the North was now not only fighting to preserve the Union but also to free the slaves. It was a direct challenge to what Southerners liked to call "our way of life."

At any rate, Bogle's wounds eventually healed without medical intervention. He survived the terrible summer at Camp Sumter and on 18 November 1864, was sent under special escort to Camp Lawton with a letter of introduction from Captain Wirz to General Winder. Bogle later described Vowles's reception of him at the prison: ["P]ut [Bogle] in the stockade—God damn him, don't register his name, he will never be exchanged, as long as I am in command of this post."[91] In fact, Major Bogle survived his time in prison and was exchanged in March 1865 at Wilmington, North Carolina. After a brief hiatus from military service, he would serve in the Army until he was discharged in 1871.

Sergeant Lyle G. Adair (111th US Colored Infantry), a white non-commissioned officer, also experienced the wrath of the Confederates against those serving with black troops when he entered Camp Lawton in November: [We] "were in the first hundred called out. And on

---

[91] Bogle's story is well summarized in William Marvel, *Andersonville: The Last Depot* (Chapel Hill: University of North Carolina Press, 1994) 33, 41, 42, 112, 221–22. McElroy, *Andersonville*, 162, also tells the story of Major Bogle, as far as Camp Sumter is concerned. The quotation is from Archibald Bogle to General Lorenzo Thomas, file of Archibald Bogle, Compiled Military Service Records of Volunteer Union Soldiers, RG 94, National Archives, cited in David J. Coles, "'Shooting Niggers Sir': Confederate Mistreatment of Union Black Soldiers at the Battle of Olustee," in Gregory J.W. Unwin, *Black Flag Over Dixie: Racial Attitudes and Reprisals in the Civil War* (Carbondale: Southern Illinois University Press, 2004) 81. See also Luis F. Emilio, *A Brave Black Regiment: The History of the Fifty-fourth Massachusetts Volunteer Infantry, 1863–1865* (New York: Da Capo Press, 1995) 428; and Anonymous, *A Voice from Rebel Prisons*, 4. The latter author, a member of the 48th New York, who was wounded and captured at Olustee, remembered Bogle being tormented by his captors. The letter from Wirz can be found in the National Archives (Wirz to Forno, 18 November 1864, National Archives, Letters Sent From Andersonville the Prison in Georgia, May 1864–March 1865, chap. 9, vol. 226, 20–21).

account of our being in a colored regt nothing was mean enough for them to call us, and no cursing hard enough."[92]

While the Bogle and Adair episodes highlight Confederate antipathy toward the use of black troops and the whites who officered them, it must be pointed out that Confederates were not the only ones who took issue with the Union utilization of black troops and the Emancipation Proclamation's promise of freedom for enslaved Americans. Reflecting an ambivalent populace on their home front, even Union soldiers were divided on the issue. Soldiers knew who their enemy was on the battlefield, and those unfortunates who became prisoners braced themselves to deal with their Confederate captors. However, the POW experience proved to be more complex. In fact, some found themselves becoming alienated from the very ones for whom they were supposedly fighting—their government and those who made up the home front.

At the moment of capture, the captive might very well have blamed himself or his military superiors for his predicament; however, once the reality of prolonged imprisonment sank in, many prisoners began to see their status in a broader context. As hopes for a quick exchange evaporated, POWs often blamed the Republican president and his administration for their woes. At times the criticism focused on the racial policies of the Lincoln administration. For example, in September of 1864, Florence inmate Private William Tritt (Company F, 21st Wisconsin) reported: "Much complaint is made against our government on account of Negro soldiers undermining our exchange. No language is too bad to use in some mouths." Tritt added later that the exchanges would have resumed except for the fact that "Old Abe and the niggers are all that is in the way."[93] Tritt's comments were echoed that same month in Savannah by Private M.J. Umstead (Company A, 13th Iowa): "[H]ere we have to stay. And pine away through the prime of life all for the Sons of

---

[92] Lyle G. Adair, Diary, Andersonville Diary Collection, Andersonville National Historic Site (ANHS), cited in Glenn Robins, "Race, Repatriation, and Galvanized Rebels: Union Prisoners and the Exchange Question in Deep South Prison Camps," *Civil War History* 53, no. 2 (June 2007): 123.

[93] William Tritt, Diary, ANHS, cited in Robins, "Race, Repatriation, and Galvanized Rebels," 123.

Africa."[94] Sergeant Howard wrote a similar statement in one of his diary entries at Camp Sumter in August: "Oh, it is very strange that the United States Government will let her soldiers lay here and live and die as they are when it is in her power to release them but we must stay here because they can't agree on some niggar question. There is a good deal of such talk here in camp."[95]

These comments stemmed from the collapse of the Dix-Hill Cartel following the issuance of the Emancipation Proclamation. The proclamation, which provided not only for the freeing of slaves in areas under Confederate control but also for the enlistment of blacks in the Union army, elicited the previously cited virulent response from Confederate authorities who discussed draconian measures to be taken against whites who officered the black units. The Federal government insisted that black troops be treated equally in the exchange process, while the Confederacy refused to recognize them as soldiers.[96]

In addition to POW letters and diary entries raising the racial issue, other signs of discontent surfaced among Union POWs in the prison camps. Both at Camp Sumter and later at the Savannah stockade, Union POWs expressed their grievances toward their own government by sending, in the former case, a letter (14 August 1864) to President Lincoln and drafting, in the latter case, a petition (28 September 1864) directed to the authorities in Washington.[97] Statements in Sergeant Howard's diary at Camp Sumter—[I] "do not see why our Government do not do something for us"—and at Camp Lawton—["I]t seems as if we were forsaken by our Government"—expressed the discontent felt by many.[98]

[94] M.J. Umstead, Diary, ANHS, cited in Robins, "Race, Repatriation, and Galvanized Rebels," 124.

[95] Howard, Diary, 3 August 1864, Vermont Historical Society.

[96] James M. Gillespie, *Andersonvilles of the North: The Myths and Realities of Northern Treatment of Civil War Confederate Prisoners* (Denton: University of North Texas Press, 2008) 71–105, provides a useful summary of the issue of black soldiers and the disruption of the exchange cartel.

[97] J.B. Dorr, T.J. Harrison, and George Stoneman to the President of the United States, 14 August 1864, *Official Records*, series 2, vol. 7, 616–18; "Mass Meeting of Federal Prisoners," 28 September 1864, *Official Records*, series 2, vol. 7, 888–89; and Jefferson Davis, *Andersonville and Other Civil War Prisons* (New York: Belford Company, 1890) 9, 11.

[98] Howard, Diary, 3 October–8 October 1864, Vermont Historical Society.

Henry Tisdale, a strong Lincoln supporter, worried about the election outcome: "We Lincoln men felt a doubt of the result as so many were bitter against the government for not effecting an exchange."[99] These actions were symptomatic of the fact that many POWS increasingly felt that the home front—the sentiment of which was divined via newspapers and letters—was not sufficiently pressuring the government to take appropriate action to free them from their imprisonment. Finally, one can assume, despite the disappointment of Confederate officials at the overall results of the mock presidential elections held in the camps, that POW votes for McClellan were often cast not so much for the Democratic candidate as against a government that was increasingly held responsible for the continued incarceration of Union prisoners under extremely difficult circumstances.[100]

A tangible result of the suffering, frustration, and disillusionment on the part of Union POWs was the numbers of prisoners who defected to the Confederate cause. Private William Tritt bitterly noted that on 29 October and 11 November, respectively, 370 and 300 Camp Lawton prisoners "took the oath to the G__ D_____ Confederacy."[101] Obviously, the motivations varied. Some simply saw it as a means of escaping conditions—hunger, cold, lack of clothing, disease—they could no longer tolerate and, perhaps, ultimately of providing a way to reach Union lines. For others it may have represented a rejection of Federal policies toward its captured soldiers.

At any rate a poem of uncertain authorship emerged from the experience of Confederate prisons that captured the feelings of many POWs:

"They Have Left Us Here to Die"
When our Country called for me we came from forge and store and mill.
From workshop, farm and factory the broken ranks to fill;

---

[99] Tisdale, 20 November 1864, "Diary."

[100] This analysis is based on the recent article by Glenn Robins's article cited above, 117–40. Also, note Marvel, *Andersonville*, 147.

[101] William Tritt, Diary, ANHS, cited in Robins, "Race, Repatriation, and Galvanized Rebels," 124.

We left our quite happy homes, and the one we loved so well;
To vanquish all the Union foes, or fall where others fell;
Now in a prison drear we languish and it is our constant cry;
Oh! Ye who yet can save us, will you leave us here to die?

The voices of slander tells you that our hearts are weak with fear.
That all or nearly all of us were captured in the rear;
The scars upon our bodies from musket ball and shell;
The missing legs and shattered arms a true tale will tell;
We have tried to do our duty in the sight of God on high;
Oh! Ye who yet can save us, will you leave us here to die?

Then are hearts with hopes still beating in our pleasant Northern homes.
Waiting; waiting; for the footstep that may never more return;
In Southern prisons pining; meager; tattered; pale and gaunt;
Growing weaker; weaker; daily from pinching cold and want;
Their brothers; sons; and husbands; poor and helpless captured be;
Oh! Ye who yet can save us, will you leave us here to die?

Just out our prison gate there is a grave yard near at hand;
Where lie twelve thousand Union men beneath the Georgia sand;
Scores and scores we lay beside them as day succeeds each day;
And this it will ever be until they all shall pass away;
And the last can say when dying with upturned and glazing eye;
Both love and faith are dead at home, they have left us here to die.[102]

Although one could spend a lot of time explicating this poem, it is difficult not to notice the author's sense of abandonment. The irony is obvious; Union POWs were beginning to blame their own government for their predicament.

Very few POW letters from Camp Lawton are known to exist, but one that survived and is in the archives of the Minnesota Historical Society is both revealing and poignant. Captured following the Battle of

---

[102] Poem cited in Robins, "Race Repatriation, and Galvanized Rebels," 132–33. The poem was apparently composed by a POW at Camp Sumter and has at least three attributions of authorship.

Brice's Crossroads in June 1864, Washington K. Latimer (Company D, 9th Minnesota) was sent to Camp Sumter and then to Camp Lawton. On 14 November, he wrote to his family:

> Dear Father:
>
> As some of the boys, sick, are going to be exchanged I will send a few lines by Corporal Pettijohn which he will mail as soon as he gets in our lines.
>
> I am in tolerable health, have beens sick some since I have been a prisoner but am better now. Think I will live through and come home all right. We all think we will be exchanged soon or at least hope so for prison life in this southern Confederacy is anything but pleasant. Our rations are very small—only ½ lb. meal; ½ lb. beef and three fourths lb. beans or rice is what we are entitled to but we do not get near that much, and not half enough wood to cook that with.
>
> When we were captured, the rebels took our many blankets and haver sacks so you may judge our clothing is rather thin for this season of the year. Out of 220 from our regiment, not 100 are alive now. James Clabaugh and Peter Miller are both dead. Also I think Goodfellow is dead. He was very low the last I heard from him. I received yours and Smith's letter of July 5th and answered them but I suppose you never got my letter. It is very difficult to get letters through to our lines. If we are not exchanged soon, send me $5.00. (I want you to write to me also.) Be very brief and write about nothing but home affairs. I have had no money since have been a prisoner. I should have written you oftener had I have had the means. It costs something to write here however do send the money if there is any prospects of exchange within two months. It takes a letter a long time to get here…. If you write tell me where the regiment is [.]
>
> Goodbye. I hope soon to be at home and see you all. Take care of yourself and not work too hard
>
> Your affectionate son,
>
> W.K. Latimer

> Dear mother and sisters:
>
> As I have a little space of paper, I will write you a few lines. I often think of you all and would like to see you very much. I dream of home every night and always in my dreams I find my way to the cupboard.

Last night I dreamt of eating a whole loaf of bread and butter and then did not get half enough. I expect I will eat you out of house and home when I get back.

How I would like to peep into the house and see how you are all getting along. I hope you are all well. I expect to find Jane fat and hearty, and Cora bustling around as good natured as ever. And Nora—I celebrated her birthday by cooking and eating a big mess of sweet potatoes, a luxury I cannot often afford. Alice, Mattie and Clara—what are they doing? I will have a big story to tell them when I get home. Yes, I always think of and pray for you all. I wonder how Ma likes Minnesota by now. [The family had moved from Illinois in 1860.] We, the 9th Regiment, think it is perfect Paradise to see the Old Flag and get to our lines. It will be the happiest day I ever saw. May it soon come is my hope and prayer. May god bless and protect you all. Goodbye.

W.K. Latimer

Latimer was not sick enough to make the list of POWs to be exchanged through the port of Savannah. However, he rode the rails to Savannah later in November when Camp Lawton was evacuated ahead of Sherman's oncoming force. Like other survivors of the final evacuation, he was shipped from Savannah down the Gulf and Western Railroad to the temporary prison at Blackshear and eventually ended up back at Camp Sumter. The poignancy of this letter for the reader derives from the fact that, despite Latimer's confidence he would "come home all right" to tell "a big story," he never made it. He died at Camp Sumter on 23 January 1865. But Latimer's letter gives some insight into the situation at Camp Lawton. For example, he says that he has received letters from home but indicates that it is "very difficult to get letters through to our lines." Therefore, some letters were getting to the prison. He also encourages his family to write but advises his family to "be very brief and write about nothing but home affairs," an indication that short letters with home news had less chance of being molested by the Confederate authorities. Yet, his request that his family send him money seems to show confidence that he would receive it. It must have been easier to receive a letter in prison than to send one out because he sent his letter by a friend who had been selected for exchange. Latimer also commented on the two items that seemed to preoccupy POWs at Camp

Lawton that fall—the lack of adequate food and the onset of cold weather.[103] Overall, the sentiments in his letter probably reflect the concerns of the typical POW at Camp Lawton.

However, as the month of November wore on, inmate worries about food and cold weather would soon be overshadowed by news and rumors of the increasing likelihood of an exchange. Sergeant Charles H. Knox (Company L, 1st Connecticut Cavalry) wrote another of the rare surviving POW letters from Camp Lawton. Dated 14 November and addressed to his to his wife in Schroon Lake, New York, which he called "God's Land," Knox was worried about his wife and son's well being in his absence, and he expressed his hope for a general exchange, "for I am tired of Cesecia" [sic].[104]

On the Confederate side concern for the exchange was complicated by news of Sherman's departure from Atlanta on 15 November. Now the more pressing issue was for the security of the prison.

---

[103] Letter of Washington K. Latimer, 14 November 1864, P939, Minnesota Historical Society Archives, St. Paul, Minnesota.

[104] Charles H. Knox, 14 November 1864, Manuscript letter to his wife. Quotation by permission of Paul Gibson, Blountville, Tennessee. The letter has since been purchased by Georgia Southern University and is in the Georgia Southern museum collection. Knox was captured on 5 May 1864, during the Wilderness campaign and was sent to Camp Sumter. He was transferred to Camp Lawton on 31 October. Paroled in North Carolina on 27 February 1865, he was hospitalized until 9 June 1865, when he was discharged from Tilton Hospital in Wilmington, Delaware.

6

The Collapse: "War Is Hell"

The beginning of the end of Camp Lawton coincided with the start of Union General William Tecumseh Sherman's march from Atlanta to Savannah on 15 November 1864. From May to September of 1864, Sherman had waged a brilliant campaign of maneuver through the difficult terrain of North Georgia against the Confederate Army of Tennessee, commanded initially by General Joseph Eggleston Johnston and then General John Bell Hood.[1] Punctuated by several sharp clashes, Sherman's mobile campaign had rendered to his forces the prize of Atlanta, the strategic Confederate rail center, on 3 September 1864. After some campaigning against General Hood, who tried to draw the Federal forces back to the north by attacks against the Union supply line to Chattanooga, Sherman proposed and received permission from Union General Ulysses S. Grant to cut loose from Atlanta, severing his supply and communications lines, and march to Savannah, a direct distance of 230 miles.[2]

As Sherman's troops emerged from their Atlanta bivouacs to begin their march to Savannah to the musical strains of "John Brown's Body," on 15 and 16 November, Confederate authorities could only guess as to

---

[1] Two books, each dealing with one of the opposing armies, together give a good overview of the Atlanta campaign: Thomas Lawrence Connelly, *Autumn of Glory: the Army of Tennessee, 1862–1865* (Baton Rouge: Louisiana State University Press, 1971), and Steven E. Woodworth, *Nothing But Victory, the Army of the Tennessee, 1861–1865* (New York: Alfred A. Knopf, 2006).

[2] Among the numerous studies of Sherman's March to the Sea, the following are good surveys: Burke Davis, *Sherman's March* (New York: Random House, 1980); Lee Kennett, *Marching Through Georgia: the Story of Soldiers & Civilians During Sherman's Campaign* (New York: Harper and Collins, 1995); Joseph T. Glatthaar, *The March to the Sea and Beyond* (Baton Rouge: Louisiana State University Press, 1995); Noah Andre Trudeau, *Southern Storm: Sherman's March to the Sea* (New York: HarperCollins, 2008); and Anne Bailey, *War and Ruin: William T. Sherman and the Savannah Campaign* (Wilmington, Delaware: SR Books, 2002).

his intentions.[3] Confederate Major General Howell Cobb wrote to his wife the next day, "That Sherman intends to move with his large army upon some point in Georgia I have no doubt, but where it will be is not so certain."[4] Was he headed toward Macon, Augusta, Savannah, or the Gulf Coast? If so, sizable Confederate POW camps were located along each axis of advance. If Macon and/or the Gulf Coast lay in his path, Camp Sumter and Camp Oglethorpe would be in danger; if he headed toward Augusta and/or Savannah, then Camp Lawton would be threatened. In addition to military prisons, significant Confederate military infrastructure lay in every direction—among them the Confederate Powder Works in Augusta, the Confederate Ordnance Laboratory in Macon, armaments and textile establishments in Athens, the Griswold and Grier armaments manufacturing complex at Griswoldville, the Confederate Naval Iron Works and Arsenal in Columbus, and the strategic railway network connecting them.

The state was convulsed with efforts to try to counter Sherman's advance, but it was faced with a fatal dearth of manpower. In a desperate but futile gesture Georgia Governor Joseph E. Brown issued a proclamation on 19 November calling for "... a *levée en masse* of the whole free white male population [of the state] between sixteen (16) and fifty-five (55) years of age [for forty days' service], except such as are physically unable to bear arms...."[5]

In his new endeavor, Sherman planned to follow the approach he had pioneered in his campaign across Mississippi the previous year.[6] From 3–14 February 1864, he had marched two army corps, plus a small cavalry force, totaling 27,000 men, from his camp near Vicksburg

---

[3] William Tecumseh Sherman, *Memoirs of General W. T. Sherman*, 2 vols. (New York: Library of America, 1990) 2:655.

[4] Howell Cobb to his wife, 16 November 1864, *The Correspondence of Robert Toombs, Alexander Stephens, and Howell Cobb*, ed. Ulrich Bonnell Phillips (repr., New York: DaCapo Press, 1972) 656.

[5] Allen D Candler, ed., *The Confederate Records of the State of Georgia Compiled and Published under Authority of the Legislature*, 6 vols. (Atlanta: Chas. P. Byrd, State Printer, 1908) 2: 800.

[6] John F. Marszalek, *Sherman's March to the Sea* (Abiliene TX: McWhiney Foundation Press, 2005) 249–55, gives an extended discussion of the Meridian raid as a precursor to the March across Georgia.

through Jackson to Meridian, Mississippi. Now, following the pattern of his Mississippi raid, he divided his army into two wings, marching the troops as much as possible along parallel routes, yet keeping them within mutual supporting distance. In this way should one of his wings run into serious opposition or should the Confederates attempt to establish a blocking position, the other wing could go to its support or flank the enemy's position.[7] The axis of his advance as he approached Millen followed the Georgia Central Railroad, and his troops destroyed it as they moved along it.[8] In their wake large stretches of the railroad were left marked by the ashes of burned crossties, the remnants of destroyed bridges, and heaps of twisted rails that were given the sartorial sobriquet of "Sherman's neckties." Using his cavalry to act as a screening force, Sherman was able in the initial stages of his March through Georgia to mask his direction. Only after his feint toward Macon ended did it become clear that Sherman was headed toward Augusta or Savannah. On 25 November when Sherman's forces were well into their march, the Augusta *Daily Chronicle and Sentinel* reported: "The whereabouts of the main body of the Yankee army is involved in mystery, and there is not a military man in this city that can definitely locate them, in our opinion."[9] The reality was that by that date Sherman had already captured Milledgeville, the state capital, and was advancing on Sandersville. In fact, this particular case of "the fog of war" did not lift for the newspaper's readership until 3 December when news of Sherman's arrival in Millen was telegraphed to Augusta, and the paper announced that Savannah was the Union commander's obvious destination.[10]

The March itself proceeded across Georgia at a steady rate—ten to twelve miles a day—with Union forces following parallel roads and

---

[7] See, for example, Henry Hitchcock's discussion of this strategy (Hitchcock, *Marching With Sherman: Passages from the Letters and Campaign Diaries of Henry Hitchcock, Major and Assistant Adjutant General of Volunteers, November 1864–May 1865*, ed. M.A. DeWolfe Howe [New Haven: Yale University Press, 1927] 135).

[8] Robert C. Black, III, *The Railroads of the Confederacy* (Reprint, Wilmington NC: Broadfoot Publishing, 1987) 258–60.

[9] *Daily Chronicle and Sentinel* (Augusta), 25 November 1864, 3.

[10] Ibid., 3 December 1864, 1.

operating across a front of twenty to sixty miles. The operations of foraging units expanded this range even farther. Units would occasionally layover as Sherman concentrated or redirected his forces. He planned the campaign in several stages, with the first objective being Georgia's capital Milledgeville, which he believed would take seven days to reach. From Milledgeville, the next objective was the strategic railroad junction at Millen, via Sandersville, Davisboro, and Louisville. The third and ultimate objective in Georgia, of course, was Savannah, where he planned to link up with the Federal blockading fleet and thus re-establish communications.[11]

In the meantime, Confederate authorities in the state were desperately trying to concentrate what meager forces were available to harass Sherman's mobile field army. There was really nothing else they could hope to accomplish. General Beauregard, Governor Brown, and all major Confederate authorities called on the Georgia populace to provide additional troops to resist the enemy. Confederate fixed installations were placed on alert to prepare to evacuate should Union units be coming their way. This was particularly true of Camp Lawton because it was along the path of Sherman's advance. In fact, on 23 November 1864, while he was in Milledgeville, Sherman had ordered General Judson Kilpatrick, who commanded his cavalry screening force, "to use all possible effort to rescue our prisoners of war now confined near Millen."[12] Later, in the final report (dated 27 December 1864) of his command's operations during the March to the Sea, Kilpatrick indicated that, following those orders, he "moved rapidly" toward Waynesboro where he learned on 27 November that the POWs had already been evacuated from Camp Lawton. Although Kilpatrick's main force did not arrive in Waynesboro until that day (27 November), in his report Kilpatrick mentioned that a scouting party of his cavalry had been in the

---

[11] Special Field Orders No. 127, 23 November 1864, United States, War Department, *The War of the Rebellion: A Compilation of the Official Records of the Union and Confederate Armies,* series 2, vol. 44 (Washington DC: Government Printing Office, 1880–1901) 527.

[12] Ibid., 527.

area the previous day, 26 November.[13] It was from this unit that Kilpatrick learned that the POWs were gone.

Because of its connection with the evacuation of Camp Lawton, this episode bears further examination. Apparently (because the official records are not explicit in the details), following Sherman's orders of 23 November, Kilpatrick sent two flying columns in advance of his main force late on the evening on 25 November. One, under the command of Captain Edward Hayes, one of Kilpatrick's aides-de-camp, was to move on Waynesboro and cut the railroad there, particularly the Brier Creek Bridge to the north of town. The second group was to advance on Camp Lawton. Described by participating trooper Julius B. Kilbourne as a "forced march to rescue Union soldiers then prisoners at Millen," the second scouting party was led by Kilpatrick's assistant adjutant-general, Captain Llewellyn G. Estes. In an 1883 *National Tribune* article, Kilbourne gave a dramatic description of the march to free the prisoners:

> [A] detail of twelve men from each company—those who had fleet horses being selected—was made and placed under the command of Major Estes, General Kilpatrick's adjutant-general, who was to start on a special expedition at 12 o'clock that night and make a forced march to rescue the Union soldiers then prisoners at Millen, seventy-five miles distant. So, after feeding, and resting our jaded horses and obtaining a fresh supply of ammunition, we got off before midnight. The command was unincumbered [*sic*] with wheels. The roads were dry, and it was a bright moonlit night. Little suspecting the object of the expedition we silently moved on during the long night through forest and towns, with nothing to break the silence save the tread of the horses or clatter of our sabers and sound of the bugle to dismount and lead our horses on coming to a stream, and then to close up and move on. So fatigued were some of the men that they would fall asleep and ride for miles quite unconscious.
>
> A little after daylight we stopped at a farmhouse where there was corn and fodder for our horses, and rested an hour or so. While the boys made coffee to soften up their "hardtack," the servants of the house brought us

---

[13] Kilpatrick to Beaumont, 27 December 1864, *Official Records*, series 2, vol. 44, 362–67; Hitchcock, *Marching With Sherman*, 124. Captain Hayes's scout mission to Waynesboro is detailed in "Report of Col. George S. Acker, Ninth Michigan Cavalry," 19 December 1864, *Official Records*, series 2, vol. 44, 396–98.

some sweet potatoes and a little bacon, which gave us a good breakfast. Shortly after sunrise we were again in the saddle, having ridden within the past twenty-four hours over sixty miles. During the night we had passed several towns, the names of which we did not know; but the negroes told us were still forty miles from Millen.

During the forenoon we made good progress meeting with no opposition. About the many plantations which we passed we saw no one but now and then some old gray-headed man walking about the house, looking at us when we passed. Their sons and sons' sons were all in the rebel service.

At noon we made another short stop to feed and water. Here we in some way got the impression that the prisoners had been sent away from Millen, but could not altogether credit the report, but as we advanced the evidence became more conclusive. About 4 o'clock we came in sight of the prison pen in which our poor boys had suffered so keenly—even death itself. How our hearts leaped with joy at the sight and at the thought that we should be able to effect their release!

Millen is situated on the Savannah and Charleston Railroad, and the stockade is some distance to the north and near the branch road running to Augusta. Maj. Estes, with his scouts, made a reconnaissance, capturing the guard—some thirty that had been left behind,—who informed us that the prisoners had been removed the Tuesday before....

After destroying the stockade and its surrounding buildings, Major Estes, with this command, as ordered, joined Kilpatrick south of Waynesboro, and participated in the engagement at that place.[14]

This reunion occurred on 27 November, when Kilpatrick's main force approached Waynesboro. Kilbourne's mentioning of "destroying the stockade and its surrounding buildings" also lends credence to the

---

[14] Julius B. Kilbourne, "The March to the Sea. Kilpatrick's Cavalry on the March through Georgia. A Scout to Millen. An Engagement with Wheeler's Cavalry near Waynesboro. Gallant Saber Charge. A Graceful Act of Courtesy Performed by General Wheeler," *National Tribune* 2, no. 40 (17 May 1883): 1; Trudeau, *Southern Storm*, 263, pieced together the story of the two advance columns. The diary of Catherine Barnes Whitehead of Ivanhoe Plantation gives local corroboration of Estes's scouting mission as the Union column stopped at Ivanhoe on 26 November. ("Diary of Civil War Days Here," *The True Citizen* (Waynesboro), 9 April 1969, 7A).

supposition that Federal forces rendered the prison unsuitable for renewed use.

But Kilpatrick was not the only one targeting the camp. While occupying Milledgeville, Major General O.O. Howard had also ordered a scouting unit under the command of Captain William Duncan to head to Millen. Captain Duncan commanded Company K, 15th Illinois Cavalry, Howard's headquarters escort unit. Duncan described the mission in a paper delivered years later (10 April 1894) to the Minnesota Commandery of the Military Order of the Loyal Legion of the United States (MOLLUS):

> Our next objective point was Millen; I started to the place with a detachment of scouts to ascertain the situation, and, if possible, to effect the release of our prisoners. We did some hard riding, but found on arriving at this place about midnight, that our prisoners had been removed. We captured a Rebel major and two men and returned with them to our army.[15]

It is difficult, though, to see how either Duncan's or Estes's small detachments of scouts could have effected the release of Union POWs from Camp Lawton had they still been there. Perhaps they could have damaged the railroad to prevent their evacuation until the trailing Union forces caught up with the scouts. Of course, this begs the question as to what Sherman himself could have done with thousands of released POWs in his van.

As for Kilpatrick, when he arrived in the Waynesboro area on 27 November, he was immediately faced with a Confederate buzz saw named General Joe Wheeler. The Confederate general's cavalry force was attempting to ascertain Sherman's direction—whether to Augusta or Savannah—as well as offering what resistance it could to the inexorable

---

[15] William Duncan, "The Army of the Tennessee Under Major-General O.O. Howard," *Glimpses of the Nation's Struggle. Fourth Series. Papers Read Before the Minnesota Commandery of the Military Order of the Loyal Legion of the United States, 1892–1897* (St. Paul MN: H.L. Collins Co., 1898) 4:168. This mission, or another one in which Duncan was involved, is mentioned in the *Official Records* (Taggart to Hitchcock, 30 November 1864, series 1, vol. 44, 578). It is not clear that Duncan actually got to Camp Lawton. He may have simply reached Millen Junction where he discovered that the POWs had already been evacuated.

Union columns. Much too small to be effective in countering the Union army, Wheeler's cavalry nonetheless was able to harass units on the perimeters of the Federal forces.

Kilpatrick stopped at Ivanhoe Plantation, northwest of Waynesboro, at mid-afternoon on that day, where he rendezvoused with Estes's scouting force that had been there since midmorning.[16] Within half an hour he was attacked by Wheeler, which initiated a running fight that drove the Union cavalry from the area. The diary of Catharine Barnes Whitehead of Ivanhoe Plantation gives local corroboration of Estes's scouting mission. In her diary entry of 29 November, she mentioned Estes's column arriving at Ivanhoe Plantation at 10 a.m. on 27 November. According to Whitehead, the Union troopers stayed at Ivanhoe Plantation until 4:30 p.m. that day, at which time they were rudely interrupted by Wheeler's onrushing Confederate troopers.[17]

When he submitted his official report of the campaign from Atlanta to Savannah, Kilpatrick returned to the issue of the failure to rescue the Union prisoners at Camp Lawton:

> Here [at Waynesboro] to my great regret, I learned that our prisoners had been removed two days previous. It is needless to say that had this not been the case, I should have rescued them; the Confederate Government could not have prevented me.[18]

Although the authorities at Camp Lawton had the advantage of military intelligence, as poor as it was, via courier and by telegraph to warn them of the Federal advance in their direction, Burke County civilians were surprised by the sudden appearance of Kilpatrick's cavalry in the Waynesboro area. In a letter to his brother James, the Rev. W.L. Kilpatrick wrote, "Before we knew that they were on this side of the Oconee (River), Waynesboro had been occupied twelve hours and

---

[16] F. Mikell Harper, *Catharine of Ivanhoe: The Civil War Journal of Catharine Whitehead Rowland of Augusta and Burke County, Georgia, with Letters from Her Husband, Charles Alden Rowland* (Macon: Indigo Publishing, 2008) 73–74.

[17] Diary of Civil War Days Here," *The True Citizen* (Waynesboro), 9 April 1969, 7A. Kilpatrick to Beaumont, 27 December 1864, *Official Records*, series 1, vol. 44, 362–67.

[18] W.L. Kilpatrick to James H. Kilpatrick, 31 December 1864, courtesy of Lyle Lansdale, 301 E. Poplar Ave., Carrboro, N.C. (a typescript copy was given to Mark H. Dunkleman who furnished it to the Burke County Genealogical Society).

some of my neighbors only four miles off were plundered."[19] Indeed, the leading elements of Kilpatrick's cavalry preceded the infantry by several days.

Meanwhile, *Harper's Weekly* was trying to penetrate the fog of war for its Northern readership by relating what was known of Sherman's progress across Georgia: "East of Milledgeville a few miles is 'Camp Lawton,' which it is not improbable that our cavalry has reached."[20] Of course, by the 10 December publication date of that issue, Sherman's forces were already investing the Confederate defenses surrounding Savannah. It would not be until the 7 January 1865 issue that the magazine's readers would learn that the Federals had reached an already-emptied prison camp more than a month earlier.[21]

On the Confederate side, Sherman's advance south and east of Atlanta had forced Confederate authorities to make provisional plans for the evacuation of whichever POW camps or other military facilities Federal troops might approach. On 18 November, Secretary of War Seddon telegraphed Winder from Richmond: "Movement of W.T. Sherman may render necessary removal of prisoners. Advise by telegraph what steps can be taken, and what you would recommend for their safe disposition."[22] The next day, Seddon again telegraphed Winder at Millen telling him to use his judgment and "best efforts for the removal and security of the prisoners as the enemy shall advance or threaten in any direction," and he indicated that he believed that Andersonville was likely the most threatened.[23] Winder responded and informed the secretary that Lieutenant General Hardee, who had been tasked with pulling together available Confederate forces to oppose Sherman, had ordered him "to remove the prisoners to Savannah for the present, and establish a prison on the Gulf Railroad at Waresboro, Ware County, Ga."[24]

---

[19] "Diary of Civil War Days Here," *The True Citizen* (Waynesboro), 9 April 1969, 7A.

[20] *Harper's Weekly*, 10 December 1864, 789.

[21] Ibid., 7 January 1864, 6.

[22] Seddon to Winder, 18 November 1864, *Official Records*, series 2, vol. 7, 1,140.

[23] Seddon to Winder, 19 November 1864, *Official Records*, series 2, vol. 7, 1,144–45.

[24] Winder to Seddon, 19 November 1864, *Official Records*, series 2, vol. 7, 1,145.

Amazingly, it was in the midst of all this chaos that Assistant Adjutant and Inspector General R.H. Chilton's original suggestion of a unified head of Confederate prisons materialized. On 21 November 1864, Cooper appointed Winder Commissary General of Prisoners. General Orders No. 84 specified the following:

> All officers and men on duty at the several military prisons are placed under his command. He is charged with the custody and care of all prisoners of war and with the discipline and general administration of such prisons east of the Mississippi River [recognizing the division of the Confederacy by the control of the Mississippi River by Union forces].... Commandants of posts in the vicinity of these military prisons are made subordinate to Brigadier General Winder in all matters necessary for the security of the prisoners. Department, army, and other commanders are required not to interfere with the prisoners, the prison guard, or the administration of the prisons.... Local and other troops doing duty at the posts herein indicated will be considered prison guards. If their immediate commander is superior in rank to the commandant of the post at which they are stationed he will, notwithstanding, detail the prison guard from his command at the request of the post or prison commander, and the detail when turned over to the last named officer, will be under his sole charge and direction.[25]

Therefore, at the very time that Camp Lawton was being evacuated in the face of Sherman's advancing columns, Winder's soon-to-be abandoned office was now the headquarters of all Confederate military prisons east of the Mississippi. On the surface, Winder's new appointment seemed to address many of the issues that had plagued the administration of Confederate military prisons—the lack of a central authority to provide consistent and standardized policies, the prison commander's murky authority vis-à-vis department and local area commanders, and the constant problems of how to secure prison guards and who then had authority over them. The reality, of course, was all of this was too late. The Confederate ship of state was sinking rapidly, and

---

[25] Cooper, General Orders No. 84, 21 November 1864, *Official Records*, series 2, vol. 7, 1,150.

there was nothing with which to plug the holes. Winder had finally been given the authority, but the always-scarce resources had evaporated.

In the summer and fall of 1864, as General Winder hurried to seek authorization to build what became Camp Lawton, then undertook to construct it, and finally worked to transport and house Union POWs there, negotiations between Union and Confederate authorities to effect POW exchanges continued.[26] The focal points of a potential exchange were Charleston and Savannah because of their respective proximity to large numbers of Union POWs. Union and Confederate forces were close to each other there, as well. Charleston was under siege, and Union forces had controlled the mouth of the Savannah River since April of 1862, when they had captured Fort Pulaski. The railroads, rivers, and coastal estuaries around the two cities provided the necessary transportation avenues for exchanging prisoners of war.

While the newly installed Union POWs at Camp Lawton desperately hoped for an exchange and grasped at every rumor of one, the actual negotiations proceeded by fits and starts, and ultimately focused on the sick and wounded. Winder received a dispatch from Confederate Commissioner of Exchange Robert Ould on 4 November, asking him to send the sick and wounded POWs in his charge to Savannah for exchange.[27] Five days later (9 November), Surgeon White wrote from Camp Lawton to his Camp Sumter counterpart, Dr. R.R. Stevenson:

> We have been quite busy for the last two days in selecting the sick to be exchanged. After getting them all ready at the depot we were notified by telegraph not to send them and had to take them back to the stockade. Many of these poor fellows, already broken down in health, will succumb through despair.[28]

One of the POWs selected for the exchange, Private William Hawkins (Company B, 154th New York), remembered this disappointing

---

[26] Foster to Wessells, 29 July 1864, *Official Records*, series 1, vol. 5, part 2, 199, and Foster to Hardee, 12 November 1864, *Official Records*, series 1, vol. 35, part 2, 327, are examples of the back-and-forth negotiations in this matter.

[27] Ould to Winder, 4 November 1864, *Official Records*, series 2, vol. 7, 1,090.

[28] White to Stevenson, 9 November 1864, *Official Records*, series 2, vol. 7, 1,114.

episode. He was among a group marched out of the prison to the railroad with high hopes, only to be returned to the stockade after a lengthy wait along the tracks. Hawkins called the return "one of the slowest, saddest processions that ever marched."[29] Once they re-entered the compound, but before they crossed the stream to their shebangs on the far slope, Captain Vowles softened the blow a bit by telling the downcast column: "Boys, I would not go over [to] the other side and mix up with the rest. You better stay together right here, for I think that in two or three days ... you will be taken out of here."

He was right. In fact, a local agreement had been reached between General Hardee, commander of Confederate forces in South Carolina, Georgia, and Florida, and Union Major General J.G. Foster, in charge of the Department of the South, headquartered in Hilton Head, South Carolina, for a special exchange in which sick and wounded POWs from Camp Lawton would be sent to Savannah where they would be traded for a like number of Confederate POWs. The exchange was conducted on the Union side by Lieutenant Colonel John E. Mulford, Assistant Agent for Exchange of Prisoners, who reported to district commander Foster as well as to Major General Benjamin Butler, Commissioner for Exchange. Employing the US steamer *New York* as a flag-of-truce ship, Mulford traveled several times up the Savannah River to meet with Confederate officials.[30] On 5 November, Robert Ould wrote John Enders, President of the Ambulance Committee in Richmond, to prepare for an exchange of the sick and wounded in Savannah.[31]

Although they occupied Fort Pulaski, which guarded the entrance to the Savannah River, an additional precaution taken by the Federals to prevent Confederate ships from reaching the sea from Savannah via the river was to extend a chain across the shipping channel. Because the exchange of POWs would involve ships ascending and descending the river, Foster requested Rear Admiral J.A. Dahlgren, commanding the South Atlantic Blockading Squadron, to remove the "chain cable."[32]

---

[29] Mark H. Dunkelman, *War's Relentless Hand: Twelve Tales of Civil War Soldiers* (Baton Rouge: Louisiana State University Press, 2006) 130.

[30] Mulford to Butler, 21 November 1864, *Offical Records*, series 2, vol. 7, 1,149.

[31] Ould to Enders, 5 November 1864, *Official Records*, series 2, vol. 7, 1,100.

[32] Dahlgren to Foster, 9 November 1864, *Official Records*, series 1, vol. 35, part 2, 326.

Meanwhile, Union authorities were gathering their Confederate prisoners for the exchange. On 11 November, Foster reported that he had 3,000 to 4,000 sick Confederate POWs downriver from Savannah and indicated that he hoped to have as many as 10,000 available for the exchange.[33] The next day, Foster informed General Halleck that Mulford had ten steamers of sick and wounded Confederate prisoners on hand.[34]

As word of the exchange reached the inmates at Camp Lawton, the old excitement returned, and speculation stirred the prison. Even though the exchange hopes of the inmates had repeatedly been disappointed, it took a steely resolve to ignore news that this time might be correct. Prison doctors examined the sick and developed a list of those to be exchanged. McElroy commented sarcastically, "The rebel surgeons took praiseworthy care that our Government should profit as little as possible from this by sending every hopeless case, every man whose lease of life was not likely to extend much beyond his reaching the parole boat."[35]

McElroy need not have been concerned that the Confederacy was taking unilateral advantage of the situation because a similar rationale was being applied to Confederate POWs in the North. General Grant wanted to make sure that any exchange did not lead to the replenishment of Confederate forces in the field and ordered Brevet Brigadier General William Hoffman, the Commissary General of Prisoners, to "exchange only men 'unfit for duty.'"[36] As a result of this policy, General Butler reported to Hoffman on 25 September, that out of a recent shipment of 500 Confederate POWs he had received, nearly thirty had died. Butler concluded, "The occurrence does not speak well either for the Government or its officials."[37] Hoffman, in turn, directed the commanding officers of Camp Chase, Camp Douglas, Camp Morton, Rock Island Barracks, and Alton Prison to select for exchange

---

[33] Foster to Hardee, 11 November 1864, *Official Records*, series 2, vol. 7, 1,120.

[34] Foster to Halleck, 12 November 1864, *Official Records*, series 2, vol. 7, 1,122–23.

[35] John McElroy, *This Was Andersonville*, edited by Roy Meredith (New York: Bonanza Books, 1957) 216–17.

[36] Cited in Charles W. Sanders, Jr., *While in the Hands of the Enemy: Military Prisons of the Civil War* (Baton Rouge: Louisiana State University Press, 2005); Grant to Butler, 18 August 1864, *Official Records*, Series II, Vol. VII, 607.

[37] Butler to Hoffman, 25 September 1864, *Official Records*, series 2, vol. 7, 872.

Confederate POWs in their custody "who will not be able to perform service in the field within sixty days," but he added a cautionary note to select only those "who are not too feeble to endure the fatigues of the journey."[38]

Actually, what each side considered underhanded behavior on the part of the enemy and despite what the negative intentions may or may not have been, the decision to exchange those unfit for duty because of illness or disability could be viewed as more humanitarian than sending the relatively healthy back home. Given the death rate in both Union and Confederate military prisons, debilitated POWs would have a better chance of recovering when returned through their respective lines. Those who were "on their last legs" might, in fact, die during transit, but their deaths would have been assured if they remained in the camps.

At Camp Lawton, the selection process for the exchange was carefully observed by the inmates. In theory, those qualified for the exchange were supposed to be sick or wounded. William Hawkins's memory of the selection reflects the extremes of the range of emotions that must have been felt by the POWs. Notes taken from an August 1880 interview with Hawkins told the story:

> The Dr. came along the line designating those whose names he had decided to exchange. He came almost to Hawkins & turned around & started to go back. H's heart sank & and he was just sinking to the ground with hope gone out of his soul when God be thanked—the Dr. turned about & came & looked at H., felt his pulse & arm mere skin & bones & said put down this man's name & joy & hope returned.[39]

However, many able-bodied prisoners developed schemes to get selected. Some resorted to the old tactic of "flanking"; others attempted to assume the identities of others. An example of the latter was depicted in a reminiscence that appeared in the 30 July 1890, issue of the *Oxford* (Pennsylvania) *Press*. The author was Captain William H. Ingram (3rd US), a quartermaster wagon master who had been captured near Baton Rouge, Louisiana. His career in Confederate military prisons carried him

---

[38] Hoffman to Richardson, 1 October 1864, *Official Records*, series 2, vol. 7, 907.

[39] Hawkins, Interview typescript, c. 7–8 August 1880, 12, Edwin D. Northrup Papers, #4190, Department Of Manuscripts and University Archives, Cornell University.

to Cahaba, Camp Sumter, Savannah, and Camp Lawton. A determined and persistent man, Ingram escaped three times and was recaptured each time. He ended up at Camp Lawton but secured his eventual release through a subterfuge. As the selection process for the exchange was taking place, Ingram, try as he may, failed to be selected to leave because he was relatively hale and hearty. Then, as he told it,

> [t]hat night I found a man about to die who had passed the doctor that day [been accepted for exchange]. I built a fire for him and cheered him up the best I could. I got his name, Wm. B. Heening, Co. B, 11th U.S. Infantry—captured at Gettysburg on July 3rd—all of which questions had to be answered at the gate. The next morning I found the poor fellow dead. I determined to pass out on this dead man's name. Every corpse that was taken out of the stockade to the dead house had to have a tag on his breast giving name, company, and regiment. My name was on Heening's body. According to rebel records I am dead and buried at Millen prison. At 10 a.m. all who had passed the doctor were ordered to the gate. I was one of the first, fixed up for the occasion. I rubbed my hands over the bottom of a camp kettle and blackened my face, arms, and legs. I had a pair of old torn drawers, a shirt and a ragged blanket around me, winding up with a pair of crutches. I remained at the gate until 2 p.m., when Heening's name was called. I answered "Here!" Some five or six others in different places also answered "here!" The sergeant who called the roll asked what it meant, so many answering? I told him they were all imposters. He asked my company, regiment, where and when captured, all of which I answered promptly. Then I was told to pass out. As I was passing through the dead-line the Captain in charge of the prison recognized me and shouted, "You, tall man with the crutches, hold on!" I heard him, but kept on; he hallooed again, "You tall man with the blanket, stop!" But I kept going ahead, when an officer in charge of the outside gate took hold of me and told me to stop. The Captain, who knew my record, studied awhile, then he told the officer to let me go, saying: "Damn him, he deserved to go." He shouted to me, "Good bye Ingram, I wish you luck!" I thanked him and passed out; none but our two selves understood what was meant.[40]

---

[40] "Nine Years in Service: A Soldier's Experience," *Oxford* (Pennsylvania) *Press*, 30 July 1890; Ingram was an Irish immigrant, and his life's story is told in Samuel T. Wiley,

Ingram made it to Savannah and to Union lines. A great story, but unfortunately neither Ingram nor Heening's names appear on any list of Camp Lawton dead. This story is either apocryphal or Heening's renamed body ended up being listed as unknown.

Still others attempted the age old tactic of "greasing" their captors' palms, and apparently some Confederate authorities were susceptible to bribery: "A surgeon would examine the sick, and take their names as those to be paroled, and then go away and sell the poor man's chance to whoever had money."[41] In particular, inmates later accused Captain Vowles of taking money for the privilege of having one's name put on the exchange list, whether able-bodied or not. Again, McElroy reported:

> The sending of our sick through gave our commandant, Captain Bowes [Vowles], a fine opportunity to fill his pockets by conniving at the passage of well men. There was still considerable money in the hands of a few prisoners. All this and more, too, were they willing to give for their lives. In the first batch that went away were two of the leading sutlers at Andersonville, who had accumulated perhaps one thousand dollars each by their shrewd and successful bartering. It was generally believed that they gave every cent to Bowes for the privilege of leaving. I know nothing of the truth of this, but I am reasonably certain that they paid him very handsomely. Soon we heard that one hundred and fifty dollars had been sufficient to buy some men out: then one hundred, seventy-five, fifty, thirty, ten and—at last—five dollars.... Captain Bowes merchandising in the matter of exchange was as open as the issuing of rations.... He dealt quite fairly. Several times when the exchange was interrupted, Bowes sent the money back to those who had paid him and received it again when the exchange was renewed.[42]

Biographical and Portrait Cyclopedia of Chester County, ed. by Winfield Scott Warner (Philadelphia: Gresham Publishing, 1893) 741–42.

[41] Robert H. Kellogg, *Life and Death in Rebel Prisons: Giving a Complete History of the Inhuman and Barborous Treatment of our Brave Soldiers by Rebel Authorities, Inflicting Terrible Suffering and Frightful Mortality, Principally at Andersonville, GA., and Florence S.C., Describing Plans of Escape, Arrival of Prisoners with Numerous and Varied Incidents and Anecdotes of Prison Life* (Hartford CT: L. Stebbins, 1865) 394. Free Lance said that if he had had five dollars he could have bought himself out (*The National Tribune*, 23 September 1882).

[42] McElroy, *This Was Andersonville*, 217.

POWs Alvis Graton and Henry Tisdale claimed that the prison doctors were also guilty of accepting bribes, while Edgar Clare (1st Vermont Cavalry) accused the captain in charge of the prison (Vowles).[43] One piece of evidence that may support the claims that prison authorities accepted bribes to put specific POWs on the exchange list is found in Sergeant Dennison's diary entries on 14 and 15 November:

> Camp Lawton, Nov. 14, 1864   C Hess dr [debtor] to JH
> Dennison $5.00
>
> ....
>
> [November 15] "they took out the sick   ten hundred for exchange
> there was a great meney bought thareself out for $5.00[44]

However, it was not only the testimony of inmates that sullied Vowles's generally good reputation among inmates because, according to Philip Cashmyer (or Cashmeyer), Winder seems to have believed Vowles to be culpable, as well.[45]

The specific arrangements for the exchange at Savannah were finally arranged at a 11 November meeting between Colonel Mulford and Captain W.M. Hatch, Confederate Assistant Commissioner for Exchanges.[46] As the exchange unfolded, the newspapers in Savannah kept their readers informed of its progress. Confederate POWs held by

---

[43] Alvis Graton, "Shanks Report," 848–50; Tisdal, "Diary"; Edgar Clare, "Shanks Report,"803–08.

[44] James H. Dennison, *Dennison's Andersonville Diary: The Diary of an Illinois Soldier in the Infamous Andersonville Prison Camp*, notes and transcript. Jack Klasey (Kankakee IL: Kankakee County Historical Society, 1987) 83.

[45] Two letters from Philip Cashmyer to Col. N.P. Chipman following the war (22 September 1865, *Official Records*, series 2, vol. 8, 753–54, and 12 October 1865, *Official Records*, series 2, vol. 8, 764–66) reported that an investigation into Vowles's involvement in such corrupt activities, "the evidence of prisoners being not acceptable," rendered no official guilty verdict, but "$60 paid by a prisoner was recovered from a clerk in Captain Vowles' office.... The suspicion was so great against this officer that General Winder declared he should have no such command in the future." Cashmyer was a long-time associate of General Winder, having served him as a detective and assistant from Winder's days in Richmond until the general's death.

[46] *Daily Morning News* (Savannah), 14 November 1864.

the Union were sent up the river to Savannah on 13 and 14 November.[47] Then, from 18–21 November, Union POWs from Camp Lawton were sent down the river to waiting Union transports.[48] The exchange site for the respective groups of POWs was the anchorage off Venus Point on Jones Island. It was nine miles downstream from the port of Savannah and two miles upstream from Federal-occupied Fort Pulaski.[49]

Many of the POW diary accounts related to Camp Lawton are very spare in their details of day-to-day events; however, those who were fortunate enough to be exchanged in November often described their departure in considerable detail. The joy of their release apparently seared the events into their memories. One of those was Sergeant Henry M. Davidson who recounted in detail how he was exchanged from Camp Lawton. Davidson was not ill, but he had assisted one of the surgeons in collecting the names of the sick for the exchange and then, as previously mentioned, had worked for several days in the camp slaughterhouse. On 20 November the "captain who commanded the post" (undoubtedly Captain Vowles), gathered twenty-four of the POW "trustees" and had them draw for the twelve spaces available for the exchange train that afternoon. Twenty-five slips of paper, twelve of which had the word "GO" printed on them, were put into a hat and shaken. Davidson drew last and found the hoped-for word on his slip of paper. He left on the exchange train that afternoon.[50]

Daniel Kelley, who was one of the sick selected for the exchange, explained the process by which the Camp Lawton POWs were taken from the stockade to the railroad. Confederate officers stood inside the gate and called out the names of those selected for exchange. When one's name was called, the acceptable response was to give one's rank, company, and regiment. Then the POW was sent to the railroad station to the east of the camp. If he were not ambulatory, he was taken in a

---

[47] *Savannah Republican*, 14 November 1864; *Daily Morning News* (Savannah), 14 November 1864.

[48] Ibid., 21 November 1864; *Daily Morning News* (Savannah), 19 November 1864.

[49] Henry Davidson, *Fourteen Months in Southern Prisons* (Milwaukee: Daily Wisconsin Printing House, 1865) 344.

[50] Asa B. Isham, Henry M. Davidson, Henry B. Furness, *Prisoners of War and Military Prisons* (Cincinnati: Lyman & Cushing, 1890) 367–69.

wagon. In fact, Kelley was one of those who could not walk and had to be transported to the station.[51]

Another, more detailed account of the selection process has been left by Private Simon Helwig (Company F, 51st Ohio Infantry):

> One evening we received word that there would be an exchange made of the worst cases [of the sick] the next morning. We were marched past a certain point where there were two surgeons stationed, and as the prisoners came up they put down the names of those they picked out to be exchanged. When I came up they looked at me and said, "Well I think you can stand it a while yet." Then I commenced to plead for liberty; I told them that I had been a prisoner fourteen months, and that my term of service had expired a month before, and as soon as I would be exchanged I would receive my discharge. So they said "Well, if that is the case with you, we will let you pass;" and they put my name down. I passed on the other side, and I felt a good deal better, but could hardly believe that we would be exchanged. I had been disappointed so often, and we were afraid it would turn out the same way again. There was considerable bustling around in camp that evening. Some of the men that had money or anything of value left, tried hard to buy off some of the other boys to stay and let them pass out under their name. But they would not sell such a chance as that. But during the night some of those died that had their names on the list, and then others passed out answering to their name. The next morning when the time arrived, the men in charge came in and called off the names, and each man answered and stepped out into the ranks, and when all the names had been called we were marched out of prison and placed on cars, and were taken to Savannah.[52]

Like the other exchangees, both Kelley and Helwig left Camp Lawton, rode the rails to Savannah, and boarded a ship on the Savannah River to reach the Federal fleet and freedom.[53] According to Kelley, "I shall ever remember the 19th of November, 1864, as one of the happiest days of my life."[54] Once transferred to a Federal deck, Helwig recalled,

---

[51] Daniel G. Kelley, *What I Saw and Suffered in Rebel Prisons* (Buffalo NY: Thomas Howard & Johnson, 1868) 78.

[52] Simon Helwig, *The Capture and Prison Life in Rebeldom for Fourteen Months of Simon Helwig: Late Private Co. F. 51st O.V.I.* (Canal Dover OH: Bixler, n.d.) 46–47.

[53] Kelley, *What I Saw*, 80-81.

[54] Ibid., 83.

"all that could hurrah, yelled with all the might they could for the old flag."[55]

On November 21, Foster and Mulford reported to Halleck and Butler, respectively, that the exchange was taking place, and Mulford indicated that he had received over 3,000 Union POWs so far. One of the exchangees from Camp Lawton described his last rail journey in Confederate custody:

> Finally the cars arrived, mostly open cars, which had apparently been used for carrying cattle, and we were put in, sixty in each car; nearly every man of which was in a helpless condition, and many who were raving in the delirium of fever. After going a few miles we stopped, and waited *five hours* for a train to pass, *the rain pouring heavily all the time,* and we soon became soaked through and through, many having no clothing but a worn-out shirt and pants. Soon after midnight, the expected train came along; and we resumed our journey, arriving at Savannah by daylight, exhausted, faint, chilled, and stiff, our hands having the appearance of having been parboiled. On unloading, many who were taken out were found to be dead, having been unable to survive this, their last day of imprisonment. Wagons and ambulances [presumably arranged by Enders] were awaiting our arrival, in which we were taken to the steam-boat landing. Those not able to walk or even crawl were taken on board by means of stretchers carried by men who had been detailed to act as nurses. As we passed through the streets on our way to the boats, large numbers of ladies came running out of the houses, bringing us baked sweet potatoes, sliced meat, and biscuit, the taste of which we had not known since our imprisonment; also buckets of water, the sight of which was as refreshing as an oasis in the desert.
>
> On arriving at the wharf, we were all put on rebel boats, and sailed down the Savannah River about ten miles, when we came in sight of the Federal fleet, one of which the *New York*, came alongside; and we were transferred on board of her, ...[56] [italics in original]

---

[55] Helwig, *The Capture and Prison Life*, 48.

[56] Anonymous, *A Voice from Rebel Prisons Giving an Account of Some of the Horrors of the Stockades at Andersonville, Milan and Other Prisons by a Returned Prisoner of War* (Boston: Rand & Avery, 1865) 15–16.

W.F. Lyon (Company C., 9th Minnesota) echoed that account: "Just before dark the train moved out and the rain began to fall at the same time, and it followed us all night. We were crowded into cattle cars, open all around, with no roof, so that as we pulled into Savannah the next day, we were wet through and so chilled we could hardly move."[57]

Another Union POW, John F. Diener (Company F, 7th Pennsylvania), remembered his trip from Camp Lawton to a wharf in Savannah, where he and fellow prisoners were sent downstream to a waiting US steamer. He related that he was so vermin infested he had to wash and change clothing three times in order to get rid of the "graybacks". His prison garb was burned.[58] One can imagine the palpable sense of relief, freedom, and homecoming that surged among both Union and Confederate exchangees as they emerged from the custody of their captors. In fact, William Hawkins witnessed a remarkable transformation among several Union POWs when they boarded Union ships: "Some who were so weak that they had to be carried on, in their joy & revived hope stood up."[59] When James Dennison finally reached a Union hospital, he wrote to his wife, Anne, to tell her that he was "in the land of the living once more."[60] Lieutenant Hodgkins put it this way:

> 27 [Nov] A beautiful morning and quite warm. This is one of the happiest days of my life. I feel very thankful to God, that he has spared my life and health through all that I have passed, and permitted me once more to look upon the dear old flag. "Long may it wave."
>
> ... After passing the Fort [Pulaski], we witnessed one of the most beautiful sights I ever saw, the setting of the sun in the water.[61]

---

[57] W.F. Lyon, *In and Out of Andersonville Prison* (Detroit IL: Geo. Harland Co., 1905) 86.

[58] Hawkins, Interview typescript, c. 7–8 August 1880.

[59] John F. Driener "A Story of Prison Life," *The War of the 'Sixties*, comp. E.R. Hutchins (New York: Neale Publishing, 1912) 199–201.

[60] Dennison, *Andersonville Diary*, 97.

[61] J.E. Hodgkins, *The Civil War Diary of Lieut. J. E. Hodgkins: 19th Massachusetts Volunteers from August 11, 1862 to June 3, 1865*, trans. Kenneth C. Turino (Camden ME: Picton Press, 1994) 111.

Sergeant Howard, who left Camp Lawton on 18 November and was exchanged at Savannah a day later, exclaimed, "It was the happiest day of my life," repeating Daniel Kelley's sentiments almost word for word.[62]

The 10 December 1864, issue of *Harper's Weekly* visually depicted for its readers the 18 November return of a group of POWs to the Union fleet. One striking illustration ("Thank God!" ...) by artist correspondent William Waud pictured a group of prisoners who have just been transferred to the deck of Colonel Mulford's dispatch boat, the *Eliza Hancock*, cheering and saluting the flag. The second print, also by Waud, featured POWs below deck on the *New York* receiving welcome rations.[63]

Upon examining the returning Union POWs, Mulford commented, "Their physical condition is rather better than I expected, but their personal [clothing?] is worse than anything I have seen—filth and rags."[64] Foster echoed Mulford's sentiment when he told Halleck, "I understand that all the rebels have been delivered and most of our men received; also, that the condition of the latter is fully as good as that of the rebels delivered."[65] The comments of the Union officers on the condition of the Union POWs they received is interesting in the light of the subsequent charges and counter charges in the war of mutual recrimination over the POW issue that followed the conflict. Mulford and Foster's comments do not necessarily mean that the Union POWs were in good shape, but they do indicate a degree of parity and some surprise. Of course, their reaction may have been conditioned by the horror stories they had heard previous to the exchange.

On the other hand, one Union POW who was selected for exchange from Camp Lawton commented on the returning Confederate exchangees that he saw:

> Whilst waiting, a train from Savannah came up, loaded with rebels just released from Northern prisons, many of whom were dressed with clothing from Uncle Sam's wardrobe, and who presented a healthy appearance compared with our pitiable condition. *They spoke to us with*

---

[62] Howard, Diary, 25 November 1864.

[63] *Harper's Weekly*, 10 December 1864.

[64] Mulford to Butler, 21 November 1864, *Official Records*, series 2, vol. 7, 1,149.

[65] Foster to Halleck, 21 November 1864, *Official Records*, series 1, vol. 44, 516–17.

compassion, and gave us tobacco and hard tack, with which they had been bountifully supplied before leaving Union lines, and which we eagerly accepted to appease out hunger.[66] [italics in original]

Mulford's last report to Butler related to these exchanges, dated 29 November, and stated that 4,600 Union POWs had been exchanged.[67] Ultimately, nearly 11,000 Union prisoners were exchanged through Savannah and other ports. Of course, Sherman's operations had ended Camp Lawton's existence by that time. Those Union POWs who had not been fortunate, sick, moneyed, or clever enough to be exchanged through Savannah found themselves in other prisons or on the road to them. Unfortunately, the delays associated with the negotiations for and the process of the 1864 exchanges contributed to the deaths of both Union and Confederate POWs who otherwise might have survived had they been exchanged. According to historian Eugene Marvin Thomas, "between August and November 1864, well over twelve thousand men died in prisons."[68]

Although the Confederates kept records of those who died at Camp Lawton, many POWs also kept careful accounts of their own, recording the names of their comrades who had died, been transferred to other prisons, or been exchanged. In some cases the exchanges from Camp Lawton passed on such information to their hometown papers which published the data, in combination with official government reports, for the benefit of an eager, but anxious readership.[69]

---

[66] Anonymous, *A Voice from Rebel Prisons*, 15.

[67] Mulford to Butler, 29 November 1864, *Official Records*, series 2, vol. 7, 1,169. As the war drew to a close, the exchanges continued and included transfer points at Charleston and the James River, as well as Savannah. On 23 March 1865, Mulford sent a tabulation indicating that from 1 November 1864 to 22 March 1865, 10,916 Federal POWs had been received from Savannah and Charleston, and 3,137 Confederate POWs had been delivered. Large numbers of prisoners from both sides were also repatriated on the James River (Mulford, "Aggregate of prisoners received and delivered at Savannah, Charleston, and in James River from 1 November 1864, to 22 March 1865, inclusive," *Official Records*, series 2, vol. 7, 424).

[68] Eugene Marvin Thomas, "Prisoner of War Exchange during the American Civil War" (PhD diss., Auburn University, 1976) 278.

[69] "List of Vermont Troops at Anapolis, MD, Recently Paroled at Savannha, Ga.," and "Deaths of Vermont Soldiers in Southern Prisons," *Vermont Watchman & State Journal* (Montpelier), 16 Deecember 1864, are examples of this.

Camp Lawton inmates who were not selected for the November sick exchanges undoubtedly felt that they were the losers in an unfair lottery. Yet, the departure of their comrades opened up an opportunity, quickly taken advantage of by those left behind, to improve their housing circumstances by moving into abandoned shebangs that were better. But the approach of Sherman's forces quickly rendered this a very temporary benefit. George Hitchcock remembered moving to a vacated shebang only to be rousted out within twenty-four hours as the entire prison was evacuated.[70]

As the sick exchange process unfolded that November, another forlorn group of POWs watched with considerable interest from the vantage point of the casemates of Fort Pulaski where they were incarcerated. Second Lieutenant Joseph Mauck (10th Virginia), a member of the "Immortal Six Hundred," Confederate POWs held for retaliatory purposes, watched wistfully as ships carrying exchange commissioners and ferrying POWs ascended and descended the river and noted in his diary: "Can see the exchange boats going up the Savannah River. Wouldn't care to be a little sick myself."[71]

The remaining, "healthy" POWs at Camp Lawton did not have to wait long after the sick and wounded were sent to the exchange port of Savannah. In the face of Sherman's advance, they were hurriedly evacuated. POW accounts tell of the precipitous closing. According to Sneden the Confederate garrison began to prepare for the possibility of transporting the prisoners away from Sherman's advancing columns as early as 17 November, when the guards began to cook three days' rations. By 22 November, all detachments of POWs had been marched to the trains. Sergeant Francis J. Hosner remembered the final evacuation of Camp Lawton:

---

[70] George A. Hitchcock, *From Ashby to Andersonville: The Civil War Diary and Reminiscences of George A. Hitchcock, Private, Company A, 21st Massachusetts Regiment, August 1862–January 1865*, ed. Ronald Watson (Campbell CA: Savas Publishing, 1997) 271.

[71] Joseph Mauck, Diary, 6–8 November 1864, Museum of the Confederacy, Richmond, Virginia, cited in Mauriel Phillips Joslyn, *Captives Immortal: The Story of Six Hundred Confederate Officers and the United States Prisoner of War Policy* (Shippensburg PA: White Mane Publishing, 1996) 155.

[A]bout nine o'clock [in the evening], the call for rations was announced. It was at such an unusual time that it told plainly that some move had been ordered and that haste must be observed. The detachments were served in the order of sequence, and when they reached my muster,—which was the last—it must have been nearly one o'clock a.m.… The rations were said to be for three days; they consisted of about a pound of fresh beef and a half pound of hard bread. This was the first, and I think, with one exception, the last bread made from wheat flour, ever issued to me, at any of their prisons.… The alacrity with which the camp was emptied at Millen, and the haste they displayed in crowding that seven thousand prisoners into Savannah, was explained later. We were in "Sherman's" way.[72]

John McElroy also referred to the suddenness of the evacuation: "About 3 o'clock in the morning the Rebel Sergeants, who called the roll, came in and around to turn us out and get ready to move."[73] Henry Tisdale's account of the final evacuation offers additional details:

On the twenty-second [November], long trains of box cars were in sight from the prison and word came to pack up and be ready to move. Cold, raw, and drizzly without, most of us were in our shelters and the order to turn out was not an agreeable one to us in our rags and tatter, with no hope of exchange to cheer us. Some tried to hide in their quarters by burying themselves in their bedding of pine boughs. This was soon discovered and a rebel bayonet thrust in their faces scattered their hopes of being left to welcome Sherman. Were hastily crowded into box cars almost at the point of bayonets for upon some of us protesting that, "this car is full," we were made to see by a bayonet charge that there was soon room for more. The cold increased as a few scattering snowflakes plainly told us. All night and until ten the next morning were getting over the

---

[72] Francis J. Hosmer, *A Glimpse of Andersonville and Other Writings* (Springfield MA: Loring and Axtell, 1896) 45.

[73] McElroy, *Andersonville*, 490–91; Henry Harmon also remembered it being early on a stormy morning ("A Year in Six Rebel Prisons"); William Smith remembered a signal gun being fired from the fort as the start of the process and the night as being cold and rainy (*On Wheels: and How I Came There: The True Story of a 15-Year-Old Yankee and Prisoner in the American Civil War*, ed. Stacy M. Haponik [College Station TX: Virtualbookworm.com, 2002] 107). Hitchcock, *From Ashby to Andersonville*, 271, indicated that it was at night, and the POWs were exposed to a windy, freezing rain.

eighty mile to Savannah—now waiting for hours at some siding or barely creeping along at some up grade.[74]

Echoing Tisdale, Martin O'Hara remembered that ["a] good many hid in the dugouts, covering themselves with rubbish, and remained until the 15th army corps came." That last phrase is problematic because, although some POWs did, in fact, try to hide in their shebangs during the final evacuation, no record exists of POWs remaining behind and rescued by Sherman's forces.[75] However, it is possible that some very ill POWs were overlooked in the hasty evacuation, which might explain several unburied bodies reportedly found by Sherman's soldiers when they reached the camp several days later.

Experienced POWs usually were very careful to keep with them what few possessions they had, but Hosmer, McElroy, and Tisdale's depictions of the urgency of camp's evacuation probably explain the wealth of POW artifacts later found by archeologists. As rushed as the evacuation might have been, McElroy remembered it as providing his comrade Andrews and him with a rare opportunity:

> As we passed through the Rebel camp at dawn, on our way to the cars, Andrews and I noticed a nest of four large, bright, new tin pans—a rare thing in the Confederacy at that time. We managed to snatch them without the guard's attention being attracted, and in an instant had them wrapped up in our blanket. But the blanket was full of holes, and in spite of all our efforts, it would slip at the most inconvenient times, so as to show a broad glare of the bright metal.[76]

Despite the shiny metal the two comrades were able to keep their ill gotten, but treasured gains on the next stage of their journey.

The suddeness of the evacuation also gave William Smith and some of his comrades another, unexpected opportunity:

> The guards had been quite careless with us that morning, And it really did not look as if we were going to be exchanged. Near the railroad track there were several large sugar kettles set up in the woods uncovered.

---

[74] Tisdale, 28 November 1864, "Diary."

[75] Martin O'Hara, *Reminiscences of Andersonville and Other Rebel Prisons: A Story of Suffering and Death* (Lyons IA: J.C. Hopkins, Printer, Advertiser Office, 1880) 47.

[76] McElroy, *Andersonville*, 491.

They would hold, perhaps, one hundred gallons each, and were, as we passed, about two-thirds full of hot mush. As we were going by them I broke ranks, and, taking my wooden plate, scooped up about a pint of hot mush, and with it got a badly burned hand. Many others, also, helped themselves to the mush in the same way, and the guards made no attempt to check us.[77]

Charles E. Walcott (21st Massachusetts) remembered leaving Camp Lawton at 4 a.m. on 22 November. It had "stormed all day," and he had just congratulated himself the day before on getting possession of a good, abandoned shebang, when he was forced to leave. At the depot he saw that POWs were not the only evacuees in Sherman path, as he witnessed "train after train pass down toward Savannah, loaded with all kinds of household goods, men with their families, and negroes of all ages, while numberless teams of all descriptions are depositing their freight alongside the railroad."[78]

Interestingly, as he boarded the train for Savannah, Private John H. Sammons (5th Indiana Cavalry) remembered General Winder remarking to a group of POWs, "If you ever go back into the service and take any of our boys prisoners, treat them well, for we have done the best we could for you."[79] One wonders what thoughts ran through the POWs' minds or what words may have been muttered under their breath in answer to Winder's comments.

Sneden left the camp on 22 November, along with Dr. White and the medical staff. They went via train to Millen and then Savannah.[80] There is some mystery, however, concerning where Winder went following the evacuation of Camp Lawton. Sneden indicates that Winder left the camp for Savannah on November 21, but Winders's last

---

[77] Smith, *On Wheels*, 107.

[78] Charles F. Walcott, *History of the Twenty-first Regiment, Massachusetts Volunteers in the War for the Preservation of the Union, 1861–1865, with Statistics of the War and Rebel Prisons* (Boston: Houghton, Mifflin & Company, 1882) 422.

[79] John H. Sammons, *Personal Recollections of the Civil War* (Greensburg IN: Montgomery & Son, n.d.) 50.

[80] Sneden, *Eye of the Storm: A Civil War Odyssey*, ed. Charles F. Bryan, Jr., and Nelson D. Lankford (New York: The Free Press, 2000) 271–72; Winder to Cooper, 22 November 1864, *Official Records*, series 2, vol. 7, 1,155.

communication from the prison is dated 25 November, and indicates that he would "await instructions at Augusta."[81] If, in fact, he left Camp Lawton as late as 25 November and went directly to Augusta from Camp Lawton via the railroad, he would have barely missed the Federal cavalry forces that were headed toward the prison and to Waynesboro to cut the rail line. On the other hand, it would have been possible for him to have gone to Savannah and from there to Charleston and then to Augusta, as Sneden recounts his movements.

Estes's scouting force indicated, when they reached the abandoned stockade on the afternoon of 26 November (Saturday), that they were told the POWs had been evacuated on the previous Tuesday (22 November). The inmates had been loaded on cars and shipped to Savannah. The weather being cold, the POWs suffered a great deal. From Savannah they were sent down the Atlantic and Gult Railroad to a holding area near Blackshear. It was literally a wooded area surrounded by guards.

The abandoned stockade remained empty and silent, waiting for its next visitors. They soon arrived in the form of Sherman's columns, several units of which in the left wing marched by the defunct prison. Numerous diary accounts by Sherman's soldiers mention seeing the abandoned prison when they arrived in the area. The ultimate disposition of Camp Lawton was in their hands. Although the *Official Records* contain nothing that specifically explains what happened to the stockade, it is clear from other accounts that it was destroyed by Union forces. With the penchant that Sherman's soldiers had for destroying anything useful to their enemy's cause, particularly one of the hated prison "pens," one could hardly expect less. Nor would they have wanted to leave such a facility behind for possible reoccupation by the Confederates once the Union forces had passed through. Kilbourne's previously mentioned account of the "scout" to Camp Lawton on 26 November claims that the flying column destroyed the stockade and

---

[81] Sneden (*Eye of the Storm*, 272). Sneden claims that Winder went to Savannah and then left on November 28 to go to Charleston and Florence (276); however, Winder's 25 November message from Camp Lawton indicates the general was going to Augusta (Winder to Cooper, 25 November 1864, *Official Records*, series 2, vol. 7, 1,160).

associated buildings. However, the destruction must not have been complete because other diary accounts mention that the stockade was burned by later arrivals. Orderly Sergeant Josiah Wilson of Company D, 1st Alabama Cavalry (US), reported that on Saturday, 3 December 1864, "Our Co. marched up the August[a] RR 6 miles to burn the stockaids the rebs kept our prisoners in."[82] Also, a member of the 149th New York wrote that he saw a portion of the prison, a smaller uncompleted stockade (most likely the hospital), in "a mass of flames, the fire having probably been set by our troops."[83] Most of the rest of Camp Lawton was burned, as well. A diary entry from Alexander G. Dowling (Company E, 11th Iowa)—"[W]e burned everything here that a match would ignite"— seems to confirm this.[84]

Although little archeological examination of the site has been done, initial findings seem also to support a fiery end to the camp. On 30 January 2007, archeologists from the Georgia Department of Transportation and Department of Natural Resources unearthed a piece of charred wood as they searched for evidence of the stockade wall line at Magnolia Springs.[85] An even more recent examination of the site begun in January of 2010 by archaeologists from Georgia Southern University has uncovered further evidence of burning. Thus, the stockade was set afire. However, the destruction apparently was still not complete. In an article in the Waynesboro *True Citizen*, dated 22 July 1893, the Lawtonville correspondent mentioned the camp twenty-nine years after its demise: "Old fortifications around Lawtonville and the remains of the stockade are to be seen to this day."[86]

---

[82] Josiah Wilson, "Diary," ed. E.D. Wilson, [http://home.houston.rr.com/heartofdixie/1stCav.html] (accessed 23 July 2008).

[83] "149th Regiment, NY Volunteer Infantry Civil War Newspaper Clippings,"
[http://www.dmna.state.ny.us/historic/reghist/civil/infantry/149thInfCWN.htm] (accessed 23 July 2008).

[84] Alexander G. Downing, *Downing's Civil War Diary: August 15, 1861–July31, 1865*, ed. Olynthus B. Clark (Des Moines IA: Historical Department of Iowa, 1916) 234.

[85] Deborah Bennett, "Possible Remnant of Camp Lawton Unearthed in Dig," *The Millen News*, 7 February 2007, 1.

[86] "Dear Citizen," July 22, 1893, *The True Citizen* (Waynesboro), cited in *Herndon and Lawtonville: A Collection of Newspaper Sources, 1883–1900* in *Occasional Studies in Sandhill*

Local traditions indicate that some of the Camp Lawton infrastructure—such as log cabins—were still standing when construction
began on Magnolia Springs State Park in the late 1930s. During the
building of the park, some of these putative Confederate vestiges were
destroyed and others were moved off the park property. However, none
of these buildings seem to have survived, and no photographs of them
are known to exist. An interesting sidelight related to this is that Union
POWs were not the only POWs to be housed near Magnolia Springs.
During WWII, German POWs worked in the area, some of them
completing work on the park buildings at Magnolia Springs. One of
them, in fact, constructed a model of one of the reputed Confederate
cabins that was still visible in the area. The model is on display in the
park museum today.[87]

The stockade was not the only thing to draw the ire of the Federal
troops. The well-documented antipathy toward dogs on the part of
Sherman's men surfaced again near Camp Lawton. Inspired by the belief
that hounds tracked and were set upon fugitive Union prisoners and
sure that packs of hounds found nearby had been used to track down
escaped POWs, the marching soldiers routinely shot dogs that came
across their path. Lieutenant Colonel Andrew Hickenlooper, chief of
staff to 17th Corps commander Major General Frank Blair, recounted
how troops who learned of a nearby plantation owner who kept a pack
of bloodhounds with a contract to hunt down any escaping prisoners "at
so much per head" destroyed his place and killed his dogs.[88]

Chaplain Stevenson of the 78th Ohio gave an even more detailed
account of Union soldiers targeting hounds:

> Yesterday we passed the plantation of Mr. Stubbs. The house, cotton
> gin, press, corn ricks, stable, everything that could burn, was in flames,
> and in the door-yard lay the dead bodies of several bloodhounds that had
> been used to track and pull down negroes and our escaped prisoners.
> And wherever out army has passed, everything in the shape of a dog has

---

History, compiled by James E. Dorsey (Swainsboro GA: Emanuel County Junior College
Library, 1980) 150–51.

[87] Interviews with Donald Perkins, 2 and 8 April 2010.

[88] Cited in William Earl Parrish, *Frank Blair: Lincoln's Conservative* (Columbia:
University of Missouri Press, 1998) 208.

been killed. The soldiers and officers are determined that no flying fugitives, white men or negroes, shall be followed by track-hounds that come within reach of their powder and ball.[89]

But the "dogs of war" were not the only ones who suffered because of their efforts to track down escaped POWs. Planters could become targets as well, as found in the post-action report of Colonel J.S. Robinson (commanding 3rd Brigade, 1st Division, 20th Corps):

> Shortly after passing Birdville [a plantation located to the west of Camp Lawton], having received reliable information that a planter named Bullard, living in that neighborhood, had made himself conspicuous for his zeal in recapturing and securing prisoners from our army escaped from rebel authorities, I dispatched an officer with authority to destroy his outbuildings and cotton. He accordingly set fire to the corn cribs, cotton gin, cotton presses, and a warehouse containing $50,000 worth of cotton. These were all consumed and the owner admonished that a repetition of his offense would bring a similar fate upon his dwelling at the next visitation of our army.[90]

Millen Junction suffered severe damage. Advanced elements of Sherman's forces reached the town on the morning of 2 December, although Captain William Duncan's scouting force had sent a small detachment into Millen on 30 November. Sherman and his staff spent 3 December in the village.[91] Millen's association with the prison camp and the fact that it was a strategic point along the railroad made it a military target, and Sherman's men made short work of it. His intention to destroy Millen Junction was made clear in his order to 17th Corps commander Major General Frank Blair in which he told Blair that he did not intend his command to march more than five miles on 3 December because he wanted him "to make the most complete and possible break

---

[89] Thomas M. Stevenson, *History of the 78th Regiment O.V.V.I. from Its "Muster-In to Its Muster-Out;" Comprising Its Organization, Marches, Campaigns, Battles and Skirmishes* (Zanesville OH: Hugh Dunne, 1865) 317.

[90] Report of Col. James S. Robinson, Eighty-second Ohio Infantry, commanding Third Brigade, 28 December 1864, *Official Records*, series 1, vol. 44, 256. This was probably Needham Bullard (1817–1876), a well-known Burke County planter.

[91] Sherman, *Memoirs*, 2:669, and Taggart to Hitchcock, 30 November 1864, *Official Records*, series 1, vol. 44, 578.

of the railroad about Millen. Let it be more devilish than can be dreamed of." Accordingly, Blair gave orders to his command to destroy the depot and the railroad bridge over Buckhead Creek, as well as the rails and ties to the east for a distance of at least six miles.[92] In addition to destroying the railroad junction, the large hotel (Gray's Inn) was burned, as was the Wayside Home. Three large Confederate storehouses along the tracks were also fired.[93] The railroad depot and the ticket office were set ablaze. Henry Hitchcock was surprised at the size of the railroad depot and estimated that it was 200 feet long. Hitchcock witnessed the scene: "Densest black smoke in immense volumes,—then broad sheets of flame licking the shingled roof and pillars, and sucked in under the eaves like a sheet of blazing fluid."[94] He watched artist T.R. Davis make the sketch, which later appeared in *Harper's Weekly*. Major Nichol's description of the burning of the railroad depot at Millen— "a wooden structure of exceedingly graceful proportions"—tallies well with that of Hitchcock: "[T]he exquisite architecture traced to lines of fire … that even the rank and file observed and made comments…. [A] circumstance that may be counted unusual for the taste of conflagrations has been so cultivated of late in the army that any small affair of that kind attracts very little attention."[95]

Five miles to the north, numerous Union soldiers, primarily men of the 20th Corps whose line of march brought them near to Camp Lawton,

---

[92] Dayton to Blair, 2 December 1864, *Official Records*, series 1, vol. 44, 606; Special Orders No. 296, 2 December 1864, *Official Records*, series 1, vol. 44, 607; and Oscar L. Jackson, *The Colonel's Diary* (Sharon PA: n.p., 1922) 169, cited in Trudeau, *Southern Storm*, 326, contains a similar version of this story. A clear, concise description of the process of destroying the railroads along the march is given in Charles Fessenden Morse, *Letters Written During the Civil War, 1861-1865* (Privately published, 1898), 203.

[93] The warehouses were reputed to have been used temporarily to house Union POWs. That this was the case is clear given the testimony of Solon Hyde, *A Captive of War* (New York: McClure, Phillips &Co., 1900) 62. A member of the 17th Ohio and a hospital steward, Hyde was captured as a result of the Battle of Chickamauga in the fall of 1863. Ultimately, he found himself on a prison train steaming across Georgia: "Arriving at Millen late in the evening, and having to change cars, we were quartered for the night in a warehouse close to the railroad." This, of course, was well before Camp Lawton was built.

[94] Hitchcock, *Marching with Sherman*, 133.

[95] George Ward Nichols, *The Story of the Great March from the Diary of a Staff Officer* (New York: Harper & Brothers, 1865) 80.

visited the prison and many noted in their journals what they saw there.[96] Not among them, however, was General Sherman. Having been informed earlier by Kilpatrick that Camp Lawton had been evacuated, Sherman remained at Millen and never saw the prison compound.

When Sherman had evacuated Atlanta, a photographer had followed, carrying his equipment. G.N. Barnard had photographed the North Georgia campaign and was going to photograph the Savannah area. He did not, however, photograph anything between the two, although he visited Camp Lawton. Hitchcock mentioned Barnard's visit to the stockade:

> Barnard went, while we were at Millen the other day, to the stockade pen where our men (prisoners) were kept. It was simply a pen, surrounded or made by stockades—high posts driven into the ground close to each other, —about 300 yards square; no shelter of any kind, no shed, nor tent, nor roof whatever, in any weather. He went into it and all over it and examined closely. Would have photographed it but did not know of it in time enough. It was about five miles up railroad from Millen—not at the Junction. There was no spring nor well nor any water inside the enclosure. He saw 750 graves,—no head board nor other designation save that each fiftieth grave was so numbered. He heard that five or six dead bodies of our men were left there unburied when they removed the prisoners,—and he saw one still lying there, unburied, himself. He said, after telling about the place, (at dinner this evening)—"I used to be very much troubled about the burning of houses, etc., but after what I have seen I shall not be much troubled about it." If B. feels so from seeing the prison pen, how do those feel who have suffered in it! The burned houses, in spite of orders, are the answer.[97]

---

[96] In addition, at least eight Union Savannah campaign unit reports mentioned passing by Camp Lawton as they marched toward the port city (*Official Records*, series 1, vol. 44, 6–417).

[97] Hitchcock, *Marching with Sherman*, 150. Had Barnard photographed the prison, some of our questions these many years hence would probably have been answered. The unburied bodies seen by Barnard (as well as several Union soldiers) may have been individuals who had been too ill to leave their shebangs and were overlooked in the hasty evacuation of the prison by the Confederates.

Barnard followed Sherman's forces to Savannah, took photographs there, and eventually published a book of them.[98] Would that he had taken photographs of the camp! If he had done so, many questions about the camp's physical layout would perhaps have been answered. His comment about there being no water in the enclosure is puzzling, however.

At least one of Sherman's soldiers, Sergeant Marcellus Darling (Company K, 154th New York) visited Camp Lawton with a sense of urgency. He had reason to believe that his brother Deloss had been there. Search as he might, Darling could find no record or trace of his sibling's presence there.[99] Another Union visitor to the stockade was 18-year-old John Ross (123rd New York). Unknown to him, his older brother Daniel (Battery F, 4th US Artillery) had been incarcerated there. What John Ross did not discover until much later was his brother's remarkable odyssey in and out of Confederate prisons. In fact, Daniel Ross went from POW to captor. He had been captured on 22 June 1864, and, by the time he arrived at Camp Lawton that fall, he was already a veteran of Camp Oglethorpe in Macon, Camp Sumter, and Charleston in turn. Following the evacuation of Camp Lawton, his all-expense-paid travel included stops at Blackshear, Camp Sumter, Charleston, Florence, and the Confederate prison at Cahaba, Alabama. He was liberated there on 2 April 1865, when Union General James H. Wilson's cavalry reached Selma.[100] Returned to active duty the following month, Ross found himself stationed in Augusta, Georgia, when on 14 May, the recently captured Confederate President Jefferson Davis and his family arrived under guard in the city. Ironically, ex-POW Private Ross was then detailed as a guard and accompanied the Davises all the way to Fortress Monroe, which they reached on 23 May. He missed the Grand Review of

---

[98] George N. Barnard, *Photographic Views of Sherman's Campaign* (New York: Press of Wynkoop and Hallenbeck, 1866). Barnard's book contains no photographs between the Atlanta area and Savannah.

[99] Marcellus Warner B. Darling, "Events and Comments of My Life" (n.p., n.d.) 17; Darling, Letter of 16 December 1864, 1.

[100] James Pickett Jones, *Yankee Blitzkrieg: Wilson's Raid through Alabama and Georgia* (Lexington: University Press of Kentucky, 1976), details Wilson's raid that not only liberated Daniel Ross but also resulted in the apprehension of Jefferson Davis' party.

Sherman's Army on 24 May in Washington, DC, and was mustered out with his regiment on 8 June.[101]

In the meantime, his younger brother John had joined the 123rd New York, and that fall John found himself marching with Sherman's 20th Corps as it approached Millen. Unfortunately neither brother knew of the other's proximity and, of course, Daniel was evacuated before John's unit arrived, thus forestalling a happy reunion. By the time John's regiment passed by the abandoned prison on 3 December 1864, his older brother had been shipped to Savannah. John and others of his unit visited the stockade.[102] Fellow regimental comrade Sergeant Rice C. Bull (Company D) echoed the feelings of many when they viewed the compound: "There were many who visited the pen and I heard them say that they would never be taken prisoner; they would prefer to be shot than put in such a place."[103]

In addition to Barnard's account, several of Sherman's soldiers who visited the abandoned prison related the finding of unburied POW bodies. Samuel H. Hurst, commander of the 73rd Ohio, for example, found two bodies in the camp.[104] Also, the Rev. J.E. Brant, in his history of the 85th Indiana recounted: "We saw the dugouts on the hillside, where our boys had sheltered themselves and in one of them we found one dead, who had been left behind too sick to be moved. There were no marks on his person to indicate who he was. He sleeps in a grave marked 'unknown.'"[105] The haste with which the prison was finally evacuated on the night, 22 November, as well as the dying conditions of some of the inmates, may account for these bodies.

Although the Union prisoners had been removed from Camp Lawton, some members of the staff remained behind because Estes's patrol captured Confederate contingents as the Federal scouts

---

[101] Ross, *Lincoln's Veteran Volunteers Win the War*, 309.

[102] Ross, *Lincoln's Veteran Volunteers Win the War*, 268–271, 282–86.

[103] Jack Bauer (ed.), *Soldiering: The Civil War Diary of Rice C. Bull* (Novato CA: Presidio Press, 1986) 193.

[104] Samuel H. Hurst (ed.), *Journal-History of the Seventy-third Ohio Vol. Infantry* (Chilicothe OH: S.H. Hurst, 1866) 159–60.

[105] J.E. Brant, *History of the Eighty-Fifth Indiana Volunteer Infantry: Its Organization, Campaigns and Battles* (Bloomington IN: Cravens Bros., 1902) 83.

reconnoitered the prison before Sherman's troop columns arrived. These Confederates, who must have been left at the camp to complete its physical closing, proved themselves unable to get away soon enough.

The last recorded official act related to Camp Lawton occurred on 21 January 1865, when General Winder sent Mrs. C.E. Jones, the lessor of the prison property, a message from his headquarters in Columbia, South Carolina:

> Madame: The occupation of Savannah by the enemy renders it inexpedient for the Confederate States to continue to occupy the stockade at Camp Lawton. It is therefore given up to you, and I will take the earliest opportunity to send an agent to arrange and settle the account between yourself and the Confederate States.[106]

That was the denouement; the "largest prison in the world" had ended "not with a bang but a whimper," to use T.S. Eliot's phrase.

On 6 February 1865, another principal of the story was gone, as well. While on an inspection trip to yet another POW stockade that came under his administration, this time at Florence, South Carolina, General Winder died suddenly of a massive heart attack as he entered the prison compound.[107] "Well," wrote prescient Confederate diarist Mary Chesnut upon hearing the news, "Winder is safe from the wrath to come."[108]

---

[106] Winder to Jones, 21 January 1865, *Official Records*, series 2, vol. 7, 111.

[107] Arch Frederic Blakey, *General John H. Winder, C.S.A.* (Gainesville: University of Florida Press, 1990) 5.

[108] Cited in Sanders, *While in the Hands of the Enemy*, 269.

7

The Aftermath:
The Trials of the Living and the Odyssey of the Dead

For those who had been involved in the Confederate POW camps—administrators, guards, and prisoners—the war's end did not necessarily provide respite from those associations. Mary Chesnut's prediction that there would be wrath to come proved prophetic. Obviously, as the camps were emptied and POWs repatriated, the relief was immediate and palpable, but in a more permanent sense the experience was not really over. Ex-POWs would carry the memories of their experiences for the rest of their lives—some bearing them silently, others regaling their families and acquaintances with colorful tales of their adventures. Many Union POWs had kept diaries of their prison sojourns, and numbers of them would go on to publish narratives that were snapped up by an eager public. These writers became the public face of the sufferings of Northern soldiers in Confederate POW camps. Still others would have their broken health and psychological scars as constant reminders of their experiences. The 1865 issues of *Harper's Weekly* were full of images relating to the Union POW experience—prints of POWs languishing in the prison camps, of POWs just released, and of Southern prisons. In the 25 February 1865, issue, one particularly poignant image was spread across two full folio pages. Entitled "Home again!—The story of life in rebel prisons," the illustration featured a returned Union POW sharing his experiences with family members who listen in rapt attention. The artist has carefully rendered his earnest face as well as the concerned, focused faces of his listeners. Looks of shock and disbelief play across their visages as they listen to his account.[1]

The fratricidal war had been a horrendous and primal experience for the nation. More than 600,000 soldiers had died, thousands more had

---

[1] *Harper's Weekly: A Journal of Civilization* 9, no. 426 (25 February 1865): 120–21.

been maimed or wounded; a president had been assassinated; slavery had come to an end; an almost incalculable amount of physical damage had occurred; both sides had harnessed their populations through conscription and centralized economic policies; habeas corpus had been suspended; and the cost of prosecuting the conflict had been unprecedented. Even though the Union had been preserved and the North was victorious, hard feelings toward the former Confederate states were not immediately erased by the surrender of the Southern armies and the capture of Jefferson Davis. Military action quickly came to an end in the spring of 1865, but the wounds of war would not be easily healed. In fact, the nation would never be the same.

During the final campaigns and in the immediate aftermath of the war, the Confederate military prisons had been captured or visited and their inmates released. The image of the Southern prisons as "hell holes" was reinforced by the POWs themselves and by books and articles and illustrations emerging in the Northern press. The result was that the operation of Confederate military prisons came to symbolize for many in the North what they saw as the moral dysfunction of the Southern cause. In the rush to locate and detain those believed responsible for the conditions in the Confederate POW camps, the administrative staff of Camp Lawton was not overlooked. As early as 4 June 1865, W.L.M. Burger, Assistant Adjutant-General at the Headquarters of the Department of the South in Hilton Head, South Carolina, issued orders to Lieutenant Colonel B.W. Thompson, the provost marshal, to arrest a number of people associated with Confederate military prisons, specifically including Captain Vowles, commandant at Camp Lawton, and Surgeon White, chief of the camp's medical staff.[2]

Although General Winder's temporal trials had ended in Florence in February of 1865, he would be tried in absentia, so to speak, not only in Wirz's trial but also in the historiographic wars to come. Some of his surviving colleagues, however, were not so lucky. Union POWs focused their accusations on the officers because, for them, most of their guards

---

[2] Burger to Thompson, 4 June 1865, United States, War Department, *The War of the Rebellion: A Compilation of the Official Records of the Union and Confederate Armies*, series 2, vol. 7 (Washington DC: Government Printing Office, 1880–1901) 639.

remained relatively anonymous. The bulk of those who had secured the prisons had been in reserve, home guard, or invalid units and, therefore, had been too young, too old, or too infirm for service in regular units. They had been pressed into service as camp guards, and when the war was over they simply went home. They were relatively powerless. Confederate officers and camp commanders, however, were more visible and powerful and, therefore, vulnerable to charges of brutality, murder, or criminal neglect.

Everyone agrees that Civil War POW camps were characterized by high mortality rates. In the partisan war of words that developed early (and continues to this day) over who was to blame for the death rates and whether conditions were intentionally created to be injurious to POWs, no one has questioned the fact that an inordinate number of prisoners on both sides died. Where authorities differ is in the specifics. Therein lies the problem because one must be cognizant that the validity of statistics is directly related to the data from which they are derived. The sheer scale of the Civil War provided ample opportunities and venues for data gathering, but record keeping was very uneven and, as is usual in war, surviving data from the losing side is even more fragmentary. Thus, authorities continue to disagree on the number of prisoners captured by each side, how many deaths occurred in the camps, and the respective death rates.

Camp Lawton presents a microcosm of these issues. We have only approximations of how many Union soldiers were incarcerated there; we do not know the exact number of deaths; and as a result we cannot calculate the precise death rate. As far as censuses of the number of POWs at Camp Lawton are concerned, the official returns are fragmentary. The only complete return is from the Camp Commandant Vowles, dated 8 November 1864, in which he stated that 10,229 POWs had been received at Camp Lawton; 486 had died; 349 had enlisted in Confederate service; and 285 were "detailed at work at post."[3] By the

---

[3] Vowles, Report to Gibbs, 8 November 1864, *Official Records*, series 2, vol. 8, 1,113–14. Interestingly, an 1869 government investigative report listed 14 escapees from Camp Lawton along with 118 enlistments by Federal POWs in the Confederate military service [U.S. House of Representatives, 40th Congress, Third Session, Report No. 25, *Report on the Treatment of Prisoners of War by the Rebel Authorities during the War of the Rebellion to Which*

date of Vowles's report, the camp was essentially completed, and few additional movements of POWs into the camp were recorded prior to its abandonment in the face of Sherman's approach.

Another source for estimates of the number of POWs who died at Camp Lawton comes from the reports of Union soldiers who saw the camp and its burial trenches during the March to the Sea. Then, there is the so-called "Camp Lawton Death Register." Sneden mentions in his diary that he kept the camp's death register in the last weeks of the prison's existence. Someone else had kept it from 1 October to 1 November. The procedure was that a POW burial detail kept a daily record of the names and units (if known) of the dead in numerical order and sent the list to Sneden who recorded the information in the official death register.[4] This squares with the account of Weston Ferris (1st Connecticut Cavalry), who indicated that he was in charge of the ten-man burial party. Ferris's testimony is that he arrived at Camp Lawton on 12 October and remained there until he was evacuated on 20 November, which overlaps with Sneden's tenure at the prison. As he recounted the experience: "I found one soldier buried when I took charge of the burying. We dug a long trench, wide enough to place the bodies side by side. We then split logs into slabs and laid over them, before covering them with earth."[5] Following the war, when the grave trenches were opened and the bodies exhumed in preparation for moving them to the newly established Lawton National Cemetery near the prison site, the bodies were, in fact, discovered lying side by side and covered with split logs.[6] Ferris said that from 15 October through 20

Are Appended the Testimony Taken by the Committee, and Official Documents and Statistics, etc. (Washington DC: Government Printing Office, 1869) 750–751].

[4] Sneden, *Eye of the Storm: A Civil War Odyssey*, ed. Charles F. Bryan, Jr., and Nelson D. Lankford (New York: The Free Press, 2000) 270.

[5] Weston Ferris, "Prison Life of Weston Ferris," cited in Bill Giles, *"The World's Largest Prison": A Camp Lawton Compendium* (Magnolia Springs State Park GA: Café Press, 2004) 173–74.

[6] United States, Department of War, Department of the Army, Quartermaster General's Office, *Roll of Honor (Vol. XVII): Names of Soldiers Who Died in Defence of the American Union Interred in the National and Public Cemeteries in Kentucky, and at New Albany, Jeffersonville, and Madison, Indiana; Lawton (Millen), and Andersonville, Georgia, (Supplementary.)* (Washington DC: Government Printing Office, 1868) 466–92.

November his crew buried 644 Union POWs. According to Ferris the most buried in a single day was 37, as the weather turned wet and cold. Interestingly, the Camp Lawton death register, found after the war, lists 488 dead.

All accounts agree that the POWs who died at Camp Lawton were buried in trenches outside the stockade and that they numbered in the hundreds. Besides the death register, the only official Confederate record of deaths at Camp Lawton is Vowles's accounting of 486 deaths in his camp census of 8 November.[7] Beyond that, there is little agreement. As indicated previously, the death register lists 488 deaths—391 named and 97 unnamed. However, Sneden gives two sets of tallies of the dead in his drawings of the camp. On one of his illustrations, he lists 450 dead buried in two trenches near the hospitals.[8] On another of his drawings of the camp, he shows two burial trenches near the hospitals and notes that there were also other burials near the railroad. On this drawing he notes that the "whole number of prisoners who died was 1,330," of which 478 were unknown. The figures he placed on this map are confusing because he lists POW deaths from 1 October through 1 November 1864: "926 prisoners died in the stockade—of these 370 were unknown—450 were buried near hospital in 2 trenches—491 buried near Rail Road 200 yds from Hospitals."[9] Totaling his figures for that period, the sum should be 941, rather than 926. Using his figure of 1,330 total burials, this leaves 389 (1,330 minus 941) POWs who died from 1 November until the prison was abandoned later in the month. Further complicating the picture is the fact that he annotates his depiction of the burial trenches near the hospital with the following phrase: "650 prisoners here buried." Perhaps the former figure (450) reflects the 1 October to 1 November period, while the latter number (650) represents the total for the duration of the prison's existence. If this were not confusing enough, Vol. XIV of the *Roll of Honor* containing a description of "Millen National Cemetery," includes these statements:

---

[7] Vowles, Report, 8 November 1864, series 2, vol. 7, 1,113–14.
[8] Sneden, Eye of the Storm, 269.
[9] Sneden, *Images from the Storm*, 228.

Originally there were two burial places here. The larger one is situated one and a half mile south of Hack's Mill, and contains three trenches, holding respectively 150, 315, and 491 bodies; in all, 960. [The total would be 956; either this is a miscalculation or it includes the four mentioned below.] The smaller was situated one mile southwest of Hack's Mill, and had but one trench, containing 682 bodies. There were also four scattered graves outside.[10]

Thus, the total here is 1,646. This account was taken from a November 1865 report by Lieutenant D.B. Chesley in which he stated that there were "1,646 bodies buried in four trenches—three at Hack's Mill and a fourth near Mrs. Jones's mill pond."[11] The total should have been 1,682, but Chesley apparently double counted the four separate burials. His report was the result of the first official post-war visit to the site by Federal officials.

Strangely, however, the complete tally of bodies, known and unknown, in Lawton National Cemetery that follows in the above-mentioned *Roll of Honor* (Vol. XIV) report of 1,646 gives a different figure. This chart, which details the name, rank, company, and regiment (where known) and the section of the cemetery where each was buried and which supposedly represents the total actual remains interred in the national cemetery after being removed from the burial trenches left by the Confederates, lists 390 known and 295 unknown for a total of 685. This figure tallies well with what Union soldiers who visited Camp Lawton during Sherman's March estimated as from 650 and 750 burials near the prison. A subsequent *Roll of Honor* (Vol. XVII) indicated that 415 known and 333 unknown Union dead were buried at the cemetery (23 of them from Sherman's March) for a total of 748.[12]

---

[10] United States, Department of War, Department of the Army, Quartermaster General's Office, *Roll of Honor (Vol. XIV): Names of Soldiers Who in Defence of the American Union Suffered Martyrdom in the Prison Pens Throughout the South* (Washington DC: Government Printing Office, 1868) 293–313; perhaps the four additional burials mentioned by Lt. Chesley may correspond to the reports of several unburied POW bodies discovered within the stockade by Sherman's troops which they then buried.

[11] Captain C.K Smith, Jr., 22 November 1865, transmits report of Lieutenant D.B. Chesley, National Archives, RG 92, Quartermaster General's Office, Remarks on Reports of Cemeteries, Book 1, 36.

[12] *Roll of Honor*, vol. 17, 466–92.

How does one make sense of this? There seem to be three streams of figures. The high group of figures—Sneden, Chesley, and *Roll of Honor* (Vol. XIV)—indicates as many as 1,300–1,600 burials; the middle group of figures—National Archives, *Roll of Honor* (Vol. XVII), Ferris, and reports of Sherman's soldiers—centers around 650–750 burials; and the lesser numbers—the death register (488 deaths) and Vowles's 8 November census (486 dead)—both of which are admittedly incomplete. There had to have been more than two deaths at Camp Lawton from 9 November until its evacuation in late November. Yet, Rogers and Saunders consider Chesley's total, which is representative of the high estimates, to be "erroneous."[13]

Should Chesley's number have been 646? Not a great deal of time elapsed between the camp's closing in November of 1864 and the establishment of the national cemetery there in the fall of 1867; therefore, it is highly unlikely that a burial trench or trenches would have been overlooked. On the other hand, we have the death register number of 488. Given the circumstances of its recovery, though, the death register may very well be incomplete. What gives one pause, however, is Sneden's claim that he kept the death register and remained at the camp until it was emptied. It is possible, however, that time had affected his recall as much as it seems to have influenced his drawings of the camp. Finally, there is the chance that some of the burials might have been those of guards. Mortality statistics for the guard force at Camp Lawton are not extant; however, even if the guards had died at the same statistical rate as the POWs, their much smaller numbers would not have generated a comparable number of deaths. At any rate, one would think that the guards who died at Camp Lawton would have been interred in a less perfunctory manner than was the case with the POWs, and many would have been transported home. The last official accounting of the number buried at Lawton National Cemetery was published in 1868 (*Roll of Honor*, Vol. XVII). As previously indicated, it gave a figure of 725 from the prison camp and 23 of Sherman's men who had been buried in the area for a total of 748 in the cemetery. Assuming that no burial trenches

---

[13] George A. Rogers and, R. Frank Saunders. "Camp Lawton Stockade, Millen, Georgia, C.S.A," *The Atlanta Historical Journal* 25, no. 2 (1981): 90.

were left unopened when POW bodies were moved to the new Lawton National Cemetery, this is probably the best estimate. The reason why Chesley's figure of 1,646 is erroneous is that he misinterpreted the markings at the original burial trenches. In the Quartermaster General Records at the National Archives there is a report describing the burial trenches that clears up the mystery: "Three trenches—300 yards south of Hack's Mills, near Lawton Ga and 150 yds west of Augusta and Savannah RR. The running numbers commenced at the north end of the eastern trench."[14] As far as the other trench was concerned:

> One trench—one and one half miles southwest of Lawton, Burke County, Ga. And 100 yards west of Mrs. Jones mill pond. The trench runs from east to west. The running number 492 commences at east end at a stake marked 492. These are interments continued from the three trenches near Hacks Mills.

Therefore, Chesley apparently had taken running numbers and added them as if they were totals—i.e., 150 + 315 + 491 + 682 + 4 (+4) = 1,682 (1,686). The separate trench that Chesley lists as containing 682 bodies was, in fact, the total number buried in all the trenches rather than the number buried in that trench.

Whatever the true number of deaths at Camp Lawton, the prisoners died from a variety of causes. Civil War POWs suffered from all sorts of maladies, many of which had exotic nineteenth-century names—i.e., ague (malarial fevers or chills), eruptive fevers (smallpox, measles, scarlet fever, etc.), flux (abnormal discharge from the bowels, diarrhea), catarrh (inflammatory infection of the mucous membranes), cholera, malaria, nostalgia (homesickness), consumption (tuberculosis), pneumonia, scorbutic diathesis (scurvy or malnutrition), yellow fever, "diseases of indulgence" (venereal diseases), and typhoid.[15] Old wounds could turn gangrenous and new ones could become infected. A mosquito

---

[14] "Records of Deceased U.S. Soldiers Reinterred at Lawton Cemetery, Lawton, GA," National Archives, Quartermaster General's Office, RG 92, Records of Cemeterial Functions, 1838–1929, Cemeteries, c. 1862–1960, Georgia: Lawton Cemetery, Vol. 14, NM 81/A1, Entry 627.

[15] Lonnie R. Speer, "Medical Glossary," *Portals to Hell: Military Prisons of the Civil War* (Mechanicsburg PA: Stockpole Books, 1997) 269.

bite, for example, could become irritated through scratching; an infection could develop; gangrene could set in; and the result could be death. Health preconditions played a role, as mentioned previously, because many entering POWs brought health impairments with them. Poor sanitary conditions complicated the situation. Even though conditions were marginally better at Camp Lawton, the death dealing illnesses continued to take their respective tolls. All of this was exacerbated by malnutrition and exposure, the latter caused by the onset of colder weather, and its accompanying freezing rain and snow. Wet weather was bad; cold weather was worse; but wet, cold weather could be deadly. Consider the experience of sitting through a cold, rainy night without the means to keep dry, adequate clothing, or food.

The camp death register seems to have been fairly carefully kept. The first ninety entries contain a listing of the decedent's name, rank, company, regiment, and service arm, if known. Beginning with number ninety-one, to the above data are added the "div"[ision], "det"[ail or achment], and "character," if known. The latter three categories seem to relate to the organization of prisoners at Camp Lawton, in particular the ration distribution system mentioned in POW accounts. As an example, entry number ninety-one reads as follows:

No.	Names	Rank	Co. Letter	Regt.	State	Arm	Div.	Det.	Character
91	G. Murray	Private	Co. F	83	Ind.	Inf.	3	2	2nd Hundred

In some cases the entries under "character" are listed as "fifties" instead of "hundreds."[16]

Although care was taken to record the names of the dead, many POWs died anonymously. They had no friends or other means of identification. Obviously, the survivability of inmates at the prison camps depended on a number of factors, but a recent statistical analysis by Dana L. Costa and Matthew E. Kahn concludes that "friends had a

---

[16] "Death Register," Camp Lawton, National Archives, RG 92, Records of the Quartermaster General's Office, Records Relating to Functions: Cemeterial, 1828–1929, General Correspondence and Reports Relating to National and Post Cemeteries ("Cemetery File"), 1865–c. 1914, Lawton National Cemetery, Box 39.

statistically significant positive effect on survival probabilities and that the close ties between friends as measured [by] such identifiers as ethnicity, kinship, and the same hometown the bigger the effect."[17] Thus, it would seem, POWs who had friends, comrades from their units, family members, or ethnic compatriots with whom they could interact and look out for one another were not only fortunate but had a greater chance of survival. The anecdotal evidence from Camp Lawton POW diaries seems to confirm this. For example, Lieutenant Hodgkins's diary entry for 21 November reported an instance of welcome assistance from unit comrades:

> Last night was another wet one for us. About midnight I had to turn out to get warm by walking about as we have to about every night and while walking about ran across two fellows of my Regiment who had a roof over them.
> They invited me in under it where there was a good fire which I was thankful to get near.[18]

Several other previously mentioned POW accounts from Camp Lawton cite the importance of friends and comrades as agents of amelioration among the inmates.

The number of unknowns listed in the Federal records of the Camp Lawton dead is tragic testimony to the loneliness and anonymity that contributed to the demise of so many POWs in Civil War prisons and that accompanied them to their last resting places. Numerous families would never know what happened to their loved ones or where their remains lay. They only knew that they never came home.

Many Union families did not find out until much later that a loved one had died at Camp Lawton; others were not sure what happened to their sons because they died anonymously. Not all of those who died at

---

[17] Dora L. Costa, and Matthew E. Kahn, "Surviving Andersonville: The Benefits of Social Networking in POW Camps" (December 2005), NBER Working Paper No. W11875. Available at SSRN: http://ssrn.com/abstract=875701.

[18] J.E. Hodgkins, *The Civil War Diary of Lieut. J. E. Hodgkins: 19th Massachusetts Volunteers from August 11, 1862 to June 3, 1865,* trans. Kenneth C. Turino (Camden ME: Picton Press, 1994) 109–10.

Camp Lawton died unmemorialized, however. Undoubtedly, some families did what Stephen N. Chandler's (Company C, 9th Minnesota) did when they received word of his November 1864 demise in Georgia. On 31 December, a funeral notice appeared in Chandler's hometown newspaper, the *Mower County Register*:

> FUNERAL SERVICES: The funeral sermon of Stephen N. Chandler of Company C 9th Minnesota Regiment, who died at Millen, Ga., as a prisoner of war, will be preached at the M[ethodist]. E[piscopal]. Church, in this place, on Sabbath morning, January 1st, 1865, at 11 o'clock."[19]

That his family in Minnesota received notification of his death in Georgia so soon after the fact probably indicates that one of his exchanged comrades had carried the news north. It might also help explain why several of the Minnesotan dead at Camp Lawton had their death dates recorded in the *Roll of Honor* (Vol. XVII).[20]

For those who survived, however, there were the hazards of the return. Numbers of Union POWs freed from Confederate prisons at war's end either did not survive their journey home or died soon after their return from the deleterious effects of their incarceration on their health. The supposed case of Elias Goff (Company K, 7th Tennessee Volunteer Cavalry) provides what may have been a particularly tragic example. According to the story, Goff, who had fought on both sides during the war—he originally enlisted in the 52nd Tennessee Cavalry—died on his return home from Camp Lawton, "when sympathetic citizens gave him a big meal."[21] The reason this story might be

---

[19] Copy of newspaper article in *Mower County Register* (Minnesota), 31 December 1864, in a Civil War notebook at Beaufort National Cemetery in Beaufort, South Carolina.

[20] *Roll of Honor*, vol. XVII, 466–92. Of the twenty men in the Minnesota regiments (9th, 164th, and 19th) who are listed in the *Roll* as having died at Camp Lawton, fourteen of them have specific death dates beside their names, and one of them has a death date (9 July 1864) that does not correspond to the dates of operation of the prison. In fact, only one other non-Minnesotan POW is given a death date, and it (Charles Link, Company I, 23rd Ohio, 3 December 1864) is well after Camp Lawton was evacuated, but it does correspond to Sherman's entry into Millen. Perhaps his was one of the bodies discovered unburied by Union forces upon entering the prison.

[21] Peggy Scott Holley, "The Seventh Tennessee Volunteer Cavalry: West Tennessee Unionists in Andersonville Prison," http://www.stjusers.com/lindas/history.html (accessed 18 August 2008); Goff's name not only appears on the death register for Camp

apocryphal is that Elias Goff's name appears on the Camp Lawton death register as decedent number 371. However, it might be possible that both stories had factual foundations. Since he was facing a Confederate charge of desertion because he was captured in a Union unit, he would have had a strong incentive to switch identities with a corpse in order to be exchanged. If such was the case, his name could have shown up in both the cemetery at Camp Lawton and as the subject of a fatal overeating episode at home. Most probably, though, Goff died at Camp Lawton, and the story of his death by overeating is a garbled tradition associated with the new rations he received after arriving from Camp Sumter. At any rate, Federal medical personnel realized that long-term nutritional deprivation rendered the returned POWs' constitutions unable to handle the immediate resumption of a normal diet, and they took pains to bring their patients along slowly.[22] The physical and/or mental health of some POWs never recovered. The author once had a teaching colleague from Iowa whose Civil War ancestor, according to his family tradition, was incarcerated at Camp Sumter and never regained his mental health upon his return home.

Tragically, some Union POWs survived combat, wounds, illness, and incarceration in Confederate prisons only to be killed or injured in the *Sultana* disaster on 27 April 1865. The *S.S. Sultana*, a paddle wheeler with a normal capacity of 376 passengers, was grossly overloaded with 2,400 people, including many former POWs, excitedly looking forward to postwar reunions with families and friends. As the steamer struggled up the Mississippi River against the strong spring currents, near Memphis, Tennessee, a boiler explosion destroyed the boat. In the ensuing fire and sinking, only 700 survived what remains the worst

Lawton but he is also on a Confederate list of galvanizers: "List of Deserters from C.S. Army Who Have Joined the 7th (Federal) Tenn. Regt. Commanded by the Renegade Hawkins and Who Are Now Prisoners of War," National Archives, RG 249, Records of the Commissary General of Prisons, General Records, Correspondence and Reports, Letters Sent from Andersonville the Prison in Georgia, May 1864–March 1865, chap. 9, vol. 227, 5; "Register" [of Deaths], Camp Lawton, National, Archives, RG 249, Records of the Commissary General of Prisons, Correspondence and Reports, 1862-67, Box 1.

[22] John H. Sammons, *Personal Recollections of the Civil War* (Greensburg IN: Montgomery & Son, n.d.) 51.

maritime disaster in American history. The rest were killed outright—fatally scalded by the boiler steam—mortally wounded from effects of the blast, or drowned as they attempted to swim to shore across the swollen river.[23]

The story of what happened to the inmates at Camp Lawton who had not been involved in the sick exchange but who were evacuated when the prison was closed involved yet another odyssey. As Sherman's forces approached Millen, those POWs remaining at Camp Lawton after the Savannah exchanges ended were moved down the Atlantic and Gulf Railroad to a wooded site near Blackshear. The commander at Blackshear, Colonel Forno, found the prison site rudimentary and incomplete. In this chaotic period, he did not know where General Winder's headquarters were, and the supply and transportation system were only what he could make them. In fact, he was on his own.

Desperately, he contacted General LaFayette McLaws in Savannah. He telegraphed from Doctortown, a stop along the Atlantic and Gulf Railroad, on 23 November requesting that his provision train from Camp Lawton be sent to him. His sense of urgency was couched in the last two sentences of his dispatch: "Send provisions from Savannah. We have nothing to eat."[24]

Some of the POWs eventually were shipped back to Savannah after Sherman had evacuated the city and ended up in South Carolina. The others were sent to Thomasville and finally wound up at Camp Sumter. Sergeant Hosmer recounted his personal odyssey:

> After being shifted about in Savannah until nearly exhausted, we were moved out on the Savannah, Albany and Gulf railroad, for what destination we were ignorant. Our progress was attended by many difficulties. Often the engine was out of wood or water, and it was necessary to stop and chop the wood and once, to fill the tender with pails. After spending nearly three days and nights on a crowded flat car without leaving it, we finally "drew rein" at No. nine station, just south of

---

[23] Alan Hoffman, *Sultana: Surviving the Civil War, Prison, and the Worst Maritime Disaster in American History* (New York: Smithsonian, 2009), is the most recent account of this catastrophe on the Mississippi river.

[24] Forno to McLaws, 23 November 1864, National Archives, RG 109, War Department Collection of Confederate Records, Papers of General Lafayette McLaws, 1861–1865.

where the railroad crosses the Altamaha river, at a place called Blackshear. Here the train stopped, the guards ordered off the cars and formed in line around the entire train, and far enough back to allow the prisoners to alight. For the first time in seventy hours we were permitted to move....[25]

Blackshear proved to be but a brief respite, and Sergeant Hosmer remembered it as "an oasis in the memory of those perilous times.... Here we were far removed from all apparent danger and the guards were more humane," and he found the rations there "sufficient." [Forno must have gotten his rations.][26] Unfortunately, Hosmer would ultimately find himself back at Camp Sumter:

> Our stay at Blackshear was short—perhaps a week.... [Then, the prisoners were transported to Thomasville, where they left the trains and marched northward.] ... [A]fter an exhausting march of three days, and a short ride by rail, we stood once more at the south gate at Andersonville on the evening of December 25, '64.

The disappointment was profound:

> What a Christmas! In the years that have followed, however merrily the bells may ring, and loving hearts may glow with peace and good will toward mankind, the withering blight of this night's memory has cast its baleful shadow over each succeeding anniversary. Why this event should leave such an impression, indelibly fixed in my mind, I am unable to explain. I only know, that of all the years, this is the Christmas that alone presents itself in retrospection,—whenever the anniversary is referred to, this, of all the number seems to insist upon stalking forward, always clothed in the same ghastly habiliments. Life has some memories which seem to be seared upon the tablets of the brain.[27]

Not all the stories had tragic endings, however. Most former POWs survived to live long lives and participate in normal peacetime activities and organizations. They picked up where they had left off, returning to friends and family. For some the war had merely been an interregnum—

---

[25] Francis J. Hosmer, *A Glimpse of Andersonville and Other Writings* (Springfield MA: Loring and Axtell, 1896) 45.

[26] Ibid., 47.

[27] Ibid., 48.

an unforgettable one to be sure—in what would have been the normal arc of their lives. For others their war experience had rendered a transformative effect on them. Ex-POWs married and fathered children; joined local chapters of veteran's organizations such as the Grand Army of the Republic (GAR), the Military Order of the Loyal Legion of the United States (MOLLUS), and the National Association of Union Ex-prisoners of War; became part of the social, economic, and political fabric of their local communities; turned out on election days; and attended funerals of their comrades. They marched in Fourth of July parades, and they "waved the bloody shirt" at election times, keeping alive the memories of what they called "the great crusade." Camp Lawton POWs came from disparate ethnic, geographic, social, and economic backgrounds. Following their common experience as inmates at Camp Lawton, most left military service at war's end and headed home, some to return to their former lives, others to begin their lives anew.

Alexander H. Ingram, the Irish-American POW who supposedly changed identities with a dead prisoner at Camp Lawton in order to secure a place on the exchange list, remained briefly in the Army following the war and was involved in the "army of observation" on the Texas border as it kept an eye on the French-installed Emperor Maximilian in Mexico. He married Anna Clark in 1866, and on his discharge from Army service, he returned to his pre-war community of Oxford in Chester County, Pennsylvania, where he re-entered the painting trade that he had begun before the conflict. Until 1880, he owned his own paint and wallpaper store. He farmed on the side and then went to work as a supervisor in charge of painting for the Pennsylvania Railroad Company. Active in civic affairs, he supported, as did many Union veterans, the Republican Party and belonged to the local GAR post (Thomson Post, No. 132) of which he became commander in 1893. From 1894 to 1896, he served a term as Sheriff of Chester County. He was also a Mason and a Presbyterian. In the 1920 census he was listed as retired and living with his second wife, Ella. As he looked back on his life early in the twentieth century, his journey—from his birth in 1841 in the Scots-Irish Presbyterian community of Ulster, Ireland, through his immigration to the U.S. in 1854, and to his status as well respected American citizen—must have seemed a long and eventful one.[28] His post-war story echoed the experiences of many of his immigrant compatriots after their return from military service. The fact that they had fought for their adopted country cemented their allegiance to it and instilled in them a sense of pride and purpose as they shaped their post-war lives.

Daniel Reid Ross, on the other hand, was a native New Yorker, having been born in Schuylerville, New York, in 1842. Following his experience of being a POW and his service as a guard for Jefferson Davis and family as they were transported to Fortress Monroe, Ross settled near the small community of Hedgesville, West Virginia, in the late summer of 1865. He was possibly drawn to the area because of his service nearby during the war. Initially, he taught school in the area, for which he had trained before entering military service. Ultimately, he decided to become a doctor and went to medical school (Starling Medical College) in Ohio and, interned there, as well. He returned to Hedgesville where he took up residence as the first doctor and practiced medicine there for the next half century. In addition to his career as a country doctor, Dr, Ross was active in community affairs. Although in private practice for his whole medical career, from 1880 to 1924, he also served as surgeon for the North Mountain District of the B&O Railroad. A strong supporter of education, he was a leader in the free schools movement and served from 1893 to 1911 as secretary of the Hedgesville Township Board of Education. He was a Royal Arch Mason, a staunch Republican, and a member of the GAR. He married, and he and his wife had nine children, six of whom lived into adulthood. When he died on 19 May 1924, he was an honored citizen of his adopted state.[29] His obituary in *The Shepardstown Register* described him as a "venerable physician [and] a native of New York State but had lived in Berkeley

---

[28] *Oxford* (Pennsylvania) *Press*, 30 July 1890; Samuel T. Wiley, *Biographical and Portrait Cyclopedia of Chester County*, ed. by Winfield Scott Warner (Philadelphia: Gresham Publishing, 1893) 741–42.

[29] Ross's life and those of his brothers are summarized in D. Reid Ross, *Lincoln's Veterans Win the War: The Hudson Valley's Ross Brothers and the Union's Fight for Emancipation* (Albany: State University of New York Press, 2008).

County for the past fifty years."[30] The beloved country doctor, whose charitable comments toward his former enemies were cited earlier, settled in what had been a border area during the war and made a successful career working with patients, some of whom had served in Confederate butternut, others of whom had enlisted in Union blue. For years he was the only white doctor in the area who would treat black patients. Ross's impressive house (c. 1885) still stands in Hedgesville, and the simple, but impressive stone marking his and his wife's grave is easily found in the village cemetery.

Whereas Dr. Ross had started a new life in West Virginia away from his native New York, other former POWs looked to the West. Following their return from war, many former POWs headed west. The vast underdeveloped region west of the Mississippi River and east of the Rocky Mountains attracted thousands of settlers from the East looking for new opportunities and adventure. Among the settlers seeking a new life in a new land was former Camp Lawton prisoner Private Edward L. Chatfield (113th Illinois). Following his discharge, he returned to his home in Kankakee, Illinois. In 1874, he went to Colorado to purchase land near Littleton where members of his extended family would move. He returned to Illinois, farmed the family land there, and married Anna E. Bates. In 1879, he and several family members moved to the new land in Colorado, where he became a successful farmer and businessman. Like many veterans he was active in the GAR, becoming the commander of the John C. Fremont Post in 1895. After a long career as a business and community leader in Littleton, failing health caused him to move to Long Beach, California, to be near his daughter. He died in 1924 at the age of eighty-two. His life and that of several members of his family have been well chronicled in *The Chatfield Story*. Edward Chatfield, like numerous Civil War veterans, North or South, trekked westward

---

[30] *The Shepherdstown Register* (West Virginia), 22 May 1924; *The Martinsburg Herald* (West Virginia), 19 May 1924. The details of Ross's life after the war in the context of Hedgesville were provided to the author courtesy of a manuscript history by his descendent and namesake, D. Reid Ross of Durango, Colorado.

looking for opportunity and not only found it but also helped domesticate a wilderness in the process.[31]

Statistically, though, the POW experience left a negative mark on many. Civil War historical statisticians Costa and Kahn concluded that, "...former POWs captured after prisoner exchanges ceased led shorter lives than those captured when the exchange system operated."[32] Whatever impact the war had on the returning POWs, they re-entered a society and political economy that was on the cusp of profound change—a change that within a quarter century would result in an urban and industrial society growing out of one that had been essentially rural and agrarian. Like veterans of all wars, the former Camp Lawton inmates were to participate in those fundamental post-war changes. Over the next half-century, Civil War veterans would provide both energy and leadership during this process.

As the war came to its conclusion, the hunt began for those deemed responsible for the travails of Union POWs. Lincoln's assassination in April 1865 accelerated the public clamor for arrests and punishments. The main target of those who sought prosecutions for crimes committed in the camps would have been General Winder, but his death at Florence eliminated that possibility. However, had he survived the war, he undoubtedly would not have escaped what would have been almost certainly a sensational trial and imprisonment and possibly worse. At any rate, his posthumous reputation was ruined. POW accounts condemning Confederate military prisons commonly paired his name with that of Captain Wirz, who became the arch villain of the camps and suffered the ultimate penalty, as a result. After a century and a half Winder is almost universally considered one of the linchpins in the problems affecting the Confederate military prison system. The reality, however, seems to be that General Winder was placed in a nearly impossible situation, and the means to remedy it were beyond his control. The documentary record details his attempts to secure an

---

[31] Terry McCarty with Margaret Ann Chatfield McCarty, *The Chatfield Story: Civil War Letters and Diaries of Private Edward L. Chatfield of the 113th Illinois Volunteers* (North Charleston, SC: Booksurge Publishing, 2009).

[32] Dora L. Costa and Matthew E. Kahn, *Heroes & Cowards: the Social Face of War* (Princeton NJ: Princeton University Press, 2008) 159.

adequate guard force, foodstuffs, and construction supplies. However, in the superheated atmosphere that prevailed in the war's aftermath, it is doubtful that these efforts would have been credited or even recognized. Yet, despite his age and the continuing frustrations of the thankless task he had been assigned, he persevered. Ultimately, he recommended that all Union POWs be paroled. Unlike so many of his officer colleagues, he never attempted to preserve his honor by resigning in the face of the increasingly insurmountable difficulties facing his command. In recent years, his biographer, Arch Frederic Blakey, and authors such as Lonnie R. Speer and Charles W. Sanders, Jr., have presented a more balanced view of Winder.

However, some of his subordinates in the Confederate military prison system would suffer. Captain Henry Wirz and Private James W. Duncan were prosecuted in the war's aftermath for their actions at Camp Sumter. Wirtz was executed for war crimes, and Duncan was sentenced to fifteen years in prison for his involvement. Other Confederate officials associated with Southern military prisons who were arrested and imprisoned pending trial included Major John H. Gee, commandant of the prison at Salisbury (tried and acquitted); Capt Richard "Dick" Turner, jailor at Libby Prison (paroled in June 1866); and captains Sidney and Richard Winder (paroled). Lieutenant Colonel John Iverson and Captain Thomas Barrett of Florence were arrested and ultimately released. Higher up the ladder of Confederate leadership, President Jefferson Davis, Vice President Alexander Stephens, Secretary of War James Seddon, and Georgia Reserves Commander General Howell Cobb spent time in prison, but all had been released by May of 1867. Others either left the country—George Alexander and Thomas Turner (commandant of Libby) fled to Canada—or were never arrested (Virginius Bossiuex, commandant of Belle Isle).[33]

A long-standing question relating to Camp Lawton is what happened to Captain D.W. Vowles, the camp commandant. After the camp was evacuated in late November of 1864, Vowles had remained behind to settle accounts and then journeyed to Augusta to await further

---

[33] This summary is derived from Speer, *Portals to Hell*, 288–93.

orders.[34] He never received his requested promotion to colonel. At that point he simply disappeared not only from the records but seemingly in a physical sense, as well. The fact that Vowles was commandant at Camp Lawton and was prominently mentioned in POW accounts placed him high on the list for possible prosecution; yet, he was nowhere to be found, and he avoided arrest. What happened to him? Did he go into hiding; did he live a life in obscurity; did he die in the chaos of the war's aftermath? No one knew. He seemed, therefore, to be lost to history until Robert Scott Davis, a prolific author and indefatigable researcher, got on the case.[35]

While examining Missouri Civil War service records, Davis discovered D.W. Vowles listed as "a Union veteran applying for admission to the Missouri Soldiers Home in 1907." The application listed his residence as Quincy, Illinois. Davis then found that the local newspaper, the *Quincy Whig*, had done a story and an obituary ("The Last of Walker's Filibusters Is Dead") on Vowles on 14 and 15 August 1919, respectively. The old soldier had celebrated his eighty-eighth birthday on 13 August. The story that unfolded was an interesting one. According to Vowles, he had moved to Washington, DC, after the war and resumed the practice of medicine, and for a time he also served as a messenger for the doorkeeper of the US House of Representatives. He lived in the nation's capital from 1874 to 1878. Although Vowles discussed his life before 1864 and after 1874, he failed to mention the years in between. He eventually moved to Quincy as his health failed and, in 1884, he married Tamantha E. Inghram. In both the interview and obituary, no mention was made of his service at Camp Sumter or Camp Lawton. To his dying day, he apparently was determined to erase that unhappy chapter of his life from the record and had carefully kept that part of his life hidden. Quincy served as a refuge for him because he had raised a company of Confederate sympathizers in the area during the war. Davis concluded:

---

[34] Winder to Cooper, 25 November 1864, *Official Records*, series 2, vol. 7, 1,160.

[35] Robert Scott Davis, "The Last Man to Get Away," *Ghosts and Shadows of Andersonville: Essays on the Secret Social Histories of America's Deadliest Prison* (Macon GA: Mercer University Press, 2006) 207–14. This summary account of Vowles's postwar career is taken directly from Davis.

Without knowing about his career at Andersonville and as commandant of Camp Lawton, the Quincy newspaper and the *New York Times*, which reprinted his obituary, failed to mention his one great notoriety, that one of the last survivors of those prisons had finally escaped from his past, from the United States government, and (almost) from history.[36]

The trail of Sneden's patron, Dr. Isaiah H. White, surgeon in charge of Camp Lawton, proved easier to follow. He ultimately was appointed chief surgeon of all hospitals attached to military prisons east of the Mississippi.[37] As such he continued to report to General Winder and in collaboration with Surgeon General Samuel Moore was able to "bring some order to the system."[38] But the end was too chaotic and near for significant results to be obtained. According to Sneden, as Camp Lawton was being evacuated, Dr. White, his staff, and the medical stores were transported by train, first to Millen and then to Savannah on 22 November; White then left Savannah for Florence on 28 November.[39] After the war, White's name was included in the indictment of Henry Wirz and others but was later dropped.[40] In the meantime, he returned to his home state of Virginia and took a position teaching at the Medical College of Virginia in Richmond in the fall of 1865. He served a term as president of the Richmond Academy of Medicine, and, in 1886, became acting assistant surgeon of the United States Marine Hospital Service.[41] At his death he was an honored member of the medical profession.

The commander of the guard at Camp Lawton, Colonel Henry Forno, was already in his sixties when the war began. A native of South Carolina and a veteran of the Mexican War, he had made his home in Louisiana and owned slaves. He re-entered military service at the

---

[36] Ibid., 214.

[37] Special Orders No. 282, 28 November 1864, *Official Records*, series 2, vol. 7, 1,169.

[38] Arch Frederic Blakey, *General John H. Winder, C.S.A.* (Gainesville: University of Florida Press, 1990) 198.

[39] Sneden, "Epilogue," *Eye of the Storm*, 300.

[40] "General Court Martial Orders, No. 607," 6 November 1865, *Official Records*, series 2, vol. 7, 784–92.

[41] R.A. Brock (ed.), *Virginia and Virginians* (Richmond and Toledo: H.H. Hardesty, 1888) 2:810.

outbreak of the war and served briefly as commander of the Fifth Louisiana Infantry Regiment before being wounded at Second Manassas (Bull Run). Late in 1864, Forno was put in charge of the POWs who were evacuated through Savannah toward Blackshear the following November. Forno was with General Winder when the general died at Florence on 6 February 1865, and he telegraphed the news to Adjutant and Inspector General Cooper in Richmond.[42] After Winder's death, Forno briefly became acting Commissary General of Prisoners. Returning to Louisiana after the war, Forno died in January of 1866.[43]

Winder's son, Captain William Sidney Winder (1833–1905), and his cousin, Captain Richard Bayley Winder (1828–94), both of whom the general had kept on his staff in the prison system, remained in Confederate service to the end. Both were at Camp Lawton, where William Sidney served as his father's aide-de-camp and assistant adjutant, while Richard Bayley held the post of quartermaster. Because of their association with the Confederate military prisons, both were also targets of retribution in the superheated atmosphere in the immediate aftermath of the war.

Following his father's death, William Sidney Winder returned to Richmond in March 1865, and took part in the evacuation of the Confederate capital in April. Assigned with eight other officers to transport and guard the Confederate treasury and archives, the mission ultimately ended in Florida on 22 May.[44] Returning northward, Winder signed an oath of allegiance and received a pardon at Hilton Head in June but fled to Canada when he heard that he was being sought for arrest. He returned to Baltimore in March of 1866, resumed the practice of law, and spent the rest of his life taking care of family and defending his reputation, as well as that of his father. He committed suicide in 1905.

Captain Richard Bayley Winder was not so fortunate in the immediate aftermath of the war. He was arrested in August 1865 and

---

[42] Telegram from Forno to Cooper, 7 February 1865, cited in Blakey, *Winder*, 201.

[43] Confederate Colonel Henry Forno," http://aotw/officers.php?officer_id=759] (accessed 14 July 2009).

[44] See Alfred J. Hanna, *Flight into Oblivion* (Bloomington: University of Indiana Press, 1959) 108–16, and "The Confederate Baggage and Treasure Train Ends Its Flight in Florida: A Diary of Tench Francis Tilgman," *Florida Historical Quarterly* 17 (January 1939).

spent time both in Old Capitol Prison and Libby Prison pending trial for charges related to his role in the Confederate prison system. In fact, no trial materialized, and by the summer of 1866 he had returned to Baltimore. He studied to be a dentist, and by 1888 was dean of the Baltimore Dental College. He also earned an MD degree from the College of Surgeons and Physicians of Baltimore. He was the founder of the National Association of Dental Faculties and was known for his efforts to equate dentistry and medicine on the professional level.[45] He died in 1894.[46] Unfortunately for the Winder family, the Civil War did nothing to rehabilitate its reputation originally besmirched in the War of 1812.

As for the Confederate guards, they would also return to family and friends. Some would participate in the Confederate counterpart to the GAR, the United Confederate Veterans (UCV), and would be honored by their respective communities for their service. Many would march in parades, raise families, and memorialize their dead compatriots. They would proclaim their loyalty to the lost cause for which they had fought, and they would struggle during Reconstruction to recover their economic and political standing. But not all of them would continue to look backward. Some would work diligently for a new future as a part of the New South movement, but others were caught up, for better or worse, in the struggle to establish a stable social system to replace the one that had been destroyed. Some would pine for the past. Most would simply try to rebuild their lives.

Although the guards at Camp Lawton are relatively anonymous, the life of one of them probably reflected the experience of many others. Private Jesse Taliaferro Carter was born in Warren County, Georgia, on 26 August 1846. In his 1919 pension application he stated that he had lived in Georgia "all my life." That is true, but he had not stayed in one place. Before the war he had moved with his family to Schley County, in the southwestern part of the state. Only fourteen when the war began, he

---

[45] T.A. Taylor, *History of Dentistry: A Practical Treatise for the Use of Dental Students and Practitioners* (Philadelphia and New York: Lea & Febiger, 1922) 100–01.

[46] The post-war biographical sketches of the younger Winders were derived mainly from Blakey (*Winder*, 202–07) who did the spadework to bring their later careers to light.

remained at home initially, even though he had two brothers who joined the Confederate service.

In April 1864, when he was seventeen, he enlisted for the duration of the war in Company F, 3rd Georgia Reserves. A recruiting advertisement in the *Columbus Daily Sun* promised "no service out of state."[47] The reserve units were notoriously poorly equipped and, according to a family tradition, he took his percussion-cap fowling piece with him when he left home, a treasured artifact that had been passed down and remains in the family today.

His military experience over the next year consisted mainly of guard service at Macon, Camp Sumter, Camp Lawton, and perhaps Savannah. Unlike many of his comrades, his health was good, as no medical records exist to indicate that he was hospitalized during his enlistment. On 11 May 1864, Company F's muster roll shows the unit posted in Macon. By 17 June his unit was at Andersonville, where it remained until at least September 1. The muster roll records ending in October 1864, list the "station of company" as Camp Lawton. Not all of his service was as a prison guard, however.

Following the evacuation of Camp Lawton in late November, the 3rd Georgia Reserves was involved in combat in South Carolina in December 1864. Hastily assembled to meet a Federal attempt to interdict the railroad connecting Savannah with Charleston, the 3rd Georgia Reserves, along with other regular and reserve units, was transported by rail to meet the threat. These units successfully blocked and repulsed the effort to cut the rail line, and in an action near Coosawhatchie Station on 6 December 1864, Carter was listed as being wounded "slightly in the neck."[48] Engaged for a time in the futile attempt to resist Sherman's advance across South Carolina, Carter's unit ended up back in Columbus, Georgia, attempting unsuccessfully to defend the city against General Wilson's Federal forces.

His unit disbanded at Columbus, and like most of his comrades, he went home, in his case to Schley County. He eventually settled in Richland in Stewart County. Postwar census records trace the outline of

---

[47] *Columbus Daily Sun* (Georgia), 16 April 1864.
[48] *Daily Chronicle and Sentinel* (Augusta, Georgia), 11 January 1865.

his life. His occupation is shown variously as farmer and grocery proprietor. He married twice, raising two families. On 21 August 1919, the then 72-year-old veteran applied for a soldier's pension based on his service. A fellow member of Company F, G.W. Rodgers, attested to his identity and his service in the war. He was approved and received a pension of $100 a year until his death on 27 February 1924. The relatively advanced age (77) at which he died attests to his strong constitution. His second wife and widow, Gussie Jones, whom he had married in 1899, then applied to receive the $100 payment due to a deceased soldier. The payment was approved. Jesse T. Carter represented so many veterans, both North and South, in that he was a common man called upon to do uncommon tasks. He did what was asked and then went home and started a new life. Although the Southern Confederacy had failed, the struggle and sacrifices in its name remained alive in the memories of the descendents of its soldiers.[49]

Interestingly, although not unexpectedly, Confederate veterans' post-war reactions to their service as prison guards on the one hand and that of Union soldiers who were POWs on the other hand differed dramatically. Prison guards seemed to minimize their experiences in the post-war period, while POWs often talked and wrote about theirs.

Actually, this was probably inversely true of Confederate POWs and Union prison guards, as well. Their families and the public wanted to hear of battlefield exploits and POW suffering and deprivation, but the role of prison guard did not meet their expectations of glorious and heroic action. The former served to buttress their belief in the nature of the enemy and to justify the cause for which they were fighting; the latter was one-sided and, therefore, did not live up to the manly code of nineteenth-century combat. Of course, former Confederates who had been prison guards had to deal with the additional onus of the "black legend" surrounding the military prison experience in the South, not to mention the real threat of possible legal prosecution in the immediate aftermath of the conflict; whereas, the same circumstances served to glorify Union POWs.

---

[49] *Schley County News* (Georgia), 7 March 1924; and Jesse T. Carter family history file, including census data, provided by Doug L. Carter.

As for Caroline Elizabeth Jones, who leased the land for Camp Lawton, her life was short and tragic. Born into a prosperous planter family of Burke County, she married twice and was twice widowed. Her first marriage, to Dr. Henry C. Hines, ended with his death in 1856 at the age of 27. She then married his first cousin, planter Batt Jones, who died in 1862 at the age of 37. Like so many women in Burke County, she participated in patriotic activities to support the war effort. She was on the 61st District Committee of the Burke Ladies' Volunteer Association, and she served on the committee that organized and ran the Wayside Home in Millen.[50] Another family tragedy struck her in the late summer of 1863, when one of her brothers, Lt. Judson C. Sapp (Company D, 2nd Georgia), died of his wounds in Virginia and another brother George (also Company D, 2nd Georgia) was captured. Caroline was childless and died in 1869, when she was only 42. She and her two husbands rest in close proximity in the Big Buckhead Baptist Church Cemetery just a few miles from the old prison site. Her lifespan and those of her husbands are illustrative of the mortality of an era in which war and disease took a frightful toll.

It is difficult not to feel some sympathy for the Widow Jones; by war's end many aspects of her early life had been destroyed. Prior to the war, according to the 1860 census, she and her husband owned 121 slaves and had an estate valued at $144,217, both figures easily placing the Jones among the elite planters of Burke County (and, in fact, the South). Now, she had lost her second husband; the value of her property had declined precipitously; the labor system to work her large landholdings had collapsed; and she was attempting, because of her collaboration with the Confederate government, to regain basic citizenship rights. In the fall of 1865, because she was still worth more than $20,000, she found herself taking the oath of allegiance to the United States and having to apply for executive clemency from President Johnson.[51] To add insult to injury, she apparently never received the

---

[50] Wayside Home (Millen), Minutes, Georgia, Secretary of State, Georgia Archives; "The William Sapp Family," http://archiver.rootsweb.ancestry.com/th/read/SAPP/2001-03/0983836423 (accessed 30 April 2012).

[51] Under the Reconstruction plan issued by President Andrew Johnson in May of 1865, persons in the former Confederacy with a personal wealth of over $20,000 had to apply for

compensation promised for the use of her land for the prison operation, and she then became embroiled in a controversy with the United States Army over the plot of her land used for a national cemetery for the Camp Lawton dead. To compound her troubles, there is a Federal report that Mrs. Jones house may have been burned.[52] Given the antipathy of Sherman's troops toward anyone associated with the prison, this would not be surprising. Within four years she was dead. One wonders if the toll of the multiple tragedies and disappointments in her life had not contributed to her early demise. Unfortunately, her post-war travails were not unique among the planters of Burke County.

At the beginning of the research for this book on Camp Lawton, the initial mystery that confronted the author was what happened to the bodies of those who died at the prison. Although the estimates of the

---

a personal pardon from the president (James M. McPherson, *Ordeal By Fire: The Civil War and Reconstruction* [New York: Alfred A. Knopf, 1982] 498); the following documents illustrate Caroline Jones's application for a presidential pardon: Application of Caroline E. Jones for Pardon under the 13th Exemption, September 18, 1865, http://search.ancestrylibrary.com/Browse/print_u.aspx?dbid=1187&iid=MIUSA1865_113 135-00406 (accessed 13 July 2009); Caroline E. Jones, Loyalty Oath, September 5, 1865, http://search.ancestrylibrary.com/Browse/print_u.aspx?dbid=1187&iid=MIUSA1865_113 135-00407 (accessed 13 July 2009); and Schedule I. Free Inhabitants of the 61st District in the County of Burke State of Georgia ... , 1860 Census of the United States, 5, http://search.ancestrylibrary.com/iexec/?htx=View&r_5542&dbid=7667&iid=GAM653_1 ... (accessed 13 July 2009). For the family connections between William Sapp, Caroline E. Jones, Henry Hines, and Batt Jones, the author interviewed family historian Robert A. Reeves of Jenkins County, Georgia (telephone interview with Robert A. Reeves, 23 March 2010). Additional family information can be found in *Burke County Folks, 1851–1900*, comp. Jo Goodson Knight (Baltimore: Gateway Press, 2004) 106; and W.L. Kilpatrick, *The Hepzibah Baptist Association Centennial 1794–1894* (Augusta GA: Richards & Shaver, 1894) 97–99.

[52] In the process of collecting the remains of Federal soldiers who were buried in the district, there is a mention of a soldier's remains located in a field across the road from Mrs. Jones "burnt home." There were many Jones in the area, but Federal references to a Mrs. Jones near Camp Lawton may very well refer to the woman who leased the land for the prison. As such, it would not be surprising, if Sherman's soldiers were aware of her role in the prison, that her house would have been a target. ["Records of Deceased U.S. Soldiers Reinterred at Lawton Cemetery, Lawton, GA," National Archives, Quartermaster General's Office, RG 92, Records of Cemeterial Functions, 1838-1929, Cemeteries, c. 1862-1960, Georgia: Lawton Cemetery, Vol. 14, NM 81/A1, Entry 627, 18]. This however runs counter to local sources that indicate what may have been her house was still standing in the early twentieth century.

numbers of dead vary (ranging from 488 to over 1,600), all the contemporary accounts that offer any detail about Camp Lawton mention that the dead were buried in trenches near the prison.[53] Yet, a cursory examination of the park revealed no surviving evidence of this. On a hunch, contact was made with the superintendent at the Beaufort National Cemetery in South Carolina, since it was the closest one to the Camp Lawton site.[54] Thinking that there might have been an effort to consolidate the burials of Union dead in the South following the war, an inquiry was made to see if the cemetery records indicated a transfer of bodies from Camp Lawton. Allen G. Farabee, at that time Superintendent of Beaufort National Cemetery, responded to the query and said that they did, indeed, have a record of reburials from Camp Lawton.[55] Subsequently, the author traveled to the cemetery to view the final resting place of the Union dead of Camp Lawton. The question that remained to be answered was how they ended up there.

It wasn't until the publication in 1981 of the excellent article on Camp Lawton by Georgia Southern University professors George A. Rogers and R. Frank Saunders, Jr., that the story of what happened to the Union dead came to light.[56] Rogers and Saunders's research in the National Archives in Washington, DC, uncovered elements of a long-lost story that chronicled a literal "odyssey of the dead" based upon extant federal records.

The story begins with the evacuation of the camp by the Confederates in the face of the Federal advance in late November of 1864. The official records of Camp Lawton, with the exception of the messages and reports sent to Richmond during the camp's brief existence, apparently did not survive the war. As camp commandant, Captain Vowles would have been responsible for seeing that they were collected, packed, and transported when the camp was evacuated. In the

---

[53] *Roll of Honor*, vol. 14, 293–313; *Roll of Honor*, vol. 18, 466–92; and numerous accounts by Sherman's soldiers.

[54] John K. Derden to Superintendent, National Cemetery at Beaufort, 20 April 1977. Author is in possession of a copy of the original.

[55] Allen G. Farabee to James [*sic*] K. Derden, 21 April 1977. Author is in possession of the original.

[56] Rogers and Saunders, "Camp Lawton Stockade."

war's aftermath, as a part of the Federal Government's effort to collect Confederate records, the US Army undertook to find the records of Confederate military prisons. Initially, nothing seemed to have survived relating to Camp Lawton. However, according to a report by Lieutenant Colonel (Brevet) and Assistant Quartermaster Edmund B. Whitman:

> A communication from a prisoner, detailed as a clerk in the office of the superintendent, early called attention to the fact that a record of the burials at this prison had been carefully kept, by means of which, if it could be found, the entire number [of dead] might be identified…. Captain Cameron [one of the prison administrators who was found after the war at nearby Alexander teaching school] states that on the approach of General Sherman's army the prisoners were hastily sent off, by railroad, to Savannah, while he was left behind in charge of the records. These comprising the muster-rolls, ration returns, and records of interments, were then packed, under his direction, in a wine box, and directed, through the adjutant general of Georgia, at Augusta, to General Winder, at Columbia, South Carolina. This box he himself took to Waynesboro', 14 miles from Lawton, on the road to Augusta, and delivered it to the railroad agent, taking his receipt for it….
>
> [In the meantime, on the night of 25 November the Federal scouting force comprised of the 9th Michigan Cavalry reached Waynesboro, "tore up the railroad, burned the depot and burned the bridge."[57]]
>
> After the passage of our army he [Cameron] returned to Lawton. Subsequently it appeared the box had never reached General Winder. In an investigation by Captain Cameron it was found that the building in which the box had been left had been burned by Kilpatrick's cavalry, and the recollection of the agent was so confused in the regard to the disposition he had made of it that no trace could be obtained…. [While a search was conducted of the area], a document was discovered among the published papers of the Unites States Christian Commission [USCC], which, if it did not at once solve the mystery of the manner in which the

---

[57] "Report of Col. George S. Acker, Ninth Michigan Cavalry," 19 December 1864, *Official Records*, series 1, vol. 44, 396–97.

documents had been preserved, at least furnished the desired information.[58]

According to the USCC, after the Confederates evacuated Savannah in December of 1864, a Presbyterian minister found a small box of blank books there, one of which contained Camp Lawton's "death register." He gave the material to the USCC, which donated the document to the National Archives. This register was transcribed and printed in 1865.[59] Listed in the death register were 488 numbered burials, 391 named and 97 unnamed.

Sneden's diary perhaps provides an explanation of how the death register ended up in Savannah while the other prison records disappeared. He reported that he accompanied Dr. White and the hospital staff to Savannah as Camp Lawton was evacuated. They left the prison on the afternoon of 22 November, and reached Savannah near dawn the next morning. They carried with them what Sneden variously referred to as hospital "stores" and "stuff." The death register may have been a part of this shipment, despite Captain Cameron's testimony. On the other hand, perhaps the agent at Waynesboro to whom Captain Cameron had entrusted the wine box full of records had shipped them to Savannah rather than Augusta on hearing that the prison staff and inmates were being transferred there. Although the POWs were sent on to other locations, the hospital staff remained in Savannah until 29 November. When they left, Sneden recounted that "[w]e had to leave all

---

[58] *Roll of Honor*, vol.17, contains a brief report on the short-lived national cemetery near the site of Camp Lawton, the issue of the death register, and tabulation of the dead.

[59] US Christian Commission, Record of the Federal Dead Buried from Libby, Belle Isle, Danville & Camp Lawton Prisons and at City Point and in the Field before Petersburg and Richmond (Philadelphia: Jas. B. Rodgers, 1865), 15968. The US Christian Commission was formed in 1861 out of the YMCA. A Protestant volunteer organization, it provided social services, medical assistance, and spiritual help to Union troops, including repatriated POWs. It is sometimes confused with the US Sanitary Commission, an agency of the Federal government that provided similar services but was a secular organization. Initially, in an effort to recover the lost records of interments at Camp Lawton, the Quartermaster General's Office authorized the payment of a reasonable fee for their purchase, if found [National Archives, RG 92, Quartermaster General's Office, Cemeterial Branch, Remarks in Reports of Cemeteries, Book 1, 36].

the stores behind us..."[60] Thus, the death register ended up in Savannah to be recovered when the Federals occupied the port city. The other prison records have never been found. As to its authenticity, in 1877, an internal Quartermaster General's Office report concluded that the document found in Savannah "was the original Burial register of the Prison at Millen Ga."[61]

Finally, there is the tale of General Winder's administrative apparatus following the closing of Camp Lawton. He had been appointed head of the Confederate military prisons in Georgia and Alabama when he was at Camp Sumter. Then, on 21 November, at the very end of the history of the camp, he was appointed Commissary General of Confederate Military Prisons East of the Mississippi.[62] After the evacuation of Camp Lawton, General Winder eventually resurfaced in Columbia, South Carolina, when he issued his first official communication in his new capacity on 5 December. He announced, "until further orders," that his headquarters would be in Augusta, Georgia, and he appointed Captain W.S. Winder as his assistant adjutant.[63] Less than a month later, Winder transferred his headquarters to Columbia, South Carolina.[64] Dr. Isaiah White had already been promoted to chief surgeon of all hospitals attached to those prisons.[65]

General Winder's new responsibilities simply increased the range of his problems. From December 1864 until 6 February 1865, when he suddenly collapsed and died, he kept up his typical hectic pace. He visited Augusta, Columbia, Florence, and Salisbury (North Carolina). He inspected the facilities under his purview, appointed staff, developed

---

[60] Sneden, *Eye of the Storm*, 272, 278.

[61] E.D. Townsend, Report, 26 October 1877, National Archives, RG 92, Quartermaster General's Office.

[62] Cooper, General Orders No. 84, 21 November 1864, *Official Records*, series 2, vol. 7, 1,150.

[63] Winder, General Orders No. 2, 5 December 1864, *Official Records*, series 2, vol. 7, 1,193; Winder to Cooper, 30 December 1864, National Archives, RG 109, War Department Collection of Confederate Records, Letters Received Adjutant and Inspector General's Office, October–December 1864, Letters W, 2,529–3,242.

[64] General Orders No. 1, 1 January 1865, *Official Records*, series 2, vol. 7, 5.

[65] Withers, Special Orders No. 282, 28 November 1864, *Official Records*, series 2, vol. 7, 1,169.

policies for the prison system (including a reporting system and rules for handling POWs' money), and sought additional prison sites.[66] As late as 6 December 1864, he even considered the possibility of a reoccupation of Camp Lawton.[67] The camp's destruction, however, eliminated that possibility. With the Federal capture of Savannah and the movement of Sherman's forces into the Carolinas, the issue of POW security came to the forefront of Winder's concerns.

But he had other ongoing concerns, as well. The lack of clothing, blankets, medicine, potable water, fuel, and food continued to undercut the ability of the prisons to operate. Even communications were difficult. For example, Colonel Forno, commanding the temporary prison at Blackshear containing the remnants of the Camp Lawton evacuees, including elements of the Camp Lawton infantry guard and the Florida Light Artillery, was not able to re-establish contact with Winder until 7 December.[68] Until then, he was literally on his own. Eventually, those 2,500 remaining POWs were sent to Thomasville. Many of them, some already veterans of Camp Sumter, would soon find themselves reoccupying those tragic grounds where they would remain until the war was over.

Sherman's advance into the Carolinas after his capture of Savannah and the continuing disintegration of the Confederacy's ability to house, transport, feed, clothe, and medically treat Union POWs brought growing and unrelenting pressure on those administering the prisons. Where to move the prisoners in the face of the Federal advance and how to feed them were problems that increasingly seemed unsolvable. A little more than a month before his death, General Winder, from his headquarters in Columbia, sent a dispatch to Adjutant and Inspector General Cooper, the tenor of which indicates his ultimate frustration with the situation:

> Under the circumstances and with my limited means of information as to the state of affairs, I am unable to fix upon any place that would be tolerably safe, and to greatly complicate the question the subject of food

---

[66] Blakey, *Winder*, 290, contains a good synopsis of these chaotic last days.

[67] Winder to Cooper, 6 December 1864, *Official Records*. series 2, vol. 7, 1,196–97.

[68] Forno to Winder, 7 December 1864, *Official Records*, series 2, vol. 7, 1,204.

enters into the calculation. I deem the question to be of so much importance that I think it necessary to send an officer to Richmond to ask if, with your extended information, you could advise me as to a suitable locality.[69]

Ultimately, Winder came to the conclusion that the difficulties were so overwhelming that the most humane solution would be for the Confederacy to unilaterally parole its prisoners. He first cautiously suggested this to Cooper on 31 December; again, on 20 January, only two and a half weeks before his death, he wrote Cooper:

I am at a loss to know where to send the prisoners from Florence. In one direction the enemy are in the way. In the other the question of supplies presents an insuperable barrier. I again urge paroling the prisoners and sending them home. I have consulted the Governor and General Chesnut, who both urge that they be paroled.[70]

Unfortunately, many POWs only found freedom when the war ended.

The most unusual odyssey of all befell the bodies of the POWs who died at Camp Lawton. The story is told in published government documents as well as in manuscript materials in the National Archives. Following the war, Quartermaster General Meigs ordered that lists and descriptions of all burial sites of Union soldiers be compiled. In November of 1865, Lieutenant D.B. Chesley (12th Maine) traveled to the site of Camp Lawton, examined the burials, and reported there were two graveyards. One was "½ mile south of Hack's Mill," and one was "1 mile S.W. of Hack's Mill near Mrs. Jones' mill pond...." Misunderstanding the markings he saw at the burial sites, he erroneously stated that there were 1,646 bodies in all. Finally, he reported that ["n]one of the above are enclosed and all are exposed to desecration."[71]

Chesley's report was supplemented by a later report that gave more precise details as to the location of the burial trenches as well as their layout:

---

[69] Winder to Cooper, 31 December 1864, *Official Records*, series 2, vol. 7, 1,302–03.

[70] Ibid., 1,304; Winder to Cooper, 20 January 1865, *Official Records*, series 2, vol. 8, 96.

[71] Captain C.K. Smith, Jr., transmits Report of Lt. D.B. Chesley, 22 November 1865, National Archives, RG 92, Quartermaster General's Office, Cemeterial Branch, Remarks on Reports of Cemeteries, Book 1, 36.

Three trenches—300 yards south of Hack's Mills, near Lawton, Ga and 150 yds west of Augusta & Savannah RR. The running numbers commenced at the north end of the eastern trench.
No. 151 commencing North of middle trench
No. 317 commencing at North end of Western trench
. . .

One trench—one and one half miles southwest of Lawton, Burke County, Ga. And 100 yds west of Mrs. Jones' mill pond. The trench runs from east to west... The running number 492 commences at east end at a stake marked 492. These are interments continued from the three trenches near Hack's Mills.[72]

Hack's Mill was one of two lumber mills located in close proximity to the prison. Perkins' Lumber Company mill, which had been purchased by the Perkins brothers in 1858, was located downstream from the stockade, undoubtedly on what was called "Mrs. Jones' mill pond." Hack's Mill, a steam-operated concern, was situated east of the prison, just west of the railroad near Lawton. Both Perkins and Hack's mills did contract work for the Confederate government. In a letter to the Perkins' Lumber Company, Captain L.S. Varnedoe, post quartermaster at Camp Sumter, requested a bill for the lumber that had been delivered to that prison and in the same letter requested that Mr. Hack also send a bill for his products.[73] The location of these two mills is germane to the study of Camp Lawton because the sites of the original POW burial trenches are described in relation to where the mills were.

---

[72] "Records of Deceased U.S. Soldiers Reinterred at Lawton Cemetery, Lawton, GA," National Archives, Quartermaster General's Office, RG 92, Records of Cemeterial Functions, 1838–1929, Cemeteries, c. 1862–1960, Georgia: Lawton Cemetery, Vol. 14, NM 81/A1, Entry 627.

[73] Captain L.S. Varnedoe to Messrs. Perkins, 5 February 1865, Sheppard Perkins" Papers, 1860-1879, Emory University, Manuscript Archives and Rare Book Library; the proprietor of Hack's Mill, George B. Hack, had been associated with the Richmond Factory, a cotton mill, near Augusta prior to moving to Lawton. He continued to operate a steam sawmill on the site until shortly after the war. See transfer of property from Caroline E. Jones to George B. Hack, which mentions a "steam saw mill" and the "George B. Hack & Co," 15 July 1866, Office of Probate Judge, Jenkins County, Deed Book B.

At any rate, the Quartermaster General's Office responded to these initial reports with an order for the creation of a national cemetery for the dead of the prison and other Union soldiers buried in the surrounding district. Accordingly, Colonel E.B. Carling negotiated the acquisition of a four-acre tract for the new cemetery with Mrs. Jones (the lessor of the prison property) through her lawyer, F.G. Godbee.[74] The bodies were exhumed from the original burial trenches and systematically re-interred in the new ground.

In an 1868 report, Brevet Lieutenant Colonel Edmund B. Whitman, Assistant Quartermaster, indicated that the Confederate prison authorities had taken some care to identify the dead through the use of a numbering system:

> At the heads of these trenches strips of split pine boards had been carefully erected, every 50th and 100th stake being numbered. From the last stake at the trenches near the railroad the numbering had been carried forward to those near the hospitals. [Apparently, then, the grave trenches near the railroad comprised the initial burials of POWs.]
>
> Through the entire number only two stakes bore any [name] inscription, and on these the inscription was carved. On the 138th board was inscribed the name of J.T. Shephard [Co. A., 10th Connecticut], and on the 257th that of J.B. Northrup [Co. G, 111 New York].[75]

One wonders if comrades of these two men had memorialized them by inscribing their names on the rough pine slabs. Their significance, however, lay in the fact that it was these two inscriptions, plus this numbering system that correlated with the names and numbers on the death register found in Savannah, that allowed many of the bodies to be identified and the graves in the new national cemetery to be marked accordingly.

Lieutenant Colonel Whitman stated that ["d]uring the two months that this prison was occupied there had occurred 725 deaths; of which 491 were buried in three trenches near the railroad, and 234 in two

---

[74] F.G. Godbee to Major General Rucker, n.d. (c. September 1867), National Archives, RG 92, Quartermaster General's Office, Cemeterial Branch.

[75] *Roll of Honor*, vol. 17, 466–92.

trenches near the hospitals." According to Whitman these hospitals were located "in a grove, on the borders of a pond, at some distance from the stockade." [76]

Whitman also described in detail the process of disinterment of the bodies from the trenches in which the dead POWs had been buried:

> On opening the trenches for the removal of the bodies to the new cemetery, a vault of about 12 inches in depth was found to extend the entire length. The bodies were laid in this vault, side by side, as they died, and strips of split logs or puncheons were laid over them, over which the earth was thrown.
>
> In the work of disinterment, as the earth was removed and the planks taken up, the bodies were exposed to view, free from the earth and plainly distinguishable from each other. They were then taken up one by one and deposited in separate coffins, and interred in the new cemetery according to the order of original burial.[77]

Ultimately, Lawton National Cemetery contained not only the bodies of the Camp Lawton dead but also the graves of Union soldiers who had died in area skirmishes, in particular the running fights between Kilpatrick and Wheeler's cavalry units. As the government began to consolidate burials of Union soldiers following the conclusion of the war, the latter bodies were disinterred and brought to the cemetery from Alexander, Catesville, Thomas's Station, Waynesboro, and other area localities.[78]

---

[76] Ibid., 466–92. Given the correspondence between the number (491) found in the original burial trenches near the railroad and the number (488) listed in the original death register as well as its dating, the death register document found in Savannah most likely represents the bodies buried there. The missing part of the records of deaths kept by the Confederate authorities at Camp Lawton is probably the list of those buried in the new burial trenches downstream from the stockade.

[77] Ibid., 466–92.

[78] Rogers and Saunders, "Camp Lawton Stockade," 90–91; Mark Hughes, *Bivouac of the Dead* (Bowie MD: Heritage Books, 1995) 50–52, 128, 130, has done yeoman work compiling these data from two publications of the Quartermaster General's Department (*Roll of Honor: Names of Soldiers Who Died in Defense of the American Union, Interred in National Cemeteries*, 23 vols., 1865–1877; and *Statement of the Disposition of Some of the Bodies of Deceased Union*

In his 1868 report Whitman also gave the general location of the new national cemetery:

> The cemetery to which these bodies have been transferred (together with others from General Sherman's army, who fell in skirmishes near this place) is located about one mile west of the Savannah and Augusta railroad, and about half a mile from the stockade. It is securely enclosed; the graves are tastefully arranged in sections, and marked by head-boards numbered to correspond to this list[79]

Interestingly, his report lists only three sections—A, B, and E. A careful perusal of the lists reveals that sections A and B contained the bodies of the Camp Lawton dead; section E mainly held the re-interred bodies of Union soldiers who initially had been buried within the district that the cemetery was to serve. Although the exact location of Lawton National Cemetery has not been ascertained, the National Archives has a copy of the cemetery plat as well as a map of the cemeterial district served by it.[80] The description above would seem to indicate that the cemetery was located to the west of the prison site. The resulting cemetery was described as follows: "A substantial board fence, well white-washed, encloses the cemetery; and suitable headboards painted white, and lettered in black, have been erected at the graves of those who could be identified."[81]

The short-lived cemetery received its first and only superintendent in August of 1867. Robert Wood was granted a warrant for the position on 6 August, and was assigned to the new cemetery near Millen a little more than a week later, on 15 August. Superintendent Wood must have taken his position quickly because he submitted the first of the required

---

Soldiers and Prisoners of War Whose Remains Have Been Moved to National Cemeteries, 4 vols., 1868).

[79] *Roll of Honor*, vol. 17, 466–92.

[80] Map "Showing section of country from which the Union dead have been disinterred and removed to the 'Lawton National Cemetery,'" National Archives, RG 92, Quartermaster General's Office, Maps and Plans of Civil War National Cemeteries and Related Areas, Cemeterial District—Dept. of Tenn., #14 Lawton, GA; Plat of Lawton National Cemetery, surveyed Sept. 8th, 1866, National Archives, RG 92, Quartermaster General's Office, Cemeterial Branch.

[81] *Roll of Honor*, vol. 17, 293–313.

monthly reports that month. The September and October reports were also dutifully submitted, but then they stopped.[82] His position must have been a lonely one, for it was a one-man position. Being on the Federal government payroll and protecting the bodies of the erstwhile and bitterly resented enemy so soon after the war, probably added to his sense of isolation. And then there was a dispute with Mrs. Jones who now demanded $1,500 for the cemetery plot. The reason for the dispute is not entirely clear, but a letter from Mrs. Jones's lawyer, F. G. Godbee, to Major General Rucker partially illuminates the issue:

> There is a National Cemetery located at Lawton on the Augusta & Savannah Rail Road in this County. It was located by Col. E.B. Carling U.S.A. and a price agreed upon; afterward there were other requirements made which altered the consideration or price of the grounds very materially, upon which I made a statement in writing to the Quarter Master then in charge in the City of Savannah, he promised me the matter should have early attention. That has been six months ago and I have heard nothing from him. The Cemetery is situated on the lands of Mrs. Caroline E. Jones of this state a Widow Lady whom I represent and she is desirous some arrangement be made. It was suggested to me by the soldier [undoubtedly Superintendent Wood] detailed to look after the grounds to write to you on the subject for the necessary information.[83]

Rather than settle, Brigadier General Rufus Saxton, Chief Quartermaster of the Third Military District in Atlanta, recommended on 23 September 1867 that the dead buried at Lawton National Cemetery be exhumed for transportation to a cemetery to be established near Savannah that would consolidate the area Union war dead.[84] Quartermaster General Meigs approved the removal of the bodies at Lawton National Cemetery on 12 October 1867.[85] However, a national

---

[82] Robert Wood, Superintendents National Cemeteries, 1867–71, National Archives, RG 92, Quartermaster General's Office, E603, 151.

[83] F.G. Godbee to Major General D.H. Rucker, n.d. (c. September 1867), National Archives, RG 92, Quartermaster General's Office, Cemeterial Branch.

[84] Brigadier General Rufus Saxton to Quartermaster General's Office, National Archives, RG 92, Quartermaster General's Office, Cemeterial Branch.

[85] Quartermaster Meigs to General Saxton, 12 October 1867, National Archives, RG 92, Quartermaster General's Office, Cemeterial Branch.

cemetery at Savannah was never created; rather, the bodies were transferred elsewhere. On 10 January 1868, the government ordered the bodies at Lawton National Cemetery to be exhumed and transferred to the national cemetery at Beaufort, South Carolina.[86]

As for Robert Wood, his career in the national cemetery service was rather brief. He was transferred to Marietta on 3 February 1868; the following April he was sent to Florence, South Carolina, where his career as a cemetery superintendent came to a sudden and inglorious end. His warrant was revoked on 29 August 1868, "on account of improper conduct."[87]

In the meantime, J.P. Low of Charleston contracted with the government to remove the bodies and headboards and re-inter them at the cemetery in Beaufort at a cost of $6 per body. Rail transport was to be furnished by the government. By the end of February 1868, Low had completed his contract. Short lived like the prison itself, Lawton National Cemetery existed for less than a year.[88] However, the closing of the cemetery and the removal of the bodies to Beaufort was not without controversy. In the 7 October 1869 issue of the *Virginia Free Press* (Charleston, West Virginia), a story appeared in which an "Eastern newspaper correspondent," while visiting the national cemetery at Beaufort, was regaled by a local guide with tales of corrupt practices in the body trade. He claimed that some of the bodies of supposed Union soldiers had been dressed in gray and others had been taken from slave cemeteries. Because the contractors were paid by the body, he said they had "dug up men, then divided them, so that a $10.00 job, by separating arms, legs, and head, was made to pay 500%.... I should not wonder," he

---

[86] Record of Superintendent's Monthly Reports on the Condition of National Cemeteries, National Archives, RG 92, Quartermaster General's Office, Cemeterial Branch, 39.

[87] Robert Wood, Record of Superintendents 1867-1875, National Archives, RG 92, Quartermaster General's Office, E606, 227.

[88] General Rufus Saxton to General D.H. Rucker, 3 January 1868, National Archives, RG 92, Quartermaster General's Office, Cemeterial Files, Box 137, Abstract of Contracts between General R. Saxton and J.T. Low; *Roll of Honor* vol. 14, 293.

mused, "if some bummer's skull was at that gate and a big toe a clean half mile away down in yonder corner."[89]

Ironically, the indication that there may have been fraud in the body count of those exhumed from Lawton National Cemetery to be re-interred at Beaufort National Cemetery argues against the higher estimates of the number of burials at Camp Lawton. One would assume, given the fact that payment was per body recovered, that a corrupt contractor would report the greatest number of bodies possible.[90] As mentioned previously, Sneden and some Federal accounts reported burials at Camp Lawton as numbering from 1,300 to over 1,600, but the grave contractors, despite their financial incentive to do so, did not report such numbers. Of course, there remains the possibility that a whole burial site or sites had been overlooked during the consolidation process. What undercuts that argument is that not much time had elapsed from the time of Camp Lawton's evacuation to the Federal grave surveys following the war. There seems hardly to have been time for any overlooked burial trenches to have been lost or obliterated by natural processes. All accounts indicate that the original Camp Lawton POW burials were marked with numbered stakes. Also, one would assume that any local landowner would have wanted buried bodies removed from their property or at the very least consolidated on one site. Another factor that should be considered is that the brevity of the period from late 1866, when the bodies were consolidated at Lawton National Cemetery, to early 1868, when they were removed to Beaufort National Cemetery, argues against the deterioration of the wooden coffins, as rudimentary as they might have been, such that the bodies would have been easily co-mingled by the contractor. Where contractors had more of an opportunity to inflate the body count by separating body parts would have been from the smaller, less well-documented burial sites of

---

[89] *Virginia Free Press* (Charleston, West Virginia), 7 October 1869.

[90] Interestingly enough, the Quartermaster General reported in 1866 that the average cost of transferring and reinterring bodies was $9.75 (US Army Military Institute, *Shrines of the Honored Dead: A Study of the National Cemetery System* [Washington DC: Department of the Army, Office of the Quartermaster General, n.d.], 16). This publication was a reprint of series of articles written by Edward Steere, Historian, Office of the Quartermaster General, in *The Quartermaster Review*, in 1953–54.

Sherman's men who had been killed in skirmishes along the route of their march.

If Vowles's 8 November prison census is accurate, and there seems to be little reason to doubt its veracity, 486 POWs died at Camp Lawton from 10 October, when the first shipments of POWs seem to have arrived, to the date of his report. Further, General Winder stated that the POWs had been evacuated by 22 November. The first period represents thirty days; the second period covers fourteen days. Therefore, if 486 POWs died in thirty days, then 227 would have died in the remaining fourteen days, assuming the death rate remained constant. Totaling these figures gives an estimate of 713 POW deaths during the camp's existence. This extrapolated figure compares well with the last official number (725) reported in Lawton National Cemetery in the *Roll of Honor* (Vol. XVII) and provides another check on the various estimates of deaths.[91] Thus, the estimates of the number of deaths at Camp Lawton ranging from 1,300 to 1,600 seem to be exaggerations. This, of course, affords no consolation for those who died and whose families may or may not have received notice that their son had died somewhere in Georgia at a place called Camp Lawton.

---

[91] *Roll of Honor*, vol. 17, 466–92.

8

The Resurrection of Camp Lawton

Camp Lawton lay dormant for nearly a century and a half—its memory erased by the passing of its principals, the records of its existence scattered among archival repositories, and the pieces of its story hidden within obscure and long-forgotten publications. The prison was publicly resurrected, so to speak, on 18 August 2010, when Georgia Southern University, the Georgia Department of Natural Resources, and the US Fish & Wildlife Service hosted a media event at Magnolia Springs State Park at which the results of archaeological work done at the site in the spring and summer of that year were unveiled for the public. What was shown to those in attendance that day was the fruit of a remarkable collaborative effort among the three governmental entities and was touted as one of the more significant Civil War finds of recent years.[1] The news was trumpeted by major news agencies—CNN, Fox News, Public Television, NPR, the Associated Press—and was picked up by local outlets nationwide, creating quite a "buzz."[2]

The term "resurrection" is appropriate because for almost a century and a half the story of Camp Lawton lay buried. Like an abandoned corpse, its remains were scattered in the aftermath of the war. The first human scavengers of the abandoned prison were Sherman's men who followed closely on the heels of the hurried Confederate evacuation. While Kilpatrick's troopers were first on the scene and began the camp's destruction, other Union troops visited it and completed rendering it

---

[1] "Camp Lawton," Special First Edition (Georgia Southern University and Georgia Department of Natural Resources, 18 August 2010); US Fish & Wildlife Service, "The Camp Lawton Archaeological Site: Bo Ginn National Fish Hatchery," http://www.fws.gov/camplawtonsite.html (accessed 1 October 2010); www.georgiasouthern.edu/camp-lawton (accessed 1 October 2010).

[2] See, for example, Phil Gast, "Major Archaeological Find at Site of Civil War Prison," CNN, 17 August 2010, http://www.cnn.com/2010/US/08/14/Georgia.civil.war.camp/index.html?iref=allsearch (accessed 7 October 2010).

useless. As official records, published accounts, and personal diaries indicate, numerous Union soldiers whose units marched or camped near the prison site wandered over the smoldering grounds to see an example of one of the "prison pens" about which they had heard so much. Some POWs carried a trinket or two away with them. Perhaps some of these survive as heirlooms in the collections of descendents of Union soldiers, their provenance long forgotten.

In the years following the war, public interest (particularly in the North) in first-person accounts of inmate travails in Confederate military prisons led to a spurt of POW publications. As the twentieth century approached, however, the number of such publications declined, and public interest in the subject dwindled. Even at the height of such interest and publication, though, scant mention was made of Camp Lawton. Moreover, early scholarly works treating the history of Civil War prisons focused little attention on the prison at Magnolia Springs.

Local citizens must also have visited the site, but with the removal of the bodies buried in the short-lived Lawton National Cemetery to Beaufort, South Carolina, Camp Lawton seems to have receded from their memory and to have been forgotten by the wider world. The surviving earthworks became a landmark (the "old fort") occasionally cited by locals when giving directions, but the area on the north side of the stream where most of the POWs had been housed slipped back into its natural state as new forest growth reclaimed the ground that had once been covered with shebangs and marked with ovens, portions of the stockade walls, and the deadline. Although the prison had been burned, some ancillary buildings may have survived to be used by locals whether remaining in situ or after having been moved to other locations.

After 1865, Magnolia Springs returned to its pre-war role serving as a recreation spot for local people. In 1924, area citizens led by Millen Mayor Walter Harrison began an effort to make the site a public park. The land package for the park was initiated when local property owner W. E. Alwood donated to the cause a 58-acre tract that included remains of Camp Lawton's entrenchments. Jenkins County then purchased more than 900 more acres to complete the property. In 1939, Magnolia Springs States Park was established, and the 175 men of Civilian Conservation Corps (CCC) Company 3465 under the direction of Albert C. Haley arrived to begin work on their assignment, Project SP16. The dollar-a-day CCC "boys" constructed 22 buildings, including five barracks, for the camp and its support. They created a swimming area by dredging, damming and widening the stream that had once supplied Camp Lawton's inmates, and they built a bathhouse, a "casino," and other early park infrastructure. The advent of World War II and the resulting deactivation of the CCC left the remainder of the construction to be completed by German POWs, one of whom made a model of an old cabin that still existed nearby and that some believed had been a part of the prison. Today, that model is on display in the small park museum.[3]

In 1948, a Federal fish hatchery (Millen National Fish Hatchery) was established on 100 acres of park property. In 1988, it was renamed the Bo Ginn National Fish Hatchery (after local congressman Howard "Bo" Ginn, who resided in Millen). The Federal hatchery closed in 1996, but plans to reopen it have been recently announced by the US Fish & Wildlife Service. Ironically, the property on which the fish hatchery was situated contained most of the portion of the Camp Lawton stockade where the Federal POWs had been located.[4] Fortunately, as the fish hatchery facilities were constructed and operated, most of the portion of the area where the POWs had lived was left in its natural, wooded state.

Ultimately, a Georgia Civil War Commission marker briefly describing the history of Camp Lawton was placed along Highway 25 near the entrance to the park, and the DNR placed a commemorative stone marker near the park office. As an aside, both the initial construction of Highway 25 and the recent expansion of the road into a

---

[3] The CCC was one of the more successful New Deal programs. Established in 1933, the CCC enrolled unemployed young men and veterans who were paid $30 a month, $25 of which went to their families. Enrollees were provided room and board, uniform clothing, and transportation and lived in quasi-military camps while they worked on government projects and engaged in self-improvement efforts. In all there were approximately 4,500 CCC camps across the nation and more than 3 million enrollees. The program was terminated in 1942, as a result of the war effort. See Stan Cohen, *Tree Army: A Pictorial History of the Civilian Conservation Corps, 1933–1942*, rev. ed. (Missoula MT: Pictorial Histories, 1980), for a good survey of this remarkable program.

[4] United States Department of the Interior, "U.S. Fish and Wildlife Service to Re-open Bo Ginn National Fish Hatchery," 28 May 2010, US Fish and Wildlife Service, http://www.fws.gov/southeast/news/2010/r10-042.html (accessed 17 July 2010).

four-lane highway cut through a portion of the prison facility. Although the bulk of the stockade, if not all of it, seems to have been to the east of the current highway, evidence of prison facilities to the west of the stockade—Confederate and POW hospitals, POW burial trenches, and perhaps an earthwork to the north—may have been compromised or destroyed.

Many people have fond memories of youthful visits to Magnolia Springs and occasionally those memories relate to Camp Lawton. A common local story is that for many years there was a wagon wheel and a portion of a skeleton visible to swimmers in the spring. Others tell of finding artifacts, one such story revolving around the discovery of a bone knife. With the advent of metal detectors based on World War II minesweeping technology, a few relic hunters sought surreptitiously to find things, apparently without much luck. Recently, a park employee recalled uncovering the remains of an old wagon wheel hub while plowing a firebreak some years ago. Overall, however, the general feeling was that there was little to find at the site.

Locals had vague knowledge of the Confederate prison, but its existence was even less known to the broader public. In Georgia, as well as across the vast landscape of interest in Confederate prisons, Camp Sumter attracted almost all of the attention because of its size, the number of deaths there, the amount of documentation related to it, the fate of Captain Wirz, and its notoriety in the history of Civil War prisons. Moreover, state park officials, understandably, were not highly motivated to publicize, develop interpretative materials for, or spend money on a park whose story centered on another prison in Georgia.

Yet, in the 1970s there were stirrings of interest. The Department of Natural Resources recovered two large, hand-hewn timbers that were submerged downstream from the spring. If, in fact, these timbers prove to have come from Camp Lawton, they are the only Civil War prison stockade timbers known to exist. Also, in 1975, Billy Townsend, a DNR staff member, authored a brief in-house study of the prison ("Camp Lawton: Magnolia Springs State Park") for the Parks and Historic Sites Division, pulling together for the first time the basic sources for its history. In the same decade several wooden signs with routed inscriptions were placed in the park denoting the prison and the earthworks on the ridge to the south. Remarkably, however, most visitors to the park remained unaware of anything but the recreational facilities there.

Camp Lawton received scholarly attention in 1981, when Drs. George A. Rogers and R. Frank Saunders, history professors at Georgia Southern University, published an article ("Camp Lawton Stockade, Millen, Georgia, C.S.A.") on the prison in *The Atlanta History Journal*. Augmenting Townsend's research, they also examined material in the National Archives illuminating what had happened to the Camp Lawton dead. In the meantime Camp Lawton had also attracted the attention of a history student at the University of South Carolina at Aiken, Roger A. McCoig, who wrote a paper on the prison that was published in the 1981–82 edition of the campus journal *Social and Behavioral Sciences*.[5]

Over the years several examinations of the Camp Lawton site had given little or no indication of the artifact-rich strata that lay below the surface. In 1981, at the request of the U S Fish and Wildlife Service, Carolina Archaeological Services surveyed portions of the Bo Ginn National Fish Hatchery and an area west of Highway 25 owned by ITT Rayonier to locate an area for additional hatchery ponds to be dug. No evidence of Civil War occupation was found. In December 1996, Jonathan Bentley tested a small area intended as a nitration field for the Aquarium. Again, no evidence of the Camp Lawton era was found. Plans for the expansion of Highway 25 from two-lanes to four lanes resulted in another survey in 1997. The road expansion ran through a portion of Magnolia Springs State Park and bordered on Bo Ginn National Fish Hatchery. New South Associates conducted the examination but found no artifacts related to the Civil War period. However, a surface feature was identified as a possible Civil War earthwork (gun battery). Further examination of that feature by Thomas Wheaton of New South Associates in 2000 concluded that it was not military in origin. The paucity of Civil War-related findings from these early investigations was probably a function of the fact that these surveys were done primarily to certify areas for construction purposes.

---

[5] Roger A. McCoig, "Camp Lawton: A Brief Chapter in the Study of Confederate States Prisons," *Social and Behavioral Sciences* (1981–82): 2–16.

A turning point in the promotion of the site as an important historical resource came with the July 1999 appointment of Bill Giles as assistant manager of Magnolia Springs State Park.[6] In March 2005, Giles was promoted to park manager. With an academic background in history, Giles developed a strong interest in Camp Lawton, a focus fueled by the discovery and publication of the Sneden materials. Displaying remarkable energy, Giles led the effort to highlight the Civil War heritage of the park, collecting source material, erecting new color signage utilizing the newly discovered Sneden illustrations, overseeing the construction of an interpretive gazebo, establishing a small museum of the park's history, developing a walking trail relating to the prison, publishing a collection of source materials for Camp Lawton in two editions, and producing an interpretive video. His perseverance and resourcefulness led to the initial use of ground-penetrating radar (GPR) at the site in the fall of 2005 by Shawn Patch of the Georgia Department of Transportation and follow-up work in the summer of 2006 to try to locate subsurface anomalies that might reveal the location of the prison's wall and gate features and, thus, point the way for future archaeological investigations. The survey revealed a square feature under the parking lot in front of the park office which, given its shape and general location, was thought perhaps to be evidence of the location of the prison gate.[7]

Based on these GPR soundings, the DNR and Georgia Department of Transportation sponsored a limited archaeological dig in 2007 that uncovered a charred wood fragment.[8] In 2009, the state of Georgia and the Federal government reached an agreement to allow Georgia Southern University archaeologists to sample the site, including both state-owned Magnolia Springs State Park land and the US Fish and

---

[6] "New Park Manager Appointed at Magnolia Springs State Park," *The Millen News*, 16 March 2005. The story of the resurrection of the prison from a local news standpoint can be traced in this local paper. See 30 March 2005; 26 October 2005; 9 November 2005; 7 June 2006; 2 August 2006; 7 February 2007; 7 April 2010; 14 April 2010; 30 June 2010; 21 July 2010; 28 July 2010; 1 August 2010; 18 August 2010; 25 August 2010; 1 September 2010; and 22 September 2010, issues.

[7] "Archeological Study in Progress at Magnolia," *The Millen News*, 26 October 2005; "Archeologists Look for 'World's Largest Prison,'" 26 August 2006.

[8] "Possible Remnant of Camp Lawton Unearthed in Dig," *The Millen News*, 7 February 2007.

Wildlife Department-owned fish hatchery property. In December 2009, the LAMAR Institute, a private archaeological research organization, was contracted to do a GPR examination of an area near where it was believed one of the stockade corners was located. The result was the discovery of an L-shaped subsurface pattern that looked very much like a corner. Under the direction of Dr. Sue Moore, Department of Sociology and Anthropology at Georgia Southern University, a team of graduate students headed by Kevin Chapman followed up with an archaeological dig beginning in January of 2010.[9]

Initial expectations were that evidence of the wall line would be found, ultimately allowing the corners of the stockade to be located and marked. In addition to the search for the wall line, a survey was conducted on the north side of the stream, an undeveloped area where the POWs had been situated in 1864. Because the prison's existence had been so brief and because it was assumed that what little might have been left had long since been picked over or destroyed by subsequent land use, the team expected to find very little physical remains of Civil War occupancy.

The exciting discoveries announced at the 18 August media day stemmed from these explorations. Chapman and his colleagues sank trenches across that L-shaped anomaly and in one discovered indications of the wall line including numerous small, charred wood fragments from the burning of the stockade in the fall of 1864. In addition, with the permission of the US Fish & Wildlife Service, on whose land the part of the stockade that held the area where most POWs were quartered was located, archaeologists conducted shovel tests and metal detectors scans the results of which, both in quantity and quality, surprised the archaeologists, who have since concluded that the area that held the prisoners' huts had been relatively untouched since the end of the Civil War. The hasty evacuation of the prison on the night of 22 November 1864, probably explains the quantity of material evidence left behind.

---

[9] Details of this work are found in "Camp Lawton," Special First Edition Georgia Southern University and Georgia Department of Natural Resources, 18 August 2010. See also James Kevin Chapman, "Comparison of Archeological Survey Techniques at Camp Lawton, a Civil War Prison Stockade" (MA thesis, Georgia Southern University, 2012)..

Camp Lawton was never reoccupied by Confederate forces, and the fact that it was little known, short-lived, and remotely located meant that it was forgotten in the broader scheme of things and did not attract the numbers of relic hunters as did other more famous or notorious Civil War locations. Many had come to assume that there was nothing of significance to find on the grounds. The 2010 archaeological team found American and Austrian coins and tokens, pieces of military and medical equipment, shebang locations, oven bricks, and personal POW items (pocket knife, spoons, knives, and forks, a harmonica frame, buttons, etc.)—all of this from a restricted survey area of the prison. The recent archeological investigation yielded a bountiful harvest; yet, it covered only a small portion of the site. Through careful spatial analysis of artifact location, the archeological investigation of the interior of the stockade may provide some insight into the location of the shebangs and "avenues," units, and even ethnic groups within the POW population. As of this writing, much more is left to be done—locating the four corners of the stockade, continuing to discover and interpret artifacts that tell the story of the prison, finding the Confederate camp and sites of ancillary administrative structures, mapping all the earthworks, locating the original burial trenches, uncovering the road network, and discovering the location of the short-lived Lawton National Cemetery. In addition to GPR and metal detectors, a high-tech tool that has and will continue to help in some of these endeavors is the use of the LiDAR (Light Detecting and Ranging) instrument by which a digital scanning system develops a 3-D model of a landscape feature. A non-invasive technology, LiDAR allows for the creation of accurate terrain and feature models with precise location data for viewing and study.[10]

The recent extraordinary measures taken by the US Fish and Wildlife Service to preserve the site by erecting a security fence, maintaining police patrols, and using electronic monitoring equipment to detect illegal activity, will help safeguard what seems to be a relatively pristine site. The relative wealth of artifacts already uncovered as well as those yet to be discovered strengthens the potential of the site to augment significantly our understanding of the operation of the prison

---

[10] Ibid.

on the macro level and of the daily lives of both captors and captives on the micro level. On the historical, textual side of the research, historians will continue to try to uncover new sources for Camp Lawton and, combining new and old documentary sources with the information derived from the ongoing archeological investigations, will be able to write a more complete, accurate history of the prison's existence.

Until other arrangements can be made, the artifacts uncovered at Camp Lawton will reside at Georgia Southern University. On 10 October 2010, a curated exhibit was opened at the GSU Museum in which the objects were displayed and interpreted for the public. Construction is underway on a facility at Magnolia Springs to display and interpret the materials for the public. For such a facility also to include exhibits related to Sherman's March would place the prison in a broader context and attract heritage tourists who travel the Atlanta-to-Savannah historic corridor.

The recent activity centered on Camp Lawton stimulated considerable interest in the local community. A local group formed a Sons of Confederate Veterans unit (Chapter 2102), the Buckhead-Fort Lawton Brigade.[11] Chartered on 13 May 2006, the chapter adopted as a project the care of the earthworks on the ridge to the south of the stockade location. In addition, local residents have vocally expressed their support for the new museum facility and hope that the news of the findings will result in more heritage tourism for their economically depressed community.

The dictum that the past is prologue was illustrated by a 16 September 2010, announcement by the Georgia Department of Corrections that the Corrections Corporation of America had been awarded a contract to operate a facility for male inmates in Jenkins County. Opened in early 2012, the new prison was built on a 107-acre tract of land in Jenkins County in the vicinity of Millen and was designed to have a capacity of 1,150 inmates with a staff of 200 full-time employees.[12] The use of a corporation to manage a prison is part of a state initiative in recent years to privatize a portion of the corrections

---

[11] "SCV Camp 2101 Hold Charter Banquet," *The Millen News*, 7 June 2006.
[12] "CCA to Build Prison Here," *The Millen News*, 22 September 2010.

system. Despite the fact that the construction of Camp Lawton a century and a half earlier had met with local opposition, this announcement was welcomed by area citizens who looked at the $56.8 million capital investment, the $8 million annual payroll, and the $1.2 million in annual property taxes and utility payments as a great boon to a depleted economy. Interestingly, not counting the jailing of local malefactors, this would be Millen's third experience with prisoners, along with the Union POWs at Camp Lawton and the German POWs at Magnolia Springs.

Conclusion

"Hallowed Ground"

The horrendous death rate and suffering of Civil War POWs led to a vigorous debate in the aftermath of the conflict. Because the Confederacy was defeated, Southern authorities were placed on the defensive as the United States Government initiated investigations into the Confederate military prisons. The arrests of prominent Confederate prison authorities, the trial and execution of Henry Wirz, the issuance of documents by the government related to his trial, and the publication of a host of accusatory Union POW accounts that flooded the market in the aftermath of the war, set the tone. Although these writings dominated the discussion, the debate over the treatment of Union POWs during the Civil War took on a life of its own and ranged from arguments blaming the death rate on a deliberate effort by Confederate authorities to kill as many Union captives as possible to publications by Confederate apologists tracing the problems to the Union termination of the exchange cartel and the failure to allow needed supplies and medicines through the Union naval blockade. A good example of the latter is represented by Jefferson Davis's booklet, *Andersonville and Other War Prisons*.[1] Partisans of each side of the debate assiduously searched supportive documents and sought corroborating testimony to secure evidence to buttress their respective arguments as the nineteenth century wore on.

The argument has never ended.[2] One only has to bring up the subject at a meeting of the Sons of Confederate Veterans, a gathering of

---

[1] Jefferson Davis, *Andersonville and Other War Prisons* (New York: Belford, 1890). Contemporary examples of the ongoing debate over the responsibility for the mortality rates in Civil War prisons include James M. Gillespie, *Andersonvilles of the North: The Myths and Realities of Northern Treatment of Civil War Confederate Prisoners* (Denton: University of North Texas Press, 2008), which defends Union treatment of Confederate POWs, and Charles W. Sanders, Jr., *While in the Hands of the Enemy: Military Prisons of the Civil War* which maintains that both sides consciously neglected their captives and share liability.

[2] Benjamin G. Cloyd, *Haunted by Atrocity: Civil War Prisons in American Memory* (Baton Rouge: Louisiana State University Press, 2010), details how the issue of Civil War prisons has proven persistently divisive to this day.

descendents of Grand Army of the Republic members, or a Civil War Round Table program to hear echoes of its lingering bitterness. In some ways the issue of Civil War prisons remains a central point of dispute among those for whom the "irrepressible conflict" remains vital. As such, the story of Camp Lawton is instructive.

The horrors of Southern prisons during the Civil War were functions of the exigencies of war rather than any overt, systematic effort to kill Union prisoners. However, many Union veterans who had been incarcerated in the camps would have vehemently disagreed with that assertion and, in fact, their memoirs are replete with cruel captors, brutal prison guards, and inhumane prison administrators. Union prisoners who had survived death-dealing battlefields often found themselves in prison camps that killed in other ways. Of course, the same can be said of Confederate captives in Northern prisons as many have pointed out. As is the case with so many Civil War controversies, this debate seems interminable. However, one of the more careful and balanced assessments of the Civil War military prison experience, *While in the Hands of the Enemy* by Charles W. Sanders, Jr., concludes: "For both the Union and the Confederacy, the treatment of prisoners during the American Civil War can only be judged 'a most horrible national sin.'" Sanders believes that both sides could have done better for their incarcerated foes if only "those who directed the prison systems of the North and the South had cared for them [POWs] as their own regulations and basic humanity required." Yet, according to Sanders, "... this was something that they very deliberately chose not to do."[3]

In many cases the layers of bureaucracy between the POWs and their captors seemed to increase antipathy and neglectful attitudes toward the prisoners. Ample evidence exists in surviving letters, diary accounts, and official records of local concern expressed toward the conditions in which the prisoners found themselves; conversely, records also often document the failure of higher echelon military and political

---

[3] Sanders, *While in the Hands of the Enemy*, 315–16. The source for "… a most horrible national sin…," cited on page 316 of Sanders's book, can be found in Dismukes to Davis, 12 October 1864, United States, War Department, *The War of the Rebellion: A Compilation of the Official Records of the Union and Confederate Armies*, series 2, vol. 7 (Washington DC: Government Printing Office, 1880–1901) 976.

officials to take strong, concerted action following reports of the plight of POWs. Typically, such reports were shuffled up and down the chain of command, often with cursory, superficial endorsements, the cumulative effect of which diverted responsibility and prevented effective action.

An example from the history of Camp Lawton is illustrative. The move from Camp Sumter to Camp Lawton did not alleviate the dire lack of funds that had plagued Confederate military prisons from the beginning. Once established at Camp Lawton, Dr. Isaiah White wrote Confederate Army Surgeon-General S.P. Moore in early November complaining bitterly about the paucity of support from the Commissary Department:

> The law of Congress creating a hospital fund to provide for the comfort of the sick and wounded is completely abrogated by the Commissary Department failing to fill requests for funds.
>
> The authority granted in your telegram of September 23, to divide the excess of funds at Andersonville among the new prisons, has been thwarted by the commissary at that post failing to supply funds. A large excess of funds at Andersonville will be turned over to the Treasury because the commissary at that post had failed to supply himself with funds to meet requisitions while thousands of sick, both at this post and Andersonville, are in a state of suffering that would touch the heart of even the most callous. Will not the Commissary-General supply the funds even after the monthly statement of hospital fund has been forwarded?

As one would expect, this accusatory letter set off a round of bureaucratic infighting. Surgeon-General Moore endorsed White's report and forwarded it to L.B. Northrop, Commissary-General of Subsistence, "asking what action would be taken." This led to a sharp retort by Northrop, at which point Dr. Moore referred the matter to Secretary of War Seddon for adjudication, adding that hospital employees and detailed men had not been paid since February of 1864, and that keeping "employed Negroes" was becoming difficult.[4] Ultimately, nothing was done.

---

[4] Isaiah H. White, "Report of the sanitary condition of the C.S. military prisons at Camp Sumter and Lawton, Ga., by Surg. Isaiah H. White," n.d. (but undoubtedly early November

This bureaucratic exchange is representative of much of the correspondence between Confederate prison administrators and the Quartermaster General's Office (of which Northrop was a part) in 1864—insistent, even desperate requests from the field followed by protestations in Richmond that everything that could be done was being done, endorsed three, four or five times by officials in various departments, and then filed. It is a tragedy that Sanders has documented with an unsparing eye.

The treatment of Union and Confederate POWs by their respective captors may also have been influenced by mutual reports of maltreatment. Although there is no evidence of retaliatory abuse of POWs at Camp Lawton, the difficulties experienced by prison authorities in acquiring money, supplies, materials, and rations may very well have been exacerbated by such thinking at the higher echelons of the Confederate government. In the final chapter ("The Real Cause of the Suffering") of *While in the Hands of the Enemy*, Sanders argues persuasively that in the case of Southern military prisons sufficient food was available to feed both the Confederate armed forces and their Union prisoners.[5] Moreover, his indictment is even broader. He concludes that, "the roots of Civil War prisoners' suffering and death [North and South] lay in decisions and directives that were deliberately chosen and implemented by Union and Confederate leaders."[6] Therefore, personal shortcomings, neglectful attitudes, and bureaucratic defensiveness among prison and government administrators proved to be a particularly deadly combination as far as both Federal and Confederate POWs were concerned.

Given these considerations, when all is said and done, what does the story of Camp Lawton tell us? The prison had been in operation for only six weeks, and its construction had taken little longer. Yet, in that

---

1864), *Official Records*, series 2, vol. 7, 1,130; S.P. Moore to L. B. Northrop, 15 November 1864, *Official Records*, series 2, vol. 7, 1,130; L.B. Northrop to S.P. Moore, 18 November 1864, *Official Records*, series 2, vol. 7, 1,131; S.P. Moore to Seddon, 20 November 1864, *Official Records*, series 2, vol. 7, 1,131. See also, similar correspondence in *Official Records*, series 2, vol. 7, 1,137–38.

[5] Sanders, *While in the Hands of the Enemy*, 300–01.

[6] Ibid., 298.

brief time span its history presents a microcosm of almost every facet of the Civil War military prison experience. Camp Lawton represented an effort on the part of the Confederate government with its dwindling resources that had the potential to alleviate the problems of Andersonville—overcrowding, lack of water, inadequate diet, poor sanitation, and the resulting horrific death rate. In its design and operation Camp Lawton was successful in alleviating the problem of overcrowding. According to General Winder the prison could hold up to 40,000 POWs. The only official census of 8 November 1864 reported an inmate population of 10,299, and POW diary accounts mention camp populations ranging from 6,000 to 10,000. Thus, the combination of prison size and inmate population combined to make conditions in the camp much more tolerable than those at Camp Sumter. Another factor, however, must be included in this discussion and that is the fact that the POWs at Camp Sumter were dispersed in the fall of 1864, not only to Camp Lawton but to other sites, as well—Charleston, Columbia, Savannah, and Florence. Others were exchanged.

The vastly superior water supply at Camp Lawton, both in quantity and quality, is a common feature reported in both the diary accounts of POWs and the observations of Sherman's troops who visited the camp. The flow and quantity of water deriving from the large spring outside the stockade made the sanitation situation an improvement over that of Camp Sumter. Because the camp builders had dammed the stream and diverted the overflow into a hand-dug channel downstream, the upper portion of the stream was reserved for drinking and washing purposes and the overflow could flush the latrines on the other end. Apparently, also, there were no camp facilities upstream of the stockade to pollute the water before it entered the camp, as had been the case at Camp Sumter. Numerous POW accounts used the term "clean" to describe Camp Lawton. However, the location of hospital facilities downstream for both guards and POWs was problematic.

Because many of the POWs brought into Camp Lawton were in poor health, prisoners continued to die. Although the worst cases of illness were left at Camp Sumter (mainly those who were not ambulatory), the health of many Union prisoners was already severely compromised by the fact that they had been at Andersonville for some time. Long-term malnourishment with the accompanying problems of scurvy and dysentery predisposed many to an imminent death. In fact, diary accounts mention that some prisoners died during transport and, although conditions at Camp Lawton were measurably better in terms of square footage per prisoner, water supply, and (at least initially) food supply, the continued lack of medicines rendered those who were already diseased more likely to succumb to their illnesses and handicapped camp doctors in their efforts to arrest their symptoms. As was the case with battlefield casualties, Civil War POWs on both sides had to hope that their immune systems could cope with the debilitating conditions to which they were exposed. Included in these factors was the wet, colder weather coinciding with the onset of fall. Thomas Aldrich summed up what many Camp Lawton POWs probably felt:

> I suffered terribly at Millen, and if I had not had an Iron Constitution, and taken an oath that they should not kill me I should have given up and died, but the thought of getting out and returning to my Regt. and having a chance to get revenge kept up my courage, and I would not give up, but we buried poor fellows all along our line of travel, and there are hundreds buried that there was never a record or account kept of.[7]

As for the food supply at Camp Lawton, the balance of POW accounts indicates that initially the diet was improved in quantity and quality over that of Camp Sumter. The local slaughterhouse, where POWs experienced in butchering could work on parole, provided a welcome source of protein that had been sorely lacking at Camp Sumter. In addition, the availability of sweet potatoes augmented the diet and helped reduce the symptoms of POWs with scurvy. The distribution system for rations seems to have been improved even if it were only because of the reduced numbers of POWs. However, POW testimony indicates that the quantity of food diminished as time went on. One can conclude, therefore, that the quality of rations at Camp Lawton was improved by its variety, but the quantity continued to be insufficient.

The death rate at Camp Lawton, as previously discussed, is impossible to calculate precisely. Because of the loss of the prison's

---

[7] Thomas R. Aldrich, Unpublished Memoir (courtesy of Patricia Wilcox of Fairport, New York) 31–32.

records, there is no daily census during the time of its operation, nor is there a precise number of deaths. However, if we assume a death total of 725 and the figure of 10,299 as the highest camp population, one arrives at a mortality rate of seven percent (total number of deaths divided by total number of POWs). These numbers are simply statistical guesses because both the numbers of POWs and the numbers of deaths are questionable. However, this calculation leaves a death rate (using the same formula as above) far lower than that of Camp Sumter (28 percent). The data indicate that the reduced mortality rate at Camp Lawton as compared to Camp Sumter was a function of several factors—less crowded conditions, marginally better rations, superior water supply, and improved sanitation. And this was in spite of the reality of a POW population that included many with weakened constitutions.

From a design and operational point of view, Camp Lawton was a new, revised version of Camp Sumter. That it was an improved version is demonstrated both by the memoirs of POWs and the mortality statistics as can be best reconstructed. Its physical advantages included better sanitation, a superior water supply, and solid (as opposed to swampy) ground. It is also true that Confederate authorities did not supply weatherproof housing. Since two lumber mills were virtually on site (Perkins and Hack's mills), one wonders why local authorities could not secure lumber for POW housing within the stockade? After all, in February of 1865, lumber was being purchased and received at Camp Sumter by Quartermaster Captain Varnedoe from the Perkins Lumber Company for construction at that prison.[8] Adequate rations and medical supplies were not provided either, but the experience of Northern military prisons demonstrated that shelter, food, and medical treatment were not panaceas in reducing the death rate among POWs.

The brief existence of the prison is also reflective of the abilities and disabilities of the Confederacy during its last days. Transportation and communications systems were still working, if barely. POWs could be brought into camp and removed when necessary, but medicines, clothing, and adequate shelter could not be provided. Dissension within

---

[8] Captain L.S. Varnedoe to Messrs. Perkins, 5 February 1865, Sheppard E. Perkins' Papers, Emory University, Manuscript Archives and Rare Book Library.

the Confederacy was reflected in General Howell Cobb's opposition to the camp's construction and in the fact that in order to build the camp Confederate authorities had to resort to impressment, or the threat of it, to obtain the necessary labor force. Moreover, correspondence received in Richmond regarding the camp's construction reveals a people divided on what to do with POWs, where to locate the prisons, and how to guard them.

Historical judgments, however, are very tricky, especially when dealing with men acting in urgent circumstances within the context of a war of survival. Much as has been made of the "gentlemanly" conduct of soldiers in the American Civil War, but cruel and even beastly behavior was not unknown. Warfare has a way of bringing out the best and the worst in its participants, and the POW experience was no exception. What rendered POWs so vulnerable was that they were in the hands and control of their enemy by whom they had also been demonized. Facing an enemy on the battlefield with equivalent weaponry was one thing; capturing and then holding a vanquished and disarmed enemy was another. It was difficult for soldiers who had been in mortal combat and who had seen comrades killed and maimed to turn off raw emotions when dealing with a captured enemy. The captive could become the face of those transgressions, real or imagined. As human beings we must fight this tendency but, at the same time, we must recognize its pull on our emotions. Imprisonment of the enemy took on a broader dimension than mere capture, one that included punishment for being on the "wrong" side, as well as the need by the captor to demonstrate the superiority of the victor and the corresponding inferiority of the vanquished. POWs, then, became *untermenschen* in the eyes of their captors.

All of these factors affected the Civil War POW story and help explain why, when faced with the pressure of making decisions in a rapidly moving and deadly contest, administrators, both North and South, often placed POW interests at the lowest priority level with tragic consequences. On the one hand, if the resources and transportation capability were insufficient to feed adequately the military, civilians, and POWs in a war for survival, one can understand that the needs of the

POWs would be given lesser consideration. On the other hand, the demands of humanity called for equity.

Even if, as Sanders argues, the Confederacy had the resources to do better for the POWs, neither the urgency of the situation nor the will to deal with it was much in evidence at the higher echelons. To be sure, the North, which clearly had the capacity and means of adequately supplying captured Confederates, also fell short of the mark. Truly, this was an American tragedy, but this was not an experience unique to our Civil War. It resonates across the history of the wars of humankind.

POWs were not the only ones to suffer and die in and around Camp Lawton. Military service took a toll on camp guards; and skirmishes, ambushes, and sickness took the lives of members of Union and Confederate units that traversed the region. Following the war, the bodies of Union dead who had fallen in the area would be collected and placed in newly established national cemeteries such as Lawton National Cemetery. And then there were the local boys. Some of those who enthusiastically left Burke County for the front to great fanfare and with well wishes would never return. Others would be brought back as corpses to receive somber and mournful receptions as their families memorialized them. Indeed, more than 100 soldiers from Burke County died in the war, and numbers of others served time as POWs in Union prisons.[9] The survivors would eventually come home in defeat. Their world would never be quite the same, and the struggle to adjust to their new environment would occupy them for the rest of their lives.

For at least one family in the area, however, the war brought real opportunity. In 1858, the Perkins family had purchased Spring Mill, located downstream from where Camp Lawton was to be. During the war they ran a lucrative business supplying the Confederate government and the railroads with lumber. Undoubtedly, given the mill's proximity to Camp Lawton, it must have supplied some of the finished lumber for its operation. After the war, with rebuilding and economic expansion stimulating the demand for wood products, their lumber business expanded into the manufacturing arena, and with headquarters in

---

[9] Albert M. Hillhouse, *A History of Burke County, Georgia: 1777–1950* (Jointly published by Swainsboro GA: Magnolia Press, 1985, and Spartanburg SC: Reprint Co., 1985) 315–24.

Augusta, it became the largest timber products operation in the Southeast.[10]

Nor did things return to "normal" for the majority of the population of Burke County—the slaves—some of whom ironically helped construct Camp Lawton to imprison those whose cause would ultimately lead to their liberation. For the slaves, as for their white counterparts, the war portended huge changes. Some of those changes, such as the full impact of emancipation, were only gradually realized; others, such as the shattering of the labor system, came more rapidly. Virtually everything we know about the great, anonymous mass of slaves in this period stems from the reports of others.[11] The almost-universal testimony of Sherman's bummers is that the slave population, to the consternation of their masters, saw the coming of the blue-coated columns as a millennial event, one that would change things forever. People generally react to great events as they perceive them within the narrower context of their lives. Slaves were no different. For them, the advent of Sherman's men had little to do with tariff levels, differential freight rates, or states' rights, but it had everything to do with freedom—their freedom. Many of them, in fact, assisted Federal forces in ferreting out items hidden by the planters. Obviously, fear often played a role in this, but so did a willingness to assist those whom they saw as liberating them. Sadly, their "liberators" were often guilty of abusing them, exploiting their labor, and stealing their possessions as well. In looking ahead, unfortunately, the initial exhilaration of freedom was most often diluted by the reality of conditions in the postwar South. Chattel slavery was gone, yes, only to be replaced by the social, economic, and political strictures of Jim Crow as the nineteenth century wore on.

Nonetheless, thousands of Georgia slaves with high hopes but uncertain prospects voted with their feet and joined large refugee columns following the track of Sherman's army. Many would never be heard from again. There are black families in the area who descend from

---

[10] Donald E. Perkins, *History of the Perkins Family of Perkins, Georgia* (Atlanta: Privately printed, 1979) 185–87.

[11] John W. Blassingame, *The Slave Community: Plantation Life in the Antebellum South* (New York: Oxford University Press, 1972) provides an interesting discussion of the stereotyping of slave behavior by Southern antebellum writers.

the slaves of that era who carry oral traditions of family members who followed the Union troops and never returned. For the soon-to-be freedmen, the long march to freedom, citizenship, education, and opportunity had just begun. Whatever their masters may have thought, the slaves saw the advent of Sherman's men in East Central Georgia as the beginning of a new, hopeful era.[12]

Within such a context, sincere memorialists of the "late unpleasantness" might look askance at the recreational venue that Magnolia Springs has become. After all, for the inmates and guards at Camp Lawton, the events in the shallow valley north of Millen involved many of the elements of suffering—separation, loss, privation, defeat, illness, and death. Perhaps, however, the ground that once teemed with thousands of Union prisoners and their Confederate guards has been and continues to be redeemed in a sense through the happy memories of later generations who have enjoyed the recreational facilities at Magnolia Springs State Park. Indeed, today's patrons know the park much more for its swimming, camping, picnicking, fishing, and other recreational activities than for either its Civil War history or Civilian Conservation Corps past.

Within the park all that remains of the "largest prison camp in the world" are three earthworks—on the south ridge overlooking the site of the camp—and an artificial channel that may have been the camp's latrine ditch. All other man-made signs of Camp Lawton are gone, but the spring still flows into the stream that runs through the small valley. Fish, turtles, and alligators ply the waterway; and waterfowl are commonly seen. Trees have reclaimed most of the once-cleared site, and one can see the remains of huge pine trees that grew up after the war,

---

[12] Slaves who left the plantations in the train of Sherman's columns saw themselves as running for freedom, but their masters considered them guilty of the crime of "self-theft," which at the very least deserved spiritual censure. (Karolyn Smardz Frost, *I've Got a Home in Gloryland: A Lost Tale of the Underground Railroad* [New York: Farrar, Straus and Giroux, 2008], 233.) This latter attitude is reflected in the March 1865 minutes of Elam Baptist Church in neighboring Emanuel County where "Hannah … and Rhoda … were excluded for 'departing from her home and master and go [sic] off with the common enemy of the state." "Elam Baptist Church: Extracts from Church Minutes," *Collections of the Emanuel Historic Preservation Society*, ed. James Dorsey (Swainsboro GA: Emanuel Historic Preservation Society, 1981) 74.

matured to live long lives, and then died, leaving depressions where their stumps had been. In recent years historical markers, a gazebo with illustrations of the camp, a walking trail, and a small museum have been established to inform visitors of the little-known story of Camp Lawton. In the small clapboard park office, patrons are offered a brochure summarizing the history of the prison, and a couple of books of collected sources for the camp are available for purchase.[13] Visitors listen as park personnel interpret the natural and human histories of Magnolia Springs. The Sons of Confederate Veterans annually run a week-long "heritage" camp for children at the site. At irregular intervals newspapers in Atlanta, Augusta, Savannah, Millen, and Waynesboro have carried short articles about Camp Lawton—upon discovery of a local diary that mentioned the prison or when the state has conducted archaeological investigations of the grounds, for example.[14] The most recent archaeological examination of Camp Lawton was initiated in January of 2010 under the auspices of Georgia Southern University in collaboration with the Georgia Department of Natural Resources and the US Fish and Wildlife Service, as a graduate research project, and is ongoing at this time. East of the park the railroad that served the camp still connects Millen with Augusta and runs along the same roadbed, but its cargoes are commercial and no longer human, and no connection between it and the old prison site exists. The depot where POWs were loaded and off-loaded has long since disappeared. After the war the prison's memory lived on in the eponymous name of a rural community of about 200 people that existed along that railroad east of the prison site. In addition to homes, churches, a post office, an academy, and a couple of stores, Lawtonville featured a railroad depot, and the activities of the community were dutifully recorded in a column of "happenings" published weekly in the Waynesboro *True Citizen*.[15] The railroad that had

---

[13] Giles, *Disease, Starvation & Death*, and *"The World's Largest Prison": A Camp Lawton Compendium* (Magnolia Springs State Park GA: Café Press, 2004).

[14] For example, Mike Toner, "Clues Found to Civil War Prison Site: Radar Images May Help Pinpoint Little-known Camp," *Atlanta Journal-Constitution*, 20 February 2007.

[15] *Herndon and Lawtonville: A Collection of Newspaper Sources, 1883–1900* in *Occasional Studies in Sandhill History*, compiled by James E. Dorsey (Swainsboro GA: Emanuel County

once transported Union POWs now carried festive passengers on day trips to the beach on Tybee Island near Savannah. A community cemetery was located across the railroad from the prison site. Located east of the railroad and fronting the Old Perkins Road, the unkempt cemetery today is bordered by a ramshackle fence, an old identifying marker, and a few scattered, neglected burials. The condition of the cemetery is symbolic because Lawtonville died in the twentieth century and, like many rural communities, it exists today only as a place name and as a faint memory of older residents.

Across the divide of nearly a century and a half, Burke and Jenkins counties have remained essentially rural in nature. Both county seats— Waynesboro and Millen, respectively—have grown but remain small towns. The railroad junction that attracted both Confederate and Union forces to Millen is still active in connecting Savannah, Macon, and Augusta, and freight trains remain a frequent sight. The economy of the region is more diverse today, but agriculture continues to predominate. Cotton is still widely cultivated, but soybeans, peanuts, corn, wheat, livestock, and pine trees add to the mix of commercial agricultural enterprises. Some of the old plantation holdings continue to exist (in some cases in the hands of the original families), but many of the old estates are no longer intact. Burke County, in particular, is noted for hunting preserves and field trials for bird dogs, and many who live in the area work in the growing Augusta metropolitan region. Plant Vogtle, a nuclear power plant near Waynesboro, adds a modern, cutting edge aspect to the county.

The road network is much changed from 1864. Sherman's forces traversed terrain that was marked with dirt roads, some of which were old, well-traveled thoroughfares running from the coast to the interior of Georgia but others of which were simple farm roads. With the advent of automobiles and trucks and all-weather roads, highways were re-engineered and often deviated significantly from the paths of the Civil War-era routes. However, a few dirt roads in the area are so little changed that they are among the best preserved of any of the Georgia

---

Junior College Library, 1980). The vibrancy of the small community of Lawtonville is very evident in these columns; Hillhouse, *History of Burke County*, 283.

roads along which Sherman's soldiers marched.[16] Across the region historical markers placed by the state over the years encapsulate Civil War history by locating for the traveler places of significance related to the Union and Confederate operations in the area. Recently, new markers placed by the Georgia Civil War Heritage Trails initiative are complimenting existing markers and highlighting the history of the war for a new generation of "heritage" travelers.

Today, Magnolia Springs is a beautiful and popular recreational area complete with rustic cabins, a swimming pool, a lake, numerous picnic sheds, a playground, an aquarium, a museum, and nature trails. The native flora and fauna are profuse. The happy murmurs of family reunions, the fellowship of church groups, the excited splashing of swimmers, and the innocent laughter of children echo across the valley floor; but, history also makes us pause to realize that long ago something quite different was witnessed here, something that makes the park much more than a recreational area. It is, in fact, "hallowed ground."

---

[16] A very good example of this is the crossroads at Birdsville Plantation in Burke County. The dirt intersection is not only intact, but it is also lined in all four directions with live oaks. The plantation house, the core of which was built in the eighteenth century, and by which Union units marched, still stands as do a number of outbuildings. The house and a portion of the land are still owned by descendents of the original family. Medora Field Perkerson's classic *White Columns in Georgia* (New York: Bonanza, 1952) contains a description of this historic home along with its connection to Sherman's March.

Appendix

Robert Knox Sneden as a Source for
the History of Camp Lawton

In 1994, a series of events began to unfold that were to enrich and challenge our understanding of the story of Camp Lawton.[1] The discovery of Union veteran Robert Knox Sneden's diary and its accompanying collection of a thousand, personally drawn illustrations opened up a fascinating new portal through which to view the Civil War. For the purposes of this study, the publication of the Sneden materials by the Virginia Historical Society was extremely significant because he had been an inmate at Camp Lawton, his diary entries covered the time he had spent there, and the illustrations contained several never-before-seen views of the compound. Heretofore, the only known representations of Camp Lawton were the rudimentary map submitted by Winder to the Confederate government, the four depictions (two each) in *Harper's Weekly* and *Frank Leslie's Illustrated Newspaper*, and the scattered illustrations in various POW accounts. Unlike Camp Sumter, Camp Lawton is thought not to have been photographed.[2] Prior to the discovery of the Sneden collection, the above-mentioned illustrations had been carefully examined, with their contradictions duly noted, and compared with the primary sources for the history of the prison. That analysis left many unanswered questions. The Sneden collection, however, contained annotated color maps of the prison and its ancillary facilities, several general scenes of the interior and exterior of the stockade, and detailed drawings of camp life.

---

[1] The story of the rediscovery of the Sneden collection and the basic facts of Sneden's life can be found at the Virginia Historical Society's Web site (www.vahistorical.org).

[2] Intriguingly, however, the famous Civil War photographer George N. Barnard, who traveled with Sherman's forces, visited Camp Lawton according to an article published on 7 January 1865 in *Harper's Weekly* 9, no. 419:6. Barnard photographed the Atlanta campaign and locations in and around Savannah but, apparently, took no photographs in between.

Sneden's materials have enlightened us and challenged our understanding of Camp Lawton, but they have not brought the story to an end. While helping us to answer some questions, the material has posed new ones. Sneden's drawings contradict several aspects of Camp Lawton that we thought we knew. For example, he consistently portrays the stockade as rectangular in shape rather than almost square as Winder's plan of the prison indicates and as several eyewitness accounts state. At least one of his drawings of Camp Sumter provides a parallel example. Although he typically drew maps of Camp Sumter that accurately showed the stockade as being rectangular with the stream running on an east-west axis bisecting the long walls, he has at least one drawing of the prison that has the stockade turned 90 degrees from its actual orientation so that the stream bisects the short walls.[3] Ultimately, only archaeology will settle this issue. As mentioned previously, he shows the large earthen fort on the ridge to the south of the stockade as irregularly shaped with a sally port on the opposite side of the prison, whereas the extant remains are pentagonal with a sally port facing the log walls of the stockade. None of his maps indicate a clearly delineated spring (Magnolia Springs) outside the stockade walls, even though Winder's map shows it distinctly, and POW accounts refer to it often. His maps also show another stream near the site to the south, running parallel to Mill Spring, but today such a stream does not exist, and it is difficult to determine if it ever did. Also, his drawings do not show a separate latrine channel as Winder's map does and POW accounts mention. Furthermore, his various maps of Camp Lawton differ from each other in some details. In addition, he provides higher numbers of prisoner deaths than typically have been reported.

How then should we deal with these problems and contradictions? In the first place one should recognize, short of conclusive archeological findings, contemporary photographs, or other documentary discoveries, that many things about Camp Lawton will never be finally determined. This study has attempted to treat each issue involving Sneden's

---

[3] William J. Miller and Brian C. Pohanka, *The Illustrated History of the Civil War: Images of an American Tragedy* (Alexandria VA: Time-Life, 2000) 352.

depictions of Camp Lawton on its own merits; however, his materials should be evaluated with two general considerations in mind.

First, Sneden says in his diary that he signed a parole and was given the job of assisting Dr. Isaiah White, chief of the medical staff at Camp Lawton. Therefore, he lived outside the stockade and was given access to areas outside of the camp. However, it was not absolute free reign because he himself says in his diary that he was refused entry to the fort on the ridge.[4] Perhaps his rendering of the defensive fortifications around the stockade was based on his view from some distance and, not being able to see them in their entirety, he drew them as they appeared to him but not necessarily as they really were. Perhaps this observation holds true for the large spring, as well. Since he claims he kept the death register for the camp, his sphere of operations seems to have centered around the stockade, the hospital for prisoners, and the prison administrative buildings.

Second, he says that he surreptitiously made sketches while in the Confederate prisons. How complete were these sketches, and when did he complete them? His diary tells us that he found drawing materials wherever he could and used all sorts of scraps of paper to make his sketches. He kept his sketches sewn into his prison clothes to avoid detection.[5] Therefore, his paintings were obviously done later, using the sketches and his memory to complete them. The question remains: How much later were they completed? Also, Sneden was incarcerated in several Confederate prisons after his capture in the late fall of 1863, at least four of which were stockades—Andersonville, Savannah, Millen, and Florence. Each of those prisons shared similarities, but each differed in detail. The passage of time and the frailty of human memory probably affected Sneden as he filled in the details and annotated his paintings from the hasty, incomplete sketches he made years before.

Sneden's illustrations and diary are an important addition to the sources we have for the Civil War. As far as the history of Camp Lawton is concerned, their overriding significance lies in the interest their

---

[4] Sneden, *Eye of the Storm: A Civil War Odyssey*, ed. Charles F. Bryan, Jr., and Nelson D. Lankford (New York: The Free Press, 2000) 269.

[5] Ibid., 268.

publication stimulated as well as the clues they provide for archeological exploration. However, as with any source material they should not be used uncritically.

Bibliography

Primary Sources

Aldrich, Thomas R. Unpublished Memoir. Courtesy of Patricia Wilcox, Fairport, New York.

Anderson, Edward C. Papers #3602. Southern Historical Collection. The Wilson Library, University of North Carolina at Chapel Hill. 6:121–28, 132–33

Anonymous. *A Voice from Rebel Prisons Giving an Account of Some of the Horrors of the Stockades at Andersonville, Milan and Other Prisons by a Returned Prisoner of War*. Boston: Rand & Avery, 1865.

Atlanta Journal-Constitution

Barber, Lucius W. *Army Memoirs of Lucius W. Barber, Company "D," 15th Illinois Volunteer Infantry. May 24, 1861, to Sept. 30, 1865*. Chicago: The J.M.W. Jones Stationery and Printing Co., 1894.

Bark Camp Church. 1859 returns. Minutes of the Hephzibah Baptist Association of Georgia. Georgia Baptist Historical Society. Stetson Memorial Library, Mercer University, Macon, Georgia.

Barnard, George N. *Photographic Views of Sherman's Campaign*. New York: Press of Wynkoop and Hallenbeck, 1866.

Bartleson, John Wool, "Memoirs of John Wool Bartleson as Transcribed and Edited by Tweed Ross." *Eye on Kansas: An Online Magazine About What Makes Kansas Our Home*. Chapter Two: Part Three, Freedom and Home! http://eyeonKansas.org/ncentral/riley/bartleson_biography/0802chaptertwo-partthree.html (accessed 15 July 2010).

Beach, Riley V. "Recollections and Extracts from the Diaries of Army Life of the Rev. Riley V. Beach of Co. 'B' 113 Ills. Inft, Vols." Typescript copy courtesy of Terry McCarty, Georgetown, Texas.

Benson, Jane. "Muster Roll of Company A," http://www.angelfire.com/tx/RandysTexas/casreserve1/page4.html (accessed 2 May 2010).

Bradley, George S. *The Star Corps or Notes of an Army Chaplain During Sherman's Famous "March to the Sea."* Milwaukee WI: Jermain & Brightman, 1865.

Brant, J.E. *History of the Eighty-Fifth Indiana Volunteer Infantry: Its Organization, Campaigns and Battles*. Bloomington IN: Cravens Bros., Printers and Binders, 1902.

Brock, R.A., ed. *Virginia and Virginians*. Richmond VA, and Toledo OH: H.H. Hardesty, Publishers, 1888.

Brockman, Charles J., Jr. "The John Van Duser Diary of Sherman's March from Atlanta to Hilton Head." *Georgia Historical Quarterly* 6, no. 53 (1969): 220–39.

Bull, Rice C. *Soldiering: The Civil War Diary of Rice C. Bull*. Edited by Jack Bauer. Novato CA: Presidio Press, 1986.

Cain, John. "John Cain's Andersonville Testimony,"
http://2Mass.omnica.com/References/cains_andersonville.htm (accessed 10 May 2009).

Candler, Allen D., ed. *The Confederate Records of the State of Georgia Compiled and Published under Authority of the Legislature.* Vol. 2. Atlanta: Chas. P. Byrd, State Printer, 1908.

Carter, Doug. File on Third Georgia Reserve Infantry Regiment,
http://files.usgwarchives.net.ga/military/civilwar/rosterss/3rdreserve.txt (accessed 5 October 2009).

Columbus Daily Sun (Georgia).

Confederate States of America. War Department. *Special Orders. Adjutant and Inspector General's Office. Confederate States.* Richmond VA, 1864.

Craham, P. *The National Tribune,* 16 May 1907.

Cunningham, George A., to Mollie Cunningham, 20 November 1864. Cunningham Family Papers. MS 2679. Hargrett Manuscripts. The University of Georgia Libraries. Athens, Georgia.

Daily Chronicle and Sentinel (Augusta).

Daily Morning News (Savannah).

Darling, Marcellus Warner B. "Events and Comments of My Life." Unknown publisher, n.d.

Darling, Marcellus Warner B. Letter of 16 December 1864. Courtesy of Mark H. Dunkelman, Providence, Rhode Island.

Davidson, Henry. *Fourteen Months in Southern Prisons.* Milwaukee: Daily Wisconsin Printing House, 1865.

Davis, Jefferson. *Andersonville and Other Civil War Prisons.* New York: Belford Company, Publishers, 1890.

Davis, Samuel B. *Escape of a Confederate Officer from Prison: What He Saw at Andersonville, How He Was Sentenced to Death and Saved by the Interposition of President Abraham Lincoln.* Norfolk VA: Landmark Publishing Company, 1892.

Dempsey, P. Letter to Mrs. Van Deusen, n.d, MSC 17698. New York State Archives. New York State Education Department, Cultural Education Center, Albany, New York.

Dennison, James H. *Dennison's Andersonville Diary: The Diary of an Illinois Soldier in the Infamous Andersonville Prison Camp.* Notes and transcription by Jack Klasey. Kankakee IL: Kankakee County Historical Society, 1987.

Derden, John K., to Superintendent, National Cemetery at Beaufort, 20 April 1977. Author is in possession of copy of the original.

Dorsey, James, editor. "Elam Baptist Church: Extracts from Church Minutes." *Collections of the Emanuel Historic Preservation Society.* Swainsboro GA: Emanuel Historic Preservation Society, 1981.

Downing, Alexander G. *Downing's Civil War Diary: August 15, 1861–July 1, 1865.* Edited by Olynthus B. Clark. Des Moines: The Historical Department of Iowa, 1916.

Driener, John F. "A Story of Prison Life." In *The War of the 'Sixties.* Complied by E.R. Hutchins. New York: Neale Publishing Company, 1912.

Duncan, William. "The Army of the Tennessee Under Major-General O.O. Howard." In *Glimpses of the Nation's Struggle. Fourth Series. Papers Read Before the Minnesota*

Commandery of the Military Order of the Loyal Legion of the United States, 1892–1897. Vol. 4. St. Paul MO: H.L. Collins Co., 1898.

Farabee, Allen G., to James [*sic*] K. Derden, 21 April 1977. Author is in possession of the original.

Frazer, C.A. "Marion County Prisoner of Rebels Kept Diary in Andersonville Prison," http://www.stkusers.com/lindas/jesse.html (accessed 24 August 2008).

Felton, Rebecca Latimer. *Country Life in Georgia in the Days of My Youth.* Atlanta: Index Printing Company, 1919.

Ferris, Weston. "Prison Life of Weston Ferris." In *"The World's Largest Prison:" A Camp Lawton Compendium.* Edited by William Giles. Magnolia Springs State Park GA: Café Press, 2004.

Frank Leslie's Illustrated Newspaper.

Free Lance (pseud). "Southern Prison Life." *The National Tribune,* 9–23 September 1882.

Glazier, Willard W. *The Capture, the Prison-Pen, and the Escape, Giving a Complete History of Prison Life in the South, Principally at Richmond, Danville, Macon, Savannah, Charleston, Columbia, Belle Isle, Millen, Salisbury, and Andersonville: Describing the Arrival of Prisoners, Plans of Escape, with Numerous and Varied Incidents and Anecdotes of Prison Life; Embracing, Also, the Adventures of the Author's Escape from Columbia, South Carolina, Recapture, Subsequent Escape, Recapture, Trial as a Spy, and Final Escape from Sylvania, Georgia.* Hartford CT: H.E. Goodwin, Publisher, 1869.

Harmon, Henry A. "A Year in Six Rebel Prisons." Part I. *The National Tribune.* 1 June 1893.

Harmon, Henry A. "Memoirs of Henry A. Harmon." In *"The World's Largest Prison:" A Camp Lawton Compendium.* Edited by William Giles. Magnolia Springs State Park GA: Café Press, 2004.

Harper, F. Mikell. *Catharine of Ivanhoe: The Civil War Journal of Catharine Whitehead Rowland of Augusta and Burke County, Georgia, with Letters from Her Husband, Charles Alden Rowland.* Macon GA: Indigo Publishing Group, 2008.

Harper's Weekly: A Journal of Civilization.

Harris, H.C. Letter, 27 October 1864. Digital Scan from Collection of Ted Berger, Courtesy Alexander Autographs, Inc., 860 Canal Street, Stamford CT 06702.

Harriss, J.C. Civil War Letter Archive. POW Andersonville. Jordan Carroll Harriss, 81st Illinois Infantry, c. 110 letters, 1862–65, http://www.banksgrandretreat.com/PDF/Harriss%2081st%20Illinois.pdf (accessed 20 December 2009).

Hart, Charles Townsend. Diary Transcript, Andersonville Diary Collection. Andersonville National Historic Site.

Hawes, Jesse. *Cahaba: A Story of Captive Boys in Blue.* New York: Burr Printing House, 1888.

Hawkins, William. Typescript of interview, c. 7–8 August 1880. Edwin D. Northrup Papers, #4190, Departments of Manuscripts and University Archives, Cornell University

Helwig, Simon. *The Capture and Prison Life in Rebeldom for Fourteen Months of Simon Helwig: Late Private Co. F. 51st O.V.I.* Canal Dover OH: Bixler, n.d.

Herndon and Lawtonville: A Collection of Newspaper Sources, 1883–1900. In *Occasional Studies in Sandhill History.* Compiled by James E. Dorsey. Swainsboro GA: Emanuel County Junior College Library, 1980.

Hitchcock, George A. *Ashby to Andersonville: Private George A. Hitchcock's Diary: The Civil War Diary and Reminiscences of George A. Hitchcock, Private, Company A, 21st Massachusetts Regiment, August 1862–January 1865.* Edited by Ronald G. Watson. Campbell CA: Savas Publishing Company, 1997.

Hitchcock, Henry. *Marching With Sherman: Passages from the Letters and Campaign Diaries of Henry Hitchcock, Major and Assistant Adjutant General of Volunteers, November 1864–May 1865.* Edited by M.A. DeWolfe Howe. New Haven CT: Yale University Press, 1927.

Hodgkins, J.E. *The Civil War Diary of Lieut. J. E. Hodgkins: 19th Massachusetts Volunteers from August 11, 1862 to June 3, 1865.* Transcribed by Kenneth C. Turino. Camden ME: Picton Press, 1994.

Holley, Peggy Scott. "The Seventh Tennessee Volunteer Cavalry: West Tennessee Unionists in Andersonville Prison." http://www.stjusers.com/lindas/history.html (accessed 18 August 2008).

Hosmer, Francis J. *A Glimpse of Andersonville and Other Writings.* Springfield MA: Loring and Axtell, 1896.

Howard, Kendrick R. Diary, 8–28 October 1864. Miscellaneous File #696. Vermont Historical Society, Barre, Vermont.

Hurst, Samuel H., ed. *Journal-History of the Seventy-third Ohio Vol. Infantry.* Chilicothe OH: S.H. Hurst, 1866.

Hyde, Solon. *A Captive of War.* New York: McClure, Phillips & Co., 1900.

Isham, Asa B., Henry M. Davidson, and Henry B. Furness. *Prisoners of War and Military Prisons: Personal Narratives of Experience in the Prisons at Richmond, Danville, Macon, Andersonville, Savannah, Millen, Charleston and Columbia.* Cincinnati: Lyman & Cushing, 1890.

Jackson, Oscar L. *The Colonel's Diary.* Sharon PA: n.p., 1922.

Jones, Caroline E. Application of Caroline E. Jones for Pardon under the 13th Exemption, 18 September 1865, http://search.ancestrylibrary.com/Browse/print_u.aspx?dbid=1187&iid=MIUSA1865_113135-00406 (accessed 13 July 2009).

Jones, Caroline E. Loyalty Oath, 5 September 1865, http://search.ancestrylibrary.com/Browse/print_u.aspx?dbid=1187&iid=MIUSA1865_113135-00407 (accessed July 13, 2009).

Jones, Caroline E. Schedule I. Free Inhabitants of the 61st District in the County of Burke State of Georgia. 1860 Census of the United States, 5, http://search.ancestrylibrary.com/iexec/?htx=View&r_5542&dbid=7667&iid=GAM653_1 (accessed 13 July 2009).

Jones, Caroline E. to George B. Hack, 15 July 1866. Deed Book 13. Office of The Probate Judge. Burke County, Georgia.

Jones, Charles C., Jr. *The Siege of Savannah in December, 1864, and the Confederate Operations in Georgia and the Third Military District of South Carolina during General Sherman's March from Atlanta to the Sea.* Albany NY: Joel Munsell, 1874.

Kellogg, Robert H. *Life and Death in Rebel Prisons: Giving a Complete History of the Inhuman and Barbarous Treatment of Our Brave Soldiers by Rebel Authorities, Inflicting Terrible Suffering and Frightful Mortality, Principally at Andersonville, GA., and Florence S.C.,*

Describing Plans of Escape, Arrival of Prisoners with Numerous and Varied Incidents and Anecdotes of Prison Life. Hartford CT: L. Stebbins, 1865.

Kelley, Daniel G. *What I Saw and Suffered in Rebel Prisons.* Buffalo NY: Thomas, Howard & Johnson, 1868.

Kilbourne, Julius B. "The March to the Sea. Kilpatrick's Cavalry on the March through Georgia. A Scout to Millen. An Engagement with Wheeler's Cavalry near Waynesboro. Gallant Saber Charge. A Graceful Act of Courtesy Performed by General Wheeler." *The National Tribune,* 17 May 1883.

Kilpatrick, W.L., to James H. Kilpatrick, 31 December 1864. Courtesy of Lyle Lansdale, 301 E. Poplar Ave., Carrboro, North Carolina. (A typescript copy was given to Mark H. Dunkleman who furnished it to the Burke County Genealogical Society.)

Kilpatrick, W.L. *The Hepzibah Baptist Association Centennial 1794–1894.* Augusta GA: Richards & Shaver, Printers, 1894.

Knox, Charles H. Letter to Mrs. C.H. Knox, 14 November 1864. Southern Museum, Georgia Southern University, Statesboro, GA.

Kurz, Elma S., ed. "The War Diary of Cornelius R. Hanleiter," *The Atlanta Historical Bulletin* 14, no. 3 (September 1969): 29–30.

Latimer, Washington K. Letter of Washington K. Latimer, 14 November 1864. P939. Minnesota Historical Society Archives, St. Paul, Minnesota.

Lightcap, William Henry. *The Horrors of Southern Prisons During the War of the Rebellion, from 1862 to 1865.* Platteville WI: Journal Job Rooms, 1902.

Lincoln, Abraham. "Memorandum Concerning His Probable Failure of Election," 25 August 1864. In *The Collected Works of Abraham Lincoln.* 9 vols. Edited by Roy P. Basler. New Brunswick NJ: Rutgers University Press, 1953–55.

"List of Vermont Troops at Annapolis, MD, Recently Paroled at Savannah, Ga." *Vermont Watchman & State Journal* (Montpelier), 16 December 1864.

"Deaths of Vermont Soldiers in Southern Prisons." *Vermont Watchman & State Journal* (Montpelier), 16 December 1864.

Long, Lessel. *Twelve Months in Andersonville: On the March—In the Battle—In the Rebel Prison Pens, and at Last in God's Country.* Huntington IN: Thad and Mark Butler, Publishers, 1886.

Lyon, W. F. *In and Out of Andersonville Prison.* Detroit: Geo. Harland Co., Publishers, 1905.

McElroy, John. *Andersonville: A Story of Rebel Military Prisons, Fifteen Months a Guest of the So-called Confederacy. A Private Soldier's Experience in Richmond, Andersonville, Savannah, Millen, Blackshear and Florence.* Toledo OH: D.R. Locke, 1879.

McElroy, John. *This Was Andersonville.* Edited by Roy Meredith. New York: Bonanza Books, 1957.

Mauck, Joseph, Diary, 6–8 November 1864. Museum of the Confederacy, Richmond, Virginia, cited in Joslyn, Mauriel Phillips. *Captives Immortal: the Story of Six Hundred Confederate Officers and the United States Prisoner of War Policy.* Shippensburg PA: White Mane Publishing, 1996.

The Martinsburg Herald (West Virginia).

Maury, Dabney H. *Recollections of a Virginian in the Mexican, Indian, and Civil Wars,* 2nd ed. New York: Charles Scribner's Sons, 1894.

Moreno, Theodore. "A Brief History of My Military Career." *Confederate Reminiscences and Letters, 1861–1865*. Atlanta: Georgia Division, United Daughters of the Confederacy, 2001.

Morse, Charles Fessenden. *Letters Written During the Civil War, 1861–1865*. Privately published, 1898.

Mower County Register (Minnesota).

Nichols, George Ward. *The Story of the Great March from the Diary of a Staff Officer*. New York: Harper & Brothers, Publishers, 1865.

Nichols, George Ward. *The Story of the Great March from the Diary of a Staff Officer*. 26th ed. New York: Harper & Brothers, Publishers, 1866.

"149th Regiment, NY Volunteer Infantry Civil War Newspaper Clippings," http://www.dmna.stae.ny.us/historic/reghist/civil/infantry/149thInfCWN.htm (accessed 7 August 2008).

O'Hara, Martin. *Reminiscences of Andersonville and Other Rebel Prisons: A Story of Suffering and Death*. Lyons IA: J.C. Hopkins, Printer, Advertiser Office, 1880.

Oxford Press (Pennsylvania).

Page, James Madison, and M.J. Haley. *The True Story of Andersonville Prison: Defense of Major Henry Wirtz*. Washington: Neale Publishing Company, 1908.

Peterson, Joe "Ida Walimaki Recalls Her Grandfathers' Daring Exploits in the Civil War." *The Issaquah Press*, http://www.issaquahpress.comn/main.asp?SectionID=25&SubSectionID=32&ArticleID=20... (accessed 24 August 2008).

Phillips, Ulrich Bonnell, ed. *The Correspondence of Robert Toombs, Alexander Stephens, and Howell Cobb*. Reprint. New York: DaCapo Press, 1972.

Platter, Cornelius C. "Cornelius C. Platter Diary," Hargrett Library, Digital Library of Georgia, http://dlg.galileo.usg.edu/hargrett/platter/006.php (accessed 9 September 2009).

Ransom, John L. *Andersonville Diary: Escape, and List of Dead with Name, Company, Regiment, Date of Death and Number of Grave in Cemetery*. Philadelphia: Douglas Brothers, 1883.

Ripple, Ezra Hoyt. *Dancing Along the Deadline: The Andersonville Memoir of a Prisoner of the Confederacy*. Edited by Mark A. Snell. Novato CA: Presidio Press, 1996.

Sammons, John H., *Personal Recollections of the Civil War*. Greensburg IN: Montgomery & Son, Printers and Binders, n.d.

Savannah Republican (Georgia).

Schley County News (Georgia).

Shearer, George M. Transcript of 17 November 1864, diary entry of George M. Shearer, provided digitally by the University of Iowa Libraries Special Collections Department, www.lib.uiowa.edu/spec-col/MSC/ToMSC100/MsC80/MsCo80_shearergeorgemarion.html (accessed 24 September 2008).

The Shepherdstown Register (West Virginia).

Sherman, William Tecumseh. *Memoirs of General W.T. Sherman*. 2 volumes. New York: Library of America, 1990.

Sherod, E. Roberts to Kiziah Roberts, 8 November 1861, transcribed by Spessard Stone, Hagan-Roberts Collection, Georgia Department of Archives and History. Atlanta, GA.

Sherwood, Adiel. *A Gazateer of Georgia; Containing a Particular Description of the State; Its Resources, Counties, Towns, Villages, and Whatever is Usual in Statistical Works,* 4th ed. Macon GA: S. Boykin, 1860; Reprint, Atlanta: Cherokee Publishing Company, 1970.

Smith, William B., *On Wheels: and How I Came There: The True Story of a 15-Year-Old Yankee and Prisoner in the American Civil War.* Edited by Stacy M. Haponik. College Station TX: Virtualbookworm.com Publishing, 2002.

Sneden, Robert Knox. *Eye of the Storm: A Civil War Odyssey.* Edited by Charles F. Bryan, Jr., and Nelson D. Lankford. New York: The Free Press, 2000.

Sneden, Robert Knox. *Images from the Storm: 300 Civil War Images by the Author of Eye of the Storm,* Edited by Charles F. Bryan, Jr., James C. Kelly, and Nelson D. Lankford. New York: The Free Press, 2001.

Stevenson, Thomas M. *History of the 78th Regiment O.V.V.I. from Its "Muster-In to Its Muster-Out;" Comprising Its Organization, Marches, Campaigns, Battles and Skirmishes.* Zanesville OH: Hugh Dunne, 1865.

Survivors' Association. *History of the 118th Pennsylvania Volunteers, Corn Exchange Regiment, from Their First Engagement at Antietam to Appomattox.* Philadelphia: J.L. Smith, Map Publisher, 1905.

Tisdale, Henry W. "Civil War Diary of Sergeant Henry W. Tisdale, Co. I, Thirty-fifth Regiment Massachusetts Volunteers," Transcribed by Margaret H. Tisdale, http://www.civilwardiary.net (accessed 12 September 2008).

Tritt, William. Diary. Andersonville Diary Collection, Andersonville National Historic Site. *The True Citizen* (Waynesboro, Georgia).

Umstead, M.J. Diary. Andersonville Diary Collection, Andersonville National Historic Site.

United States Bureau of the Census. *Eighth Census of the United States. Agriculture of the United States in 1860, Compiled from Original Returns of the Eighth Census, under the Direction of the Secretary of the Interior, by Joseph C.G. Kennedy, Superintendent of the Census.* Vol. 2. Washington DC: Government Printing Office, 1864.

United States Christian Commission. *Record of the Federal Dead Buried From Libby, Belle Isle, Danville & Camp Lawton Prisons and at City Point and in the Field before Petersburg and Richmond.* Philadelphia: Jas. B. Rodgers, 1865.

United States. Department of the Army. Quartermaster General's Office. *Roll of Honor. (No. XIV) Names of Soldiers Who Died in Defence of the American Union Interred in the National and Public Cemeteries in Kentucky, and at New Albany, Jeffersonville, and Madison, Indiana; Lawton (Millen), and Andersonville, Georgia, (Supplementary).* Washington DC: Government Printing Office, 1868.

United States. Department of the Army. Quartermaster General's Office. *Roll of Honor (No. XVII) Names of Soldiers Who Died in Defense of the American Union Interred in the National and Public Cemeteries in Kentucky, and at New Albany, Jeffersonville, and Madison, Indiana; Lawton (Millen), and Andersonville, Georgia, (Supplementary).* Washington DC: Government Printing Office, 1868.

United States. Department of the Army. Quartermaster-General's Department, *Statement of the Disposition of Some of the Bodies of Deceased Union Soldiers and Prisoners of War Whose Remains Have Been Moved to National Cemeteries.* 4 vols. Washington DC: Government Printing Office, 1868.

United States. Department of War. *The War of the Rebellion: A Compilation of the Official Records of the Union and Confederate Armies*. 128 vols. Washington DC: Government Printing Office, 1880–1901. Series 1, vols. 44 and 39; series 2, vols. 5–8.

United States. Department of the Army. Quartermaster-General's Office. US Army Military Institute. *Shrines of the Honored Dead: A Study of the National Cemetery System*. Washington DC: Quartermaster-General's Office, n.d.

"U.S. Fish and Wildlife Service to Re-open Bo Ginn National Fish Hatchery," 28 May 2010, http://www.fws.gov/soputheast/news/2010/r10-042.html (accessed 17 July 2010).

United States House of Representatives. 40th Congress, 3rd Session. *Report No. 45: Report on the Treatment of Prisoners of War by the Rebel Authorities During the War of the Rebellion to Which Are Appended the Testimony Taken by the Committee, and the Official Document and Statistics, etc.* Washington DC: Government Printing Office, 1869.

United States. National Archives and Records Administration, Record Groups 77, 92, 109, and 249.

Urban, John W. *Battlefield and Prison Pen, or Through the War, and Thrice a Prisoner in Rebel Dungeons*. Philadelphia: Edgewood Publishing Company, 1882.

Vance, James. "Andersonville Diary of James Vance." Transcribed by Donald A. Huntslar. Collections of the Ohio Historical Society.

Varnedoe, Captain L.S., to Messrs. Perkins, 5 February 1865. Sheppard E. Perkins Papers, 1810–79. Manuscript Archives and Rare Book Library. Emory University, Atlanta, GA.

Vaughter, J.B. *Prison Life in Dixie. Giving a Short History of the Inhuman and Barbarous Treatment of Our Soldiers by Rebel Authorities, by Sergeant Oates*. 3rd ed. Chicago: Central Book Concern, 1881.

Virginia Free Press (Charleston, West Virginia).

Walcott, Charles F. *History of the Twenty-first Regiment, Massachusetts Volunteers in the War for the Preservation of the Union, 1861–1865, with Statistics of the War and Rebel Prisons*. Boston: Houghton, Mifflin and Company, 1882.

Waters, Thaddeus L., *The Terrors of Rebel Prisons by and Old Andersonville Prisoner*. Newaygo MI: E.O. Shaw, Publisher, 1891.

Wayside Home (Millen). Minutes. Georgia Secretary of State. Georgia Department of Archives and History.

W.R. Crites to Ruth Blair, 15 September 1922, Georgia Department of Archives and History.

White, George. *Statistics of the State of Georgia*. Savannah: W. Thorne Williams, 1849.

Whitaker, Levi. Diary Transcription. Andersonville Diaries. Andersonville National Historic Site.

Wilson, Josiah "Diary." Edited by E.D. Wilson, http://home.houston.rr.com/heartofdixie/1stCav.html (accessed 23 July 2008).

Yeakle, Amos E. Diary Transcription. Andersonville Diaries. Andersonville National Historic Site.

Secondary Sources

"Andersonville: Prisoner of War Camp." Teaching with Historic Places Lesson Plans, National Park Service. http://www.nps.gov/history?NR/twhp?wwwlps/lessons/11andersonville/11facts1h tm (accessed 18 September 2008).

Bailey, Anne. *War and Ruin: William T. Sherman and the Savannah Campaign*. Wilmington, DE: SR Books, 2002.

Bennett, Deborah. "Possible Remnant of Camp Lawton Unearthed in Dig." *The Millen News*, 7 February 2007, 1.

Black, Robert C., Jr. *The Railroads of the Confederacy*. Reprint. Wilmington NC: Broadfoot Publishing, 1987.

Blakey, Arch Frederic. *General John H. Winder, C.S.A.* Gainesville: University of Florida Press, 1990.

Blassingame, John W. *The Slave Community: Plantation Life in the Antebellum South*. New York: Oxford University Press, 1972.

Bollet, Alfred Jay. *Civil War Medicine—Challenges and Triumphs*. Tucson AZ: Galen Press, 2002.

Brannen, Edmund. "Magnolia Springs State Park—Jenkins County's Playground; Once Site of World's Largest Prison Camp." *The Millen News*, 24 September 1955, section C, 1.

Bryan, T. Conn. *Confederate Georgia*. Athens: University of Georgia Press, 1953.

"Camp Lawton." http://www.georgiasouthern.edu/camplawton (accessed 1 October 2010).

"Camp Lawton." Special First Edition. Georgia Southern University and Georgia Department of Natural Resources, 18 August 2010.

Carpenter, Kenneth J. *The History of Scurvy and Vitamin C*. Cambridge: Cambridge University Press, 1988.

"Casualties and Costs of the Civil War." Civil War, Digital History. http://www.digitalhistory.uh.edu/historyonline/us20.cfm (accessed 19 November 2009).

Chapman, James Kevin. "Comparison of Archeological Survey Techniques at Camp Lawton, a Civil War Prison Stockade." MA thesis, Georgia Southern University, 2012.

Civil War Records of Sebastian Glamser. Translated by Nina J. Raeth. June 2010.

Cloyd, Benjamin G. *Haunted by Atrocity: Civil War Prisons in American Memory*. Baton Rouge: Louisiana State University Press, 2010.

Cohen, Stan. *Tree Army: A Pictorial History of the Civilian Conservation Corps, 1933–1942*. Revised edition. Missoula MT: Pictorial Histories Publishing, 1980.

Cole, Gerald. *Civil War Eyewitnesses: An Annotated Bibliography of Books and Articles 1986–1996*. Columbia: University of South Carolina Press, 2000.

"Confederate Colonel Henry Forno." http://aotw/officers.php?officer_id=759 (accessed 14 July 2009).

Connelly, Thomas Lawrence. *Autumn of Glory: the Army of Tennessee, 1862–1865*. Baton Rouge: Louisiana State University Press, 1971.

Costa, Dora L., and Kahn, Matthew E. "Surviving Andersonville: The Benefits of Social Networking in POW Camps," (December 2005). NBER Working Paper No. W11875. Available at SSRN: http://ssrn.com/abstract=875701 (accessed 23 June 2010).

Costa, Dora L., and Kahn, Matthew E. *Heroes & Cowards: The Social Face of War*. Princeton: Princeton University Press, 2008.

Coulter, E. Merton. *A History of the South*. Vol. 7, *The Confederate States of America 1861–1865*. Baton Rouge: Lousiana State University Press, 1950.

Davis, Burke. *Sherman's March*. New York: Random House, 1980.

Davis, Robert Scott. *Ghosts and Shadows of Andersonville: Essays on the Secret Social Histories of America's Deadliest Prison*. Macon GA: Mercer University Press, 2006.

"Diamond Jubilee Issue," *The Millen News*, 2 October 1980, no. 1.

Dixon, Matt, "Building the Central Railroad of Georgia." *The Georgia Historical Quarterly* 45, no. 1 (March 1961): 1–21.

Drago, Edmund L., "How Sherman's March through Georgia Affected the Slaves," *The Georgia Historical Quarterly* 42, no. 3 (Fall 1973): 361–75.

Dunkelman, Mark H. *War's Relentless Hand: Twelve Tales of Civil War Soldiers*. Baton Rouge: Louisiana State University Press, 2006.

Emilio, Luis F. *A Brave Black Regiment: The History of the Fifty-fourth Massachusetts Volunteer Infantry, 1863–1865*. New York: Da Capo Press, 1995.

Fabian, Ann. *The Unvarnished Truth: Personal Narratives in Nineteenth Century America*. Berkeley: University of California Press, 2002.

Freeman, Douglas Southall. *R.E. Lee: A Biography*. Vol 3. New York: Charles Scribner's Sons, 1963.

Futch, Ovid. *History of Andersonville Prison*. Gainesville: University of Florida Press, 1968.

Garlick, Julia. "Reminiscences of Federal Prison at Lawtonville." *The True Citizen* (Waynesboro), 4, 7 June 1924.

Gast, Phil, "Major Archaeological Find at Site of Civil War Prison." CNN, 17 August 2010. http://www.cnn.com/2010/US/08/14/Georgia.civil.war.camp/index.html?iref=allse arch (accessed 7 October 2010).

Giles, Bill, ed. *Disease, Starvation & Death: Personal Accounts of Camp Lawton*. Raleigh NC: Lulu Press, 2005.

Giles, Bill, ed. *"The World's Largest Prison": A Camp Lawton Compendium*. Magnolia Springs State Park: Café Press, 2004.

Gillespie, James M. *Andersonvilles of the North: The Myths and Realities of Northern Treatment of Civil War Confederate Prisoners*. Denton TX: University of North Texas Press, 2008.

Glatthaar, Joseph T. *The March to the Sea and Beyond*. Baton Rouge: Louisiana State University Press, 1995.

Hallock, Hiram, Philip Steele, and Richard Selin. "Comparing Lumber Yields from Board-Foot and Cubically Scaled Logs," Research Paper FPL 324, Forest Products Products Laboratory, Forest Service, US Department of Agriculture, Madison WI, 1979. http://www.fpl.fs.fed.us/documnts/fplrp/fplrp234.pdf (accessed 3 March 2010).

Hanna, Alfred J. *Flight into Oblivion*. Bloomington: University of Indiana Press, 1959.

Hanna, Alfred J. "The Confederate Baggage and Treasure Train Ends Its Flight in Florida: A Diary of Tench Francis Tilgman." *Florida Historical Quarterly* 17, no. 3 (January 1939): 159–80.

Hesseltine, William Best. *Civil War Prisons: A Study in War Psychology*. New York: Frederick Ungar Publishing, 1964.

Hillhouse, Albert M. *A History of Burke County, Georgia: 1777–1950*. Jointly published by Swainsboro GA: Magnolia Press, 1985, and Spartanburg SC: The Reprint Company, 1985.

Holley, Peggy Scott, "The Seventh Tennessee Volunteer Cavalry: West Tennessee Unionists in Andersonville Prison." http://www.stjusers.com/lindas/history.html (accessed 18 August 2008).

Hoffman, Alan. *Sultana: Surviving the Civil War, Prison, and the Worst Maritime Disaster in American History*. New York: Smithsonian, 2009.

Hughes, Mark. *Bivouac of the Dead*. Bowie MD: Heritage Books, 1995.

Jones, James Pickett. *Yankee Blitzkrieg: Wilson's Raid Through Alabama and Georgia*. Lexington: University Press of Kentucky, 1976.

Kennett, Lee. *Marching Through Georgia: The Story of Soldiers & Civilians During Sherman's Campaign*. New York: Harper and Collins, 1995.

Knight, Jo Goodson, comp. *Burke County Folks, 1851–1900*. Baltimore: Gateway Press, 2004.

Leyman, Marvin V. *Bartlesons of Grand Chain*. Tulsa OK: True Image Printing, 1995.

McCarty, Terry, with, Margaret Ann Chatfield McCarty. *The Chatfield Story: Civil War Letters and Diaries of Private Edward L. Chatfield of the 113th Illinois Volunteers*. North Charleston SC: Booksurge Publishing, 2009.

McCoig, Roger A. "Camp Lawton: A Brief Chapter in the Study of the Confederate States Prisons." *Social and Behavioral Sciences* (1981–82): 3-16.

McPherson, James M. *Ordeal by Fire: The Civil War and Reconstruction*. New York: Alfred A. Knopf, 1982.

"Magnolia Springs State Park." http://www.gastateparks.org/info/magspr/ (accessed 19 November 2009).

"Magnolia Springs State Park." http://www.georgiaencyclopedia.org/nge/Article.jsp?id=h-2929 (accessed 19 November 2009).

Marvel, William. *Andersonville: The Last Depot*. Chapel Hill: University of North Carolina Press, 1994.

Marvel, William. "Johnny Ransom's Imagination." *Civil War History* 39 (September1995): 181–89.

Marszalek, John F. *Sherman's March to the Sea*. Abiliene TX: McWhiney Foundation Press, 2005.

Melton, Tracy Matthew. *Hanging Harry Gambrill: TheViolent Career of Baltimore's Plug Uglies, 1854–1860*. Baltimore: Maryland Historical Society, 2005.

"Millen," *The New Georgia Encyclopedia*. http://www.georgiaencyclopedia.org/nge/Article.jsp?id=h-2929 (accessed 21 November 2009).

Miller, William J., and Pohanka, Brian C. *The Illustrated History of the Civil War: Images of an American Tragedy*. Alexandria VA: Time-Life, 2000.

"Norwegians in the Civil War: Knude Olson." Vesterheim Norwegian-American Museum, http://vesterheim.org/CivilWar/db/o/ols/index.html (accessed 25 November 2009).

Parks, Joseph E. *Joseph E. Brown of Georgia*. Baton Rouge: Louisiana State University Press, 1977.

Parrish, William Earl. *Frank Blair: Lincoln's Conservative*. Columbia: University of Missouri Press, 1998.

Perkerson, Medora Field. *White Columns in Georgia*. New York: Bonanza, 1952.

Perkins, Donald E. *History of the Perkins Family of Perkins, Georgia*. Atlanta: Privately printed, 1979.

Perkins, Donald E. Interview. 2 and 8 April 2010.

Perkins, Donald E. "Old Lawtonville." *Jenkins County 1905-2005 Centennial History: The Millen News Centennial Edition* (24 August 2005): 55–58.

Prince, Richard E. *Central of Georgia Railway and Connecting Lines*. Millard NE: Privately printed, n.d.

Reeves, Robert A. Interview. 12 May 2010.

Robins, Glenn. "Race, Repatriation, and Galvanized Rebels: Union Prisoners and the Exchange Question in Deep South Prison Camps." *Civil War History* 53, no. 2 (June 2007): 117–40.

Rogers, George A. and R. Frank Saunders. "Camp Lawton Stockade, Millen, Georgia, C.S.A." *The Atlanta Historical Journal* 25, no. 4 (1981): 81–94.

Ross, D. Reid. *Lincoln's Veterans Win the War: The Hudson Valley's Ross Brothers and the Union's Fight for Emancipation*. Albany: State University of New York Press, 2008.

Sanders, Charles W., Jr. *While in the Hands of the Enemy: Military Prisons of the Civil War*. Baton Rouge: Louisiana State University, 2005.

Smardz Frost, Karolyn. *I've Got a Home in Gloryland: A Lost Tale of the Underground Railroad*. New York: Farrar, Straus and Giroux, 2008.

Smith, Gerald J., Jr. "'Satisfaction Wherever He Served': The Career of Alexander Robert Lawton, 1818–1862." MA thesis, Georgia Southern University, 1991.

Speer, Lonnie R. *Portals to Hell: Military Prisons of the Civil War*. Mechanicsburg PA: Stackpole Books, 1997.

Springer, Paul J. *America's Captives: Treatment of POWs from the Revolutionary War to the War on Terror*. Lawrence KS: University Press of Kansas, 2010.

Stahura, Barbara. *Sons of Union Veterans of the Civil War*. Edited by Gary Gibson. Paducah, KY: Turner Publishing Company, 1996.

Taylor, T.A. *History of Dentistry: A Practical Treatise for the Use of Dental Students and Practitioners*. Philadelphia and New York: Lea & Febiger, 1922.

The Millen News (Millen, Georgia.)

Thomas, Eugene Marvin. "Prisoner of War Exchange during the American Civil War." PhD dissertation, Auburn University, 1976.

Toner, Mike. "Clues Found to Civil War Prison Site: Radar Images May Help Pinpoint Little-known Camp." *Atlanta Journal-Constitution*, 20 February 2007.

Townsend, Billy. "Camp Lawton: Magnolia Springs State Park." Atlanta: Recreation and Programming Section, Parks and Historic Sites Division, Georgia Department of Natural Resources, July 1975.

Trudeau, Noah Andre. *Southern Storm: Sherman's March to the Sea*. New York: HarperCollins, 2008.

Underwood, John Levi. *The Women of the Confederacy*. New York and Washington: Neale Publishing, 1905.

Unwin, Gregory J.W. *Black Flag Over Dixie: Racial Attitudes and Reprisals in the Civil War.* Carbondale: Southern Illinois University Press, 2004.

United States Army Military Institute. *Shrines of the Honored Dead: A Study of the National Cemetery System.* Washington DC: Department of the Army, Office of the Quartermaster General, n.d.

United States Government. Department of the Interior. US Fish & Wildlife Service, "The Camp Lawton Archaeological Site: Bo Ginn National Fish Hatchery." http://www.fws.gov/camplawtonsite.html (accessed 1 October 2010).

Virginia Historical Society. http://www.vahistorical.org (accessed 25 February 2011).

White, Ronald C. *A. Lincoln: A Biography.* New York: Random House, 2009.

Wiley, Bell Irwin. *The Road to Appomattox.* New York: Athenuem, 1971.

Wiley, Samuel T. *Biographical and Portrait Cyclopedia of Chester County.* Edited by Winfield Scott Warner. Philadelphia: Gresham Publishing, 1893.

Wilson, Leonard G. "The Clinical Definition of Scurvy and the Discovery of Vitamin C." *Journal of the History of Medicine and Allied Sciences* 30, no. 1 (1975): 40–60.

Woodworth, Steven E. *Nothing But Victory, the Army of the Tennessee, 1861–1865.* New York: Alfred A. Knopf, 2006.

Index